Teaching Young Children

This book was made possible through the understanding, patience and support of my husband, Jerold, and our daughters, Cheryl and Jeryl – to whom it is dedicated with love.

Teaching Young Children

BEATRICE D. MARTIN

Jeanne Machado — Consulting Editor

Isaac Rodriguez III — Photographer

Elinor Gunnerson — Early Childhood Education Series Editor

DELMAR PUBLISHERS • **ALBANY, NEW YORK 12205**
A DIVISION OF LITTON EDUCATIONAL PUBLISHING, INC.

Preface

Today, at last, teachers of young children are being recognized as vital to the educational progress of the child. Early childhood education experiences affect life-long attitudes toward learning. Quality early childhood education can prevent many of the education problems evident today. Those who are preparing the teachers of young children must accept responsibility for a comprehensive approach toward this important part of the educational system.

Teaching Young Children discloses the author's philosophy as an eclectic — composed of compatible parts from the philosophies of many famous educators and behavioral scientists including Jean Piaget, Jerome Bruner and R.M. Gagné. This philosophy is stated simply, and where possible, without the use of "educationese."

Three major premises undergird the philosophy of education expressed in this book.

- Individuals are unique; therefore, alternatives must be available for students and for teachers.

- Many of today's problems in education are preventable.

- The role of communication in education must be understood.

These ideas appear repeatedly throughout the book. The writer has attempted to ingrain these thoughts in the student's mind.

The primary purpose of *Teaching Young Children* is to guide the student who is learning to become a teacher of young children. The broadness of its scope may make it useful, also, to the experienced teacher as a review and as a supplementary or evaluation tool.

This collection of helps for teachers of young children is the result of the author's varied experiences — in a church-related school, a commercial day-care center, a Headstart Child Development Center and a public school district early childhood education center — as well as much research. In all these situations, the following areas of knowledge are necessary to the truly effective teacher of young children:

- Child growth and development: awareness of "the whole child."

- A personal philosophy of education.

- A concept of "readiness" for learning.

- How children learn: learning theories.

- How to teach: strategies and curriculum.

- Communication techniques.

- Parent involvement.

- The role of the teacher as a model.

Since the teacher models behavior throughout the school day, the text encourages introspection on part of the reader. Students are encouraged to become actively involved in early childhood education through use of the Suggested Activities at the end of each unit. These activities are designed to place the student in closer touch with the real world of early childhood education in action. A major purpose of the activities is to motivate the student to think about his/her observations in terms of what has been learned from the text and of what the individual knows about himself. Three major categories of activities are suggested for the student: research, problem-solving, and individual professional development.

For the student to benefit maximally from the use of this text, it is necessary that he/she have access to a variety of early childhood education programs for specific observation experiences. It is also suggested that observation of parent meetings, staff meetings, and inservice training meetings should be possible. This, of course, places responsibility on the instructor for creating opportunities for these activities.

At the end of each unit, review material is provided. Usually all the information needed to complete the Review can be found within the body of the unit. Acceptable responses are given however, in a special section, for those who may need help. Thus, there is no need for students to wait for further class discussion to clarify difficult points or to evaluate for themselves their grasp of the unit objectives.

Beatrice D. Martin feels that one who successfully teaches young children is a Very Important Person in the truest sense. She wrote *Teaching Young Children* to help students grow educationally and professionally so that they may become these VIPs. Mrs. Martin's vast experience — as teacher of young children, director of child care centers, teacher of inservice and paraprofessional teachers and, presently, as Curriculum Development Specialist for Early Childhood Education in the Edgewood Independent School District, San Antonio, Texas — qualifies her to write such a book. Her active involvement in research, writing, and several professional associations shows her dedication to quality education for the very young.

Other texts in the current Delmar Early Childhood Education Series are

Early Childhood Experiences in Language Arts — Jeanne Machado

Creative Activities for Young Children — Mayesky, Neuman, and Wlodkowski

Administration of Schools for Young Children — Phyllis Click

ACKNOWLEDGMENTS

The words in this book have come alive through the efforts of Isaac Rodriguez III, the photographer; the author is grateful for his utmost cooperation.

Appreciation is expressed to the leaders, staff members, children and parents of the two San Antonio schools where most of the photographs were taken:

Cardenas Early Childhood Center, Edgewood Independent School District; Teresa Z. Dent, principal.

Jefferson United Methodist Day-Care and Kindergarten; Hazel Sublett, director.

The author gratefully acknowledges the help of Joyce Coleman, coordinator of the Bilingual Early Childhood Program for the Southwest Educational Development Laboratory, Austin, Texas and her staff; Jacqueline Galindo and Sarah Solis, who typed the original manuscript; John Wesley for several photographs (figures 10-1 and 10-4); and the staff at Delmar Publishers.

Publications Director — Alan N. Knofla

Editor-in-Chief — Marjorie A. Bruce

Source Editor — Elinor Gunnerson

Reviewer — Elizabeth Eames

Director of Manufacturing/Production — Frederick Sharer

Illustrators — Anthony Canabush, Michael Kokernak, George Dowse

Production Specialists — Jean Le Morta, Betty Michelfelder, Lee St. Onge, Patti Barosi, Sharon Lynch

Contents

Section I How Children Learn

unit 1 human development

OBJECTIVES

After studying this unit, the student should be able to

- List and explain five characteristics of human development.

- State four ways that a teacher can use knowledge of developmental patterns.

- Define the following terms: reflexive behavior, environment, motor skills, socialization, cognition, frustration tolerance, emotional catharsis, percept, critical period, self-motivation.

How a newly fertilized egg inside a mother's abdomen becomes an *autonomous* (self-directed) intelligent adult is the story of human development. Scientists offer proof that human development follows a predictable pattern. Some of the characteristics of the pattern are listed.

- Development is similar for all human beings: all babies stand before walking.

- Development proceeds from the general to the specific in both mental and *motor* (body) activities: baby waves his whole arm in random movements before he is able to pick up a pin.

- Development is continuous change from the moment of *conception* (the uniting of the male sperm and the female ovum) until death.

- Development proceeds at different rates: permanent teeth are functioning in the body before the sex organs mature. Kinds of intelligence also develop at varying rates: the ability to know one object from another comes before learning to recognize one series of objects from another series, or sequence.

- There is positive correlation in development: as one kind of development occurs, other kinds of development become possible. An infant must develop physically before he can learn to solve abstract problems.

Each aspect of human development, physical, social-emotional and intellectual, has its own pattern. A teacher of young children must know and understand these patterns in order to know what to look for. Knowing the sequences helps in recognizing normal and abnormal change in children. The patterns can serve as guides for planning curriculum. They are used in determining standards or measurement of child growth and development.

All human development needs guidance. The infant must be given nutritious foods if he is to physically mature successfully. He must have proper amounts of rest and exercise. Adults must guide the child's social-emotional development. He must learn to get along with others. Skillful direction provided by parents and teacher can make the process less painful and more efficient. Intellectual growth or *cognitive* growth (the increase of knowledge) has always been recognized as a prime function of schooling. A child does not know about those things that are not in his experience. Related new ideas must be presented to him when he is ready.

Understanding developmental patterns helps the teacher in wisely guiding the young child through maximum physical, social, emotional, and intellectual development during the time that they are together. Each kind of growth in the very young child should be examined individually so that the effects of each on the others can be understood. In this way, the human resources of the future depend on the schools.

PHYSICAL DEVELOPMENT

Physical development is characterized by changes that are seen in the external body and by unseen internal changes in the organs, muscles, blood, bones, and nervous system.

Variations in body size exist at birth and become more pronounced as children grow. Growth in body size is internally controlled by a hormone secreted by the pituitary gland at the base of the brain. Growth is externally controlled by the food, water, exercise, and rest given the body. Poor nutrition may cause an overweight or underweight child. Improper exercise can cause fatigue, poor muscular development, poor circulation of blood, and poor excretion of waste matter.

At birth the child has only simple reflexive behaviors. These are spontaneous responses to the needs of his body and to his environment, which is all the world outside himself. He can cry, grasp, suck, and move his head, arms, and legs in jerks. The human infant automatically reacts to his internal needs. If he is in pain, he cries. If he is tired, he sleeps. The human infant also reacts to his external surroundings. When given food or drink, he sucks it into his body. If the room is too hot or too cold, he cries to let someone know he is uncomfortable. If a pin sticks him, he yells. If light is too bright, he closes his eyes.

An infant reacts to all that happens to him. Thus the child's innate behaviors indicate his internal

General	Specific
Physical	
Random arm movements.	Reaching.
Random leg movements.	Walking.
Takes all foods by sucking.	Sucks, drinks, uses a spoon to take foods.
Mental	
Says "doggie."	Says "Snoopy," "Scamp."
Says "birdie."	Says "blackbird," "airplane," "helicopter."
Social	
General fear response is loud crying	Fear response may become throwing, running away, saying "bad" words.
Emotional	
Shows fear response to any unusual thing, person, or place	Shows fear response to an unusual thing, person, or place only if it is completely strange to him — army tank, monster, jail.

Fig. 1-1 Human development proceeds from general to specific responses.

Physical Development	Mental Development	Social-Emotional Development
Learns to ride a kiddy-car (large muscles of legs and arms).	Learns which table is too low to ride under, which surface is easier to pedal on, that he cannot ride down steps.	Learns to ride to persons for attention, to share, to take turns riding.
Learns to throw a hand-size object (large muscles of arms, some of hand).	Learns that an object does not come back unless a person is there to return it.	Learns to use throwing as a new way to express strong feelings and to play "I'll throw and you hand it back to me" with another person.
Learns to catch a ball.	Learns rules of a simple ball game for two or three persons.	Learns to be a member of a ball team for more complex ball games and higher level socialization.

Fig. 1-2   One level of physical development leads to further mental development; this allows further social-emotional development.

Age	Developmental Characteristics	Implications for Curriculum
2	Prefers to play alone; is very dependent; has poor motor coordination.	Needs much space; needs toys with comfortably large pieces to hold. Requires much individual attention; requires more adults per number of children (1 to 4).
3	Likes to play alone, but near another child. May not be ready to share with others all of the time. Short attention span.	Requires duplicates of many toys and materials enjoyed by one child at a time. Wide variety of activities should be available. Any group activities should be for small groups of two or three children and be very brief. Picture books and stories must be brief.
4	Likes to play with others. Attention span is increasing. Very active; talks readily.	Ready for learning activities in groups of four to eight. Can concentrate longer on one idea, so may go into greater depth on any subject. Activities may be longer (15 - 20 minutes). Concept development should be through physical activities, not sitting at tables. Ready for group discussions if not too long. Stories may be longer.
5	Great concentration when interested. Likes games and team work. Fine-motor development rapid. Eye-hand coordination rapidly improving.	Ready for larger group games and class activities. Can sit at tables for twenty minutes or longer. Interested in printed matter: labels, books, captions, newspaper comics, his own printing. Should be encouraged to initiate discussions, ask many questions, describe what he sees. Can play ball games and use equipment with small pieces (pegs, 12-piece puzzles).

Fig. 1-3 How developmental patterns serve as guidelines for planning curriculum.

Age	Motor Skills
3	Walks sideways and backwards, upstairs and downstairs, on tiptoe; runs with few falls; hops with two feet together. Can cut roughly, paste, finger paint, use fat crayons, work puzzles with four parts. Can partially dress self, brush teeth, feed self using spoon and fork.
4	Jumps from height of twelve inches; makes standing jump of two feet; skips to music; rides a tricycle; swims with simple strokes; uses alternate legs on stairs. Shows left-handedness or right-handedness. Can cut soft food with knife, fasten zippers and large buttons, throw and catch a large ball, paint with a large brush, swing high, and use a hammer.
5	Can use a balance board and a seesaw; marches in time to music; jumps over small objects; throws a beanbag accurately four to six feet; can saw wood on a line, weave; butter bread, and make sandwiches; brushes and combs hair; bathes self; prints letters and name well; makes some numerals.
6	Can dance in time to music; jumps rope and rides bicycle well; ice skates; swims several strokes; plays team ball games. Can cut most foods with knife; washes back and neck without help; prints sentences with pencil; sews with a large needle.

Fig. 1-4 Approximate ages at which children achieve certain motor skills.

needs and are the means by which he interacts with with his world. These result in his first physical growth and motor development.

The child's first effective motor control is over the major muscles that lift the baby's head from the surface when he is lying down. Then he gains power over the arm, shoulder and abdominal muscles that he uses to lift his whole torso. Later, legs and arms obey commands, and then fingers and toes. Control of the large muscles usually precedes control of small muscles.

Many lists of the approximate ages at which motor skills appear are available. Because of internal differences and the variety of environments, even children of the same age enter school at varying levels of physical development. Sex, too, makes a a difference. During the early childhood years, the physical development of girls is greater than that of boys. The needs of every child must be met, however.

Fig. 1-5 The needs of each child must be met; small group or one-to-one activities are best sometimes.

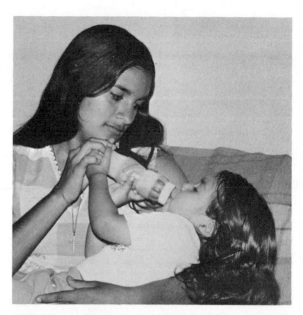

Fig. 1-6 A child's trust in other human beings develops according to the way his needs are met.

It is essential that the teacher closely watch each child and write down what is seen. Activities should be planned to test motor abilities in games and simple exercises. The child's record may be compared with the sequences of normal skill development. When the child's developmental level has been determined, plans for the child may be made.

Motor experiences should be planned for the group when these will be beneficial to all the children. Special activities should be planned to meet the unique needs of small groups or individuals.

SOCIAL AND EMOTIONAL DEVELOPMENT

Social and emotional development, including the use of language, is essential if the child is to learn to live successfully with other people. This process, *socialization,* begins at birth and lasts until death.

A young baby is totally dependent upon adults to see that his hunger and thirst are satisfied. As he matures physically, he gains a new power over his life. If he is hungry and sees food, he can reach for it, pick it up, and eat it. Thus a certain degree of physical development leads to new kinds of social behavior. The child can now begin and influence, if not completely control, some of his experiences. He is no longer totally dependent upon other people.

Living amid the social interaction of other human beings, the child hears voice sounds. The infant's babbling, cooing, and crying are forms of vocal exercise. In time, these help to prepare the sound-making parts of the body for meaningful speech. The child imitates the words he hears. Soon he attaches meanings to the words. He is then able to tell his mother what his needs are. He says "Wa-wa" when thirsty, and mother gives him a drink. He has become part of the social interaction.

During his first two years, the infant develops a sense of trust in other human beings. How much trust depends on how well his needs are met. Failure to receive tender loving care (TLC) may create a distrust of others that is critical to his personality for life. Many research studies have shown that some children have died from lack of love in institutions where there was not a large enough staff to give sufficient attention to individuals. In other studies, babies who were not given affection had delays in physical and cognitive development. Such infants responded well when individual affectionate attention was shown them.

Before he is able to speak, the infant communicates his positive or negative feelings by smiling, clapping, crying, showing excitement, thrashing his arms and legs. When he learns to speak, he soon develops a vocabulary that expresses his likes and dislikes. His motor skills continue to be a part of his emotional behavior. He hits or throws in anger; he hugs or jumps in glee.

Age	Perceptions, 3-Dimensional Objects	Perceptions, 2-Dimensional Objects	Abstractions
5			fanciful science fiction ideas, thunderstorms, violence associated with war, being hit by a car.
4		wild animals (zoo animals, on TV and in pictures)	"robbers," loss of affection, too much deviation from routine
3	most live animals		bogeyman, ghosts, sudden unexpected change of any kind, of being left behind
2	pets; farm animals dark room	face masks	sudden displacement, insecure footing, fear of being dropped
1	domestic animals; strange persons, places, things; high places		
0	loud noises, pain		

Fig. 1-7 Fears of the very young child (0-5 years).

The nervous system and the glands in the body are functioning at birth. It is natural for the child to respond to his experiences emotionally. It is important that these feelings be expressed. Physicians say that persons who are taught to hide their emotions frequently develop ulcers and many *psychosomatic illnesses* (those that begin in the mind, not in the body). Children must be taught to show their feelings in ways that are socially acceptable and to deal with the frustrations that cause some of the negative feelings. This is a task for both parents and teachers of young children.

Appropriate ways to express strong feelings may differ for the child and his adult models. He cannot imitate these as he did their speech. Therefore, he must be able to remember the acceptable forms of expression he is taught. He must learn the limits placed on his means of expression. Thus, this level of social and emotional development must wait until adequate cognitive skills have been developed.

Teaching acceptable methods of revealing joy, approval, or acceptance is seldom a serious problem in school. Fear, jealousy, frustration, and anger are more frequently inappropriately expressed.

Some fears have been identified as typical of certain periods of the child's development. Any fear a child feels is worthy of his teacher's attention. Fear is always based on a real *stimulus* (something that initiates the fear as a response): a barking dog, a "snake," a person in a doctor's white jacket.

Fear in the very young child

- Is learned

    from a bad experience ("white coat means pain in arm").

    through imitation (mother shows fear of thunder).

    by association of experiences ("loud music is like thunder").

    by vicarious experience (seeing a car crash on TV).

- Is developmental in nature

    Stimuli change as the child grows.

    Early fears come from perceptual experience (loud noise, pain).

    Gradually the bases become abstract in nature (ideas).

Worries may be longer lasting and vague and are sometimes based on imaginary ideas. Prolonged worries can have bad effects on young children.

Jealousy over a real or imagined incident or person is usually caused by a feeling of the loss of

1.	Spank a doll	11.	Hammer nails into wood
2.	Bounce a ball hard	12.	Cry
3.	Pound clay	13.	Throw a ball at a wall
4.	Tear paper	14.	Draw a picture of how he feels
5.	Hit a stuffed toy	15.	Run in a safe outdoor area
6.	Scrub or mop the floor	16.	Throw rocks in a safe place
7.	Talk about what happened	17.	Pound dough
8.	Beat a drum	18.	Kick a football
9.	Play in water	19.	Hit a croquet ball with a mallet
10.	Dig in soil	20.	Jump rope

Fig. 1-8 Acceptable ways for a young child to get rid of anger.

some person's affection. It is frequently cured with large doses of TLC and enough success experiences to give the jealous child a good self-image.

Expressing anger is probably the most common problem in dealing with emotions of young children. Socially acceptable ways of expressing anger include physical exercise (pounding on a doll or throwing pebbles in a safe place). At other times, just verbalizing the anger seems to end it. Every teacher should be prepared with materials and ideas for expressing anger that are appropriate for children.

When a child's anger becomes so great he cannot control it, he has exceeded his *frustration tolerance.* It is necessary to help him develop an increasingly higher tolerance of frustration for three reasons:

- His frustrations can only increase as he grows older.

- Patterns of emotional behavior set firmly early in life tend to persist as the child grows older.

- The mental aspects of a negative emotion must be considered as much as the positive physical aspects. The child must learn to mentally cope with the stimulus that caused the anger.

Emotional distress generates excess body energy. This energy must be spent acceptably to keep the classroom climate suitable for learning. For very young children, this emotional *catharsis* (getting rid of the feeling) is frequently achieved by these methods:

- Verbalization: calling names, epithets, yells.

- Doll play therapy: spanking the doll in lieu of hitting the true cause of the anger.

- Testing a frustration to see if it is real: Was the barking dog by the door or on a television show?

Fig. 1-9   Preschool children can be taught many acceptable ways to express anger.

- Discussing his feelings to give the child insights on the problem. This requires some degree of maturity in the child, but it usually works well.

Personality traits and the bases of good mental health are instilled in the child during his early childhood years. For good results, it is helpful for an adult to remember these needs of the child:

- Strenuous physical exercise daily.

- The development of a good sense of humor.

- The understanding that crying is not always "being a baby."

- A close, affectionate relationship with at least one family member.

- A close friend to whom he can say things he would not say to an older person.

- A willingness to talk about his problems.

- A respect on the part of others for his emotions.

Social and emotional development in the very young child has long-lasting effects. It is highly dependent on physical maturation and intellectual development. It is a serious responsibility of the teacher.

INTELLECTUAL DEVELOPMENT

For many years it was believed that heredity decided how intelligent a person could become. *Heredity* is the sum of the characteristics given a child by both parents. There is no reason to believe that people are born genetically equal in potential; there is evidence, however, that human beings develop intelligence after birth by interacting with the environment. There is also much evidence that the most learned human beings only develop a portion of the brain. So far as is known, no one ever achieves his maximum potential. (Today men are struggling to learn how to come closer to such a goal.) Educational,

biological, and psychological researchers have provided many conclusions about how intelligence develops. Some of the major theories are discussed in the unit *Theories of Learning*. Some generally-agreed-upon understandings about intellectual development will be helpful at this point, however.

- Cognition (cognitive development) is defined as the act or process of knowing, including both awareness and judgment.

- Cognition occurs when the human organism (a complex structure of elements that act as a whole) interacts with the world through the five senses: he sees, hears, touches, tastes, and smells.

- The impressions from the sensory acts, called "percepts," are recorded in the brain. The child *perceives* them.

- The information is processed in the brain and grouped by categories called *concepts*. "things I taste, things that fly, things that hurt." This is similar to programming a computer; the more information that is put in, the more that can come out or be recalled for use at a later time.

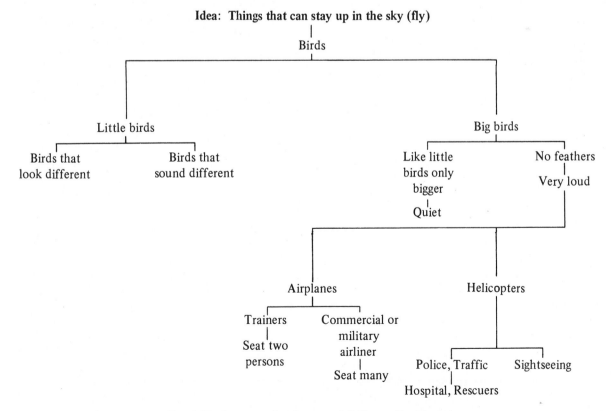

Idea: Things that can stay up in the sky (fly)

Fig. 1-10 Concepts develop as a child learns to categorize.

- The development of *cognitive structures,* or concepts from percepts, begins at birth and is sequential. New learning must be only slightly more complex than existing cognitive structures, so that it can be plugged in. If the percept cannot be *assimilated* (thoroughly comprehended) this way, it is *accommodated* (accepted) by a new structure being formed. There is a limit to the speed with which new structures can be formed.

- The period from birth to six years contains most of the critical periods for intellectual development. A *critical period* in child development is that time in a child's life when the presence or absence of certain things is of the utmost importance to normal development. The effects of not having a necessary factor often cannot be overcome. This will be discussed at greater length when theories of learning are presented.

- Intellectual development, like physical and social-emotional development, depends on things inside the child as well as things outside him. *Self-motivation,* which means curiosity, a natural desire for *competence* (doing things well), and a natural desire for variety affect the value of learning experiences. Exposure to sensory stimuli is not enough. How much a child cares affects how much he learns.

- Teachers can increase the intellectual development of each child by creating a stimulating learning environment, analyzing the needs of each child, and then meeting the needs.

- Maximal intellectual growth depends upon physical and social-emotional development as well.

SUMMARY

Each kind of development — physical, social-emotional, and intellectual — depends upon internal factors (within the person) and external factors (the environment, outside the person). Each kind of development has its own sequential pattern but is similar for all persons.

Physical development depends upon inherited characteristics and upon health care. Muscular control begins over the large torso muscles — neck, shoulders, abdomen — and then spreads outward toward the extremities, the hands and feet. Knowing the most likely sequences in which motor skills are acquired helps the teacher plan the motor training that is best for young children.

Social-emotional development — including the use of language — is critical to personality development from birth until age two. The socialization process occurs relatively slowly during the preschool years until language development occurs. The young child must be taught to express negative feelings in socially acceptable ways. The foundation for good mental health in adulthood is laid in childhood. Parents and teachers are responsible for this kind of development.

Intellectual development is the result of the mental processing of percepts acquired from interaction with the environment. The percepts are acquired through sensory experiences.

It is not known exactly how cognition occurs but there is evidence to support a variety of theories of learning. Knowing how a child probably learns helps a teacher to make it easier for him to learn.

Behavioral evidence indicates that input to the brain is organized there into concepts. These are related groups of information. The development of a concept is sequential from the least complex to the most complex part.

From birth until age six is a critical period for the intellectual development of a human being. If development during this period is inadequate, the total maximum potential for this kind of development may be limited, although some degree of development continues.

Self-motivation and caring about the learning experience affects the amount of benefit received from it. Physical and social-emotional development must accompany intellectual development. The whole child is involved in the process.

From conception until death the human organism is developing physically, socially, emotionally, and intellectually. These changes are interdependent and occur at the same time.

SUGGESTED ACTIVITIES

- Observe two young children (aged three or four) in a classroom for thirty minutes. List behaviors that reflect each child's physical, social-emotional, and intellectual development. Indicate which child shows greater development of each kind.

a. For one of the children, list some preschool motor activities that would probably be too advanced for the child because of the level of his social-emotional development.

b. List some preschool activities for cognitive development that would probably be too advanced for him because of the level of his physical development.

• Observe a classroom of five-year-olds. State how one of the classroom activities is providing physical, social-emotional, and cognitive development for the children.

REVIEW

A.   Define the following terms.

1. Reflexive behavior
2. Environment
3. Socialization
4. Cognition
5. Frustration tolerance
6. Percept
7. Critical period (as it refers to human development)

B.   List and briefly explain five characteristics of human development.

C.   In what four ways does a knowledge of the developmental sequence assist the teacher of young children?

D.   Answer each of the following questions briefly.

1. In what way can both parents and teachers make the process of getting along with others (a part of social-emotional development) more efficient for the young child?

2. What internal control is exercised by the growth hormone secreted by the pituitary gland?

3. By what means does the very young child reflect his internal needs and inter-act with his environment?

4. During the preschool years, is the physical development of girls equal to that of boys?

5. What adverse effect may result if an infant does not receive adequate affection?

6. What illnesses may result from not expressing one's feelings?

7. What name is given that time when a child must have a specific element (such as good nutrition) in order for normal development to take place?

8. What two factors are included in cognition, the act or process of knowing?

9. What can teachers do to increase the intellectual development of each student?

E.   Select all the correct choices for each of the following statements.

1. Motor development proceeds from the general to the specific.

a. A child is ready for toe dancing before he is ready for roller skating.

b. A child can throw a ball before he can lace and tie his shoes.

c. A child can make small pegboard designs before he is ready to learn to play piano.

d. A child can climb the ladder of a slide before he can thread a needle.

e. A child can dress a doll before he can push a doll buggy.

2. There is positive correlation among the kinds of human development.

   a. A new level of physical development slows down the child's intellectual development.

   b. Social-emotional development positively waits for the child's physical development to reach a new level before proceeding.

   c. As intellectual development occurs, further social-emotional and physical development becomes possible.

   d. Physical, social-emotional and intellectual development all occur at the same time.

3. The following is an acceptable manner in which a preschool child may express anger.

   a. Talking about it.   c. Kicking a ball.

   b. Hiding behind a door.   d. Spanking a doll.

4. Perceptual experience

   a. Is recorded in the brain.

   b. Occurs in interaction with the environment.

   c. Changes concepts.

   d. Prevents socialization.

F. Select the letter of the term in Column II that best matches each concept expressed in Column I.

Column I	Column II
1. Developmental levels	a. Frustration tolerance
2. Perceptual experience	b. 0-6 years
3. Body growth and motor skills	c. Sequence patterns
4. Critical period for social-emotional development	d. Physical development
	e. 0-2 years
5. Curiosity, competence-drive	f. Listening to music
6. Cognitive structure composed of related ideas	g. Concept
7. Socially acceptable expression of feelings	h. Self-motivation
8. Critical period for intellectual development	

unit 2 theories of learning

OBJECTIVES

After studying this unit, the student should be able to

- Briefly explain Piaget's theory of how learning takes place.
- Briefly explain and give examples of intrinsic and extrinsic motivations for learning and explain how these can be further developed.
- Describe and explain at least five kinds of experiences that a child may have in a good learning environment.

A theory of learning is a set of ideas that helps explain how learning takes place. In many of the several learning theories, there are similar ideas. Teachers and parents need these ideas so that they can plan experiences that help the children learn the most in the least time.

Adults need to know what happens to the information that a child receives through his five senses. It is important to understand why two children who share an experience act differently as a result of it. Since adults provide the child's environment, they need to know how it affects his learning. It is important to find out how the human mind processes information, how children are motivated to learn, and which kinds of activities to plan to provide a good learning environment for very young children.

INFORMATION PROCESSING

A child arrives in this world with a built-in readiness to learn. Soon he can see, hear, taste, touch, and smell. He is naturally curious. This pushes him to learn. It makes him use his five senses.

Soon after birth, a baby learns to make sounds. These later develop into speech. Curiosity is then shown by a stream of questions. "Who," "why," "where," "what," and "when" help the eyes, ears, nose, mouth, and fingers. All of these pour information into the child's brain. What happens there cannot be seen, but by observing the behavior of many children, scientists and educators have been able to develop ideas on the ways that the child processes the information.

Fig. 2-1 Children keep busy responding to their natural curiosity.

Fig. 2-2 A small child imitates the smile of an adult.

Many of the child's sensory experiences result in *primary learning,* or imitating what he sees and hears. When baby smiles and makes the first sounds that have meaning to adults ("wa-wa" for "water") he is imitating what he sees and hears. He cannot imitate all that he perceives, however.

There is much evidence that the child sorts his impressions as he receives them. Classifying percepts is one of the first stages of thinking that can be recognized in the young child. The infant reacts differently when a new food is added to his diet. It may be fruit juice or cod liver oil. The look on his face shows that he knows the food is a new kind and that he is surprised. In his mind he adds this to a category: "food that I eat." He *assimilates* this new experience into the food group, enlarging it and possibly dividing it into two parts: "What I like when I'm hungry" and "what I like when I'm thirsty." Of course, an infant does not think in words, but words are needed to explain what goes on in the child's mind.

In a child's play, a teether finds its way into his mouth. He sucks but nothing goes into his throat. If he is hungry, the toy does not help his hunger. If he is thirsty, it does not relieve his thirst. He cannot assimilate this percept into the food category. He can *accommodate* (make a place for) this new impression by making a new category for it. This might be "things I can put into my mouth that do not help if I need food or water." His fingers, toys, shirt, and blanket may fit this group.

The learning theory that is based on assimilation and accommodation of percepts is the one most widely accepted today in the United States. It is the work of a Swiss scientist-educator, Jean Piaget. He has been active in Europe for more than fifty years. He continues to work in educational research.

The child classifies new sensory input every day. He tries to assimilate all new percepts. Obviously, this can cause errors. A child's first brown animal with four legs may be a "dog." Then a brown cat, cow, and horse may be "dog" to the child unless there is someone there to tell about several kinds of brown animals with four legs. It is easy to understand, then, why each child needs interaction with older persons each day. An adult or older child is needed to help him accommodate what he cannot assimilate. He also needs someone to correct his errors in classifying.

Another important part of Piaget's theory is the concept of equilibration. This means that there must be *equilibrium* (balance) between the amounts of assimilation and accommodation if the child is to become an intelligent person. Too much assimilation will cause him to learn some things in great detail, but he will know about too few things. Too much accommodation causes too little knowledge of very many things. Only when the two processes are in balance does the child grow into a person with reasonable depth of understanding of as many concepts as he needs to learn.

It has been shown how cognitive, physical, and social-emotional growth depend on each other. Information processing depends on levels of growth. The physical development of the body's sensory organs determines how the child perceives. Until the eyes and ears are fully matured, the child does not react to

---

Natural Errors Children Make in Classifying Percepts
1. Mother gives me a ball. I can drop it from my highchair. It comes up to me. It is round in my hand. This orange is round. If I drop it, it will come up to me. It is a ball.
2. There is a loud noise outside my home. They say it is a police car. So the other noise I heard was a police car. . . . (Note: It may have been an ambulance or a helicopter.)
3. Birds and airplanes have wings. They can fly. Anything that has wings can fly. If I put on some wings, I can fly.
4. Bang, bang, bang. On TV that noise is a gun shooting. I heard that noise out in the street. There is a gun out there. (Note: It may have been a car backfiring or fireworks.

Fig. 2-3   When making new perceptions, the child always tries to assimilate them into existing cognitive structures.

Developing Visual Perceptual Skills		
Actions	**Images**	**Symbols**
Builds with blocks randomly, labels later.	Builds a structure like one he sees or remembers seeing.	Draws a picture of a block structure (or tells/writes about it.)
Recognizes foods, eats them.	Points to pictures, identifies familiar foods, states ones he likes.	Draws/cuts pictures of foods, prints labels on them, writes the names of foods.
Matches a three-dimensional model of a design on a pegboard.	Matches a pegboard design he sees on paper.	Represents objects by making a design, shapes, or letters on paper with pencil.

Fig. 2-4 Visual perceptual skills are developed by first experiencing a skill through manipulation of the body and objects, then through images in the mind or on paper, later through symbols such as representative drawings, numerals, letters, spoken words.

what he sees and hears in the way that he will later. The child cannot recognize fine differences with these organs until they mature. A three-year-old can easily tell that salt and sugar do not taste the same, but he may not be able to tell the taste of lettuce from that of watercress. The very young child soon learns to tell the sound of the phone from that of the doorbell. It may be years later before he can tell if a b flat musical tone is higher or lower than a b natural. Whether or not a child enjoys playing a game with a group depends upon his social skills. Unless he has learned to share, he will classify the experience as a negative one. Each child's cognitive organization and discrimination skills are unique because his experience, before and after birth, is different from that of any other child.

By learning how a child processes sensory information, an adult can understand how the child's mind develops concepts. By knowing the need for a balance between the two processes, the need for an adult's awareness is seen. If an imbalance is noticed, plans can be made to restore balance by planning the kinds of learning needed to do this.

A famous American educator Jerome Bruner has agreed with Piaget's theory. He has added some of his own ideas. He feels that information is processed in three ways.

- The way in which man responds to his world through motor responses *(enactive representation)*. An example is a child's smile when he sees a smile.

- The way in which images stand for events in his mind *(iconic representation* or *imagery)*. For example, a child sees a bathtub and mentally relives the soaping, scrubbing, and splashing.

- The way symbols, such as letters and numerals, have meaning for the child *(symbolic representation)*. A good example is when a child sees his name in print (symbols) and realizes that it means him.

Bruner states that the three modes of processing information are learned in order:

- Enactive: child smiles back at mother who is smiling.

- Iconic: child smiles at mother when she is not smiling because he associates loving care with the sight of her.

- Symbolic: child smiles at the sight of the word *mother* because he associates loving care with the thought represented by the word.

Piaget agrees that there is a fixed order of the stages of cognitive development. Learning more about these stages will help in planning curriculum for the very young child.

MOTIVATION

There are many theories of how a child is motivated to learn. One theory states that at first it is curiosity that pushes the child to learn. This drive may last for a lifetime.

Fig. 2-5   A child learns from daily experiences.

Fig. 2-6   When children are prepared, a well-planned field trip is a sure way to stimulate curiosity and to develop oral language.

Many educators and psychologists agree with Robert C. White, who believes that human beings are born with a desire to be *competent,* to do things well. This is not a sign of competitiveness. The child may not want to do things better than another child. He wants to do well enough to please himself.

Having a positive self-image means to think of one's self as a person of worth or value. A child's drawing may look like scribbling to an adult. It may look like "pretty lines" to the child and be pleasing to him. To lack a feeling of self-worth can lead to emotional ill health. A child's self-satisfaction must not be spoiled by unnecessary adult criticism. It is easy to destroy a young child's *competence drive* (motivation).

For the young child, daily living is daily learning. He does not require any other specific motivation at first. Every day he records percepts, groups them, develops concepts, and therefore is able to take in still more the next day. If he cannot assimilate them, he can accommodate them by beginning new concepts.

In school not every child seems strongly motivated to learn. It is important to discover why. In many cases a child's curiosity has been reduced by adults who consider it a nuisance and often say "No, no, don't touch!"

The emptiness of a child's surroundings may be caused by poverty, neglect, or a mistaken idea that all a baby needs is food, warmth, and dry clothing. The bareness means fewer things to be curious about, fewer percepts to assimilate, and fewer concepts to be developed. The result is slower cognitive growth.

Research has disclosed that a child may receive too much or too little stimulation. Too much can be seen in the child's physical condition. Frequent fatigue, unexpected changes in habits of eating, sleeping, or elimination of body wastes may indicate over-stimulation. Occasionally a child becomes tense or socially withdrawn; he "tunes it out." These same conditions may result from other causes, however. Only by checking carefully can the true cause of these conditions be found.

In extreme poverty, when a large family lives in a little space, overstimulation may not be preventable. For a child from such a home, motivation for learning may come from a little privacy, personal space and materials, and one-to-one interaction with an adult.

The development of a skill must be in small steps and in order. To motivate a child to continue to learn, each step must be only slightly more difficult than the preceding one. If the task is too easy, he will be bored. If it is too hard and steps are omitted, the child will fail. This destroys motivation and slows his mental growth.

From birth on, a child needs daily sensory experience. Daily living provides some of these, but planned activities can advance the child's development at every age. The teacher makes the child's growth possible by creating a learning environment that meets all his needs. This allows his natural motivation for learning to grow.

THE LEARNING ENVIRONMENT

Natural curiosity and a desire to do a thing well are considered *intrinsic* (from inside one's self) *motivation.* They are found in different amounts in all individuals. Each person is also stimulated by *extrinsic* (people and things outside of one's self) *motivation.*

It is hard to change what is inside a person, but the environment can easily be changed. This then becomes a vital factor in motivating a child to learn.

Learning theorists agree that a child learns through a variety of experiences or interactions with the things around him. The following have been identified as experiences that provide learning for a very young child.

- Exploring a new place is a great learning experience. The new place may be a supermarket, a friend's backyard, or a park. Exploring means seeing, touching, hearing, smelling, and perhaps tasting. This is a sure way to stimulate curiosity, develop language, and promote cognitive growth.

- Imitating the actions of others helps a child learn many behavior patterns, good or bad according to his models. If a teacher puts away materials when she is through, she is helping the child learn to be neat. When a teacher shows respect for a child by listening attentively to him and responding, he is teaching the child to be a good listener. All children learn by imitating. Therefore it is vital for the learning environment to include interesting and worthy actions for children to imitate.

- Making mistakes is a valuable way for a child to learn. There should be materials with which a child can safely make mistakes. Putting too much water in his paint will make it runny. After a few such errors he will carefully add water a little at a time to get a mixture that will not run. Learning that it is all right to make mistakes helps a child learn to accept himself and others.

- Being part of the action is the fastest way for a child to learn many new things. A child does not learn to play a game by just listening to the rules. He must play the game.

Kinesthetic learning (learning which involves the whole body) is often used in teaching mentally retarded children. It is effective with all very young children. Writing a large imaginary letter B in the air is a good way to help a child visualize the letter so that his body helps him remember the shape when he must recognize or write the letter.

- *Communicating* by talking and by other means is needed in the learning environment. Communication is a two-way thing. Unless a message is received and responded to, there is no communication. The teacher must be aware of all the ways the child speaks to him:

  a. APPEARANCE may tell of poverty or affluence, illness or health.

  b. BODY LANGUAGE may show rebellion, fear, love.

  c. ORAL LANGUAGE may reveal past experience or lack of it, curiosity, shyness.

  d. BEHAVIOR may show good models at home, emotional upsets, onset of illness.

Only when the teacher receives the messages and acts upon them is there any communication. Also, the teacher speaks to the child in all of the same ways. The child must be helped to learn to communicate and to receive communication from others.

- *Being disabled,* whether temporarily (a scraped knee) or permanently (hearing loss), is an experience from which a child learns. Having a disabled child in a class is an opportunity to develop good character in all the children. The disabled child may learn patience coping with a different set of problems and perseverance. Other children may learn being considerate, helpful, and sympathetic.

- Having fun promotes learning quickly. If learning is made fun, children retain the learnings, seek more of them, and develop good attitudes toward school. If a game of "same and not the same colors" is fun for the child, he is more likely to stay interested in "same and not the same" until he can tell a "d" from a "b". The learning environment should always provide some activities that are enjoyable for the learner.

SUMMARY

In order to plan the best possible learning experiences for the child, there is a need to know how he learns. Piaget and Bruner help meet the need with their theories of learning.

Both intrinsic (internal) and extrinsic (external) motivations affect the child's cognitive development. The teacher can encourage his natural motivations — curiosity and a desire to do well — by providing materials and helping the child develop a positive self-image. The teacher can further motivate the child by giving him a learning environment in which he can learn from (1) exploring new places, (2) imitating good behavior models, (3) making mistakes, (4) being part of the action, (5) being disabled or being with someone who is, and (6) having fun.

SUGGESTED ACTIVITIES

- Visit a classroom of very young children. Observe and list evidence of three behaviors that are intrinsically motivated and three that are extrinsically motivated.

- Observe a very young child in a class. Describe ten behaviors observed. Next to each behavior, note whether the motivation was intrinsic or extrinsic. Then for each behavior note the kind or kinds of learning that result from it: cognitive, motor, and/or social-emotional.

- Look up at least one other theory of how children learn. Briefly explain it to the group.

REVIEW

A. Briefly explain the following statement.

"Daily living is daily learning for the very young child."

B. Answer the following questions briefly.

1. In learning theory, what does assimilation mean?

2. In learning theory, what does accommodation mean?

3. In learning theory, what does equilibration mean?

4. a. How can a child's intrinsic motivation for learning be encouraged?

b. How can it be discouraged?

5. a. How can a child's extrinsic motivation for learning be encouraged?

b. How can it be discouraged?

6. To whom must the learning theory of assimilation, accommodation, and equilibration be credited?

C. Give examples of three ways information is processed according to Jerome Bruner.

D. State five kinds of helpful experiences in a good learning environment for a very young child.

unit 3 readiness

OBJECTIVES

After studying this unit, the student should be able to

- Define the concept of readiness.
- Explain the best way to use charts of developmental skills.
- Explain how to determine for which physical, affective and cognitive skills a young child is ready.

In the schools of today, specific activities are called "reading readiness." They are chosen to prepare children to learn to read. Readiness needs to be looked at in a wider scope, however.

Physical, social-emotional, and cognitive skills are developed from very low levels to very high levels step by step. A child must reach the easiest goal before he is ready for a harder task. When he has mastered a set of these tasks he is in a *developmental stage.* (This is a normal period of growth in which a child has a specific set of abilities.) Then the child is ready for higher-level tasks. So *being ready* may be defined as having had all the experiences necessary to be able to try a higher-level task with reasonable hopes of success.

READINESS FOR PHYSICAL DEVELOPMENT

There is an old saying: "You must walk before you can run." This is true. Yet the rate of physical development of each child varies according to his own body: his motor skills, his health, and the food he eats. Not every child learns to run at the same age.

Developmental Motor Skills

There are many charts of developmental tasks that show the ages at which young children usually acquire sets of motor skills. It is better to consider the order in which the skills appear than the ages given. Figure 1-4, page 3, lists various motor skills.

Before enrolling in a preschool class, most children can feed and dress themselves, wash their faces and hands, and have control of the bladder and bowels. Also, they have learned to run, go up and down stairs, and to push and pull toys.

The rate of body growth slows during the preschool years, so the child has more energy and sleeps less. He may need a rest after lunch each day. He may or may not be ready to give up his nap.

Fig. 3-1   Children develop many large-muscle motor skills before they are ready to master fine-muscle motor skills.

Observing Motor Skills

It is helpful for the teacher to observe and write down each child's motor skills during the first weeks of school. When complete lists of each child's motor abilities (both large muscle and fine muscle skills) are available, they may be compared with several developmental task charts. Answers to the listed questions help determine the motor skills for which each child is ready.

- Does he run without falling?
- Can he pedal a tricycle?
- Does he jump with two feet or on one foot?
- Can he throw a large lightweight ball?
- Will he walk, march, or move freely to music?
- Does he prefer to build with large or small blocks?

Fig. 3-2 Available materials used creatively often make excellent playground equipment

Fig. 3-3 The tremendous energies of very young children require many outlets.

- Does he use toys that have small pieces?
- Can he work a six-part puzzle? Eight part?
- Can he control a crayon on paper?
- Can he fasten his zipper or buttons?

Every young child may be expected to be very active. Four-year-olds often are more active than threes or fives. All very young children need uncrowded spaces, indoors and outdoors, for physical development.

Equipment for Motor Skills

Playground equipment of all kinds motivates children to have active fun together. Homemade equipment is just as useful for developing muscles as costly commerical kinds.

Each room needs open spaces for action on rainy days. Physical readiness for harder tasks can be building up in any kind of weather.

To meet the needs of all the boys and girls, games, balls, wheel toys, records for dancing and exercising are needed. Young children are ready to move freely to the music. Older preschoolers can learn dances (follow directions), give directed motor responses, and match the beat of a simple rhythm. Mature four-year-olds and fives may be expected to follow directions from a record, tape, or cassette.

Motor Activities

The three-year-old likes to clap to music and to push and pull toys. He may or may not like to

"draw" with fat crayons. Whenever he is ready to use crayons, he has a "scribble" stage in which he just learns the feel of the crayon in his hand. Later he begins to control his moves on the paper. Much later he draws "pictures" that have meaning to him. Only then is he ready to draw pictures that can be recognized by others.

The child goes through these same stages with each new art medium: clay, paint, chalk. He is also learning to turn the pages of a book, roughly at first, then carefully.

Most four-year-olds are ready for all the motor activities just named. Outdoors, the four can pump a swing high, climb a slide and slide down, and keep a tricycle on a path.

At age five, a child is ready for more of the fine muscle skills. He can learn to use a pencil and write letters and numerals. He can handle pets skillfully. He can throw and catch a medium-size ball, ride a merry-go-round, and climb a fence or tree.

Perceptual Motor Skills

The muscles and functions of the eyes are maturing in the five-year-old. His visual skills are improving quickly. His ability to detect fine differences in things he sees indicates that he may soon be ready to tell a *d* from a *b*.

The parts and functions of the ear are well developed now. He needs much practice but usually he can learn to tell the sound of the word "pin" from

1.	Identifying very different sounds (made by objects)	seesaw, cutting paper; airplane, cow; siren, bell
2.	Identifying sounds not as different (made by objects)	tricycle, bicycle; chicken, duck; ambulance, firetruck
3.	Identifying sounds that are the same (made by objects)	cat, cat; drum, drum; hammer, hammer
4.	Identifying sounds that are similar (made by objects)	hen, rooster; mockingbird, robin; ambulance, firechief's car
5.	Identifying rhyming words	duck, truck; pan, fan; fish, dish

Fig. 3-4   Auditory discrimination skills can be developed gradually.

the sound of "pen." This *auditory* (hearing) skill is developed by first using sounds that have a gross difference, such as the sounds of a cat and a car. When he can recognize the difference in many pairs of such sounds, he is ready to discriminate sounds that are not so different, for example, the sounds of a chicken and a duck. Later he is ready for *phonics* (the sounds represented by letters) and first grade language arts and reading lessons.

The Disabled Child

The child with physical disabilities of any kind (visual, auditory, weight, loss of limbs) may or may not be ready for the usual motor tasks for a child his age. Such a child should be permitted to progress in his skills at his own rate. He should not be pressured to keep up with any other children. If he is given the time he needs to get ready for each skill, the disabled child will develop as far as he can.

It is enough for every child to continually improve his physical skills even if very slowly. Bettering his own record is as much challenge as any very young child needs. This is especially important to remember in designing motor activities for the disabled child.

READINESS FOR AFFECTIVE DEVELOPMENT

Affective development is the changing of the child from a self-centered infant into a social-emotional being who can live in a friendly way with other people. There are many levels of social skills between a newborn child and a mature adult. These skills begin to develop soon after birth.

Meeting Emotional Needs

The first two years of a child's life is a critical period for the development of a healthy personality.

In this period, specific needs of the child must be met if he is to have normal emotional and social experiences later in life. If these needs are not met during this period, the child is more susceptible to social and emotional problems as he grows older.

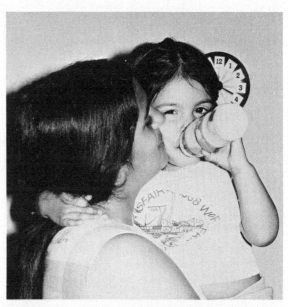

Fig. 3-5   Every effort should be made to see that very young children experience pleasant emotions.

The infant depends on others near him. The only way he can help himself is to cry to let them know he is in need of one or more things: food, drink, dry clothes, cool or warm air, attention or love.

Having someone to anticipate his needs and respond to his tears is a part of tender loving care that helps a baby become a happy and active toddler. Soon he is *less egocentric*. (He no longer sees himself as the whole world.) Now he is aware of the people, places, and things that are near him. He is ready to

Social Skills			
Three-year-old	**Four-year-old**	**Five-year-old**	**Six-year-old**
Plays parallel to another child	Plays best in small groups of three or four children	Functions well in groups of six to eight children	Plays with a large group; likes team games
Rapid expansion of vocabulary, especially nouns and verbs	Uses language socially; learns good manners	Uses language as a tool of thinking and of socializing	Communicates well with words; still not good at verbalizing his deep feelings
Needs help in feeding self	Feeds self and imaginary playmates/dolls with very little help	Independent eater	Can cut most meats and salads, can use a knife
Poor at sharing and taking turns	Shares with a child he likes	Takes turns; respects rights of others	Has a strong sense of territoriality; may be strongly protective of his own possessions
Plays well beside a boy or a girl	Plays with boys and girls in very small groups and in role-playing	Can play in larger groups of both sexes and settles arguments without adult help; changes groups often	Best friends are of same sex; friendships are longer lasting
Is not aware if playmate is same or different	Likes variety in his playmates	Socially conforming; prefers playmates who are also conformists	Develops awareness of "doing it like my friends do"

Fig. 3-6 During early childhood years, social skills are constantly changing

trust others. He knows that they will take care of him — because that is what they are doing. Now he is ready to play near others of his age group part of each day.

Social Interaction

Older children interact with the toddler just as adults do, but a *peer* (a child of his own age group) may not behave this same way. A peer or a child near his age may want to use a toy "now" instead of taking turns. If there is only one cookie, a peer may grab it if he is hungry. For the time being, there is a moment of unhappiness. Sometimes loud reactions are heard. An adult usually finds a second cookie, substitutes a toy, or diverts attention. The happening ends quickly and with no ill effects.

It is different if a child's emotional needs are not met during those first two critical years. Then he is not ready for the social problem of how to get along with another toddler. If he has been "let down" before, this neglect will show in an overreaction to a normal incident with another child, such as cookie grabbing. This child will rebel too long, too loudly,

and will cause the offender to become equally upset. The child with unmet emotional needs in infancy is not yet ready to play with another child.

Developmental Social Skills

Social skills are also developmental tasks in early childhood. Specific sets of them are usually acquired in each developmental stage. Again, children vary in the rates at which they grow socially. Knowing the sequences for developing social skills helps in planning experiences for the children.

Observing Social Skills

When a child is new at school, observations of his social skills should be made and recorded. These notes on the child's social and emotional behavior tell the planner for what the child is and is not ready.

Oral language ability assists social-emotional development. Socialization can occur without this assistance but the process is speeded by verbal interaction. A child's speech gives clues about his level of social skills. These should be carefully noted so that appropriate language experiences are planned.

- Does he prefer to play alone, beside another, or with a small group?
- Does he take turns?
- Does he dominate other children?
- Is he usually friendly and outgoing?
- How does he express anger?
- Can he follow a direction?
- Does he show or express fear of anything?
- Is he affectionate?
- Is he cooperative or rebellious?
- Does he frequently exaggerate?
- Does he accept small responsibilities?
- Does he seem to trust adults?

Answers to the listed questions help in assessing a child's social skills, enabling a teacher to plan for his affective development.

Affective Behavior

Affective behavior is that behavior by which the child shows how his interaction with his environment affects him. These interactions make him laugh, cry, scream, sing, hug, pat, be silent, throw, stomp, and clap to express his feelings about what happens to him.

- The child who prefers parallel play (beside a peer) should not be expected to do much group work. He is not ready for this.
- The shy timid child should not be expected to perform before a large group. He is not socially ready for this.
- The child who has no responsibilities at home should not be placed in charge of caring for the classroom pet. He is not ready for this higher-level task until he learns to be responsible for simpler tasks, such as giving out napkins at snack time.

Learning new social skills for which he is ready is a major area of affective development. Expressing feelings in acceptable ways and learning to be cooperative in a group are desirable goals for every child in his preschool years.

READINESS FOR COGNITIVE DEVELOPMENT

Cognitive development occurs daily through the mental processes of assimilation and accommodation. The preschool child is ready for beginning-level tasks to develop important skills. He can learn to:

- Concentrate: keep his mind on a task.
- Remember: expand concepts by assimilation.
- Classify: categorize foods, animals, toys.
- Reason: draw logical conclusions and see relationships.
- Use oral language as a tool: ask questions to get information and for social interaction.

Observing Cognitive Skills

To give each child opportunities to expand his cognitive skills, his readiness must be assessed. Written records of observations of each child in the first few weeks is essential. These notes should reveal what length stories to read to him, how many parts should be in his puzzles, and whether to teach colors, shapes, and sizes. The child's concepts of *categories* ("families" of things that belong together) and "same" and "different" need to be evaluated. His skills in using simple logic and language are to be expanded.

Observation based on the listed points reveal the level of the child's present cognitive development; then experiences can be planned for which he is intellectually ready.

- Does he pay attention throughout a short story?
- How long?
- Does he usually complete his puzzles?
- Does he remember to put away each toy where it belongs?
- Does he usually remember classroom rules?
- Can he group objects by color? by shape? by size?
- Can he select all the foods from non-foods?
- Does he solve simple problems independently (get something out of reach)?
- Does he ask questions when he needs information?
- Are his answers usually labels, phrases, or sentences?

Careful observing and listening to children should take place all during the year. This information should be reflected in curriculum plans and in goals set for each child.

SUMMARY

Being "ready" for any new activity means having had all the previous learnings needed to be able to benefit or learn from the new activity. Since physical, affective, and cognitive skills in the early years usually develop in a known order, there must be no gaps in the sequences of a child's learning. Gaps can mean that the child will not be ready for his next school experience.

Teachers of young children must learn to carefully observe students to determine for which kinds of experiences each child is ready. These observations should be used in planning curriculum. In this way, each child learns from his new experiences because he is ready for them.

SUGGESTED ACTIVITIES

- Observe a five-year-old child as if you were to plan activities for him/her. Make a list of ten preschool activities for which you think the child is ready. Justify your choices.

- Using your same notes, make a list of ten preschool activities for which the child is not ready. Explain why you think he is not ready for these activities.

- Observe a three-year-old child. Compare the observations with those of the five-year-old. Can you see any possible "gaps" in the development of the older child? Explain briefly.

REVIEW

A.   Define each of the following.

1.   Readiness.

2.   Developmental skills chart.

3.   Large muscle activities.

4.   Critical period for mental health and personality development.

5.   Affective behavior.

6.   Parallel play.

7.   Categories.

B.   Briefly explain each of the following.

1.   How to determine which motor activities to teach a three-year-old girl.

2.   How to determine which level of cognitive tasks should be given a four-year-old boy.

3.   How to determine the needs of a five-year-old girl in developing affective skills.

unit 4 a theory of instruction

OBJECTIVES

After studying this unit, the student should be able to

- Define a theory of instruction, its rationale, teaching strategies, and teaching techniques and explain how they are related.

- Discuss a rationale for early childhood education.

- Discuss planning strategies and teaching strategies for three kinds of learnings for very young children in school.

A teacher must have a *theory of instruction,* a set of ideas that is the basis for plans of what to teach the child, how to teach the child, and why it should be done in a particular way. These ideas give purpose to the teacher's plans and behavior. They are individual, personal beliefs about the best ways to help the very young child learn.

Each teacher needs to develop an individual theory of instruction. It should have in it a rationale, teaching strategies, and teaching techniques. A *rationale* is a set of guidelines a teacher can use in making decisions. The guidelines are helpful in designing curriculum and when deciding school or classroom policies.

Teaching strategies should be based on the teacher's rationale. When she has decided on what to teach, she needs to know a variety of ways that she can teach any particular skill or concept. All of the ways must be in agreement with her rationale. For example, if her rationale states that levels of skill are always learned best in a fixed order, then one strategy would be to list and teach the steps of a skill in order, easiest to hardest. She would not omit steps nor start on the third level of difficulty. She would always teach the skill according to her rationale.

When the teacher has decided on what she believes and on strategies based on her beliefs, then she is ready to develop *techniques* to be used in the school for applying the strategies. These procedures may vary according to the situation. Therefore, a teacher needs to know many techniques for motivating children to learn, for developing a good relationship with each child, and for having methods of reaching the mind of each child while helping him to grow physically and socially as well.

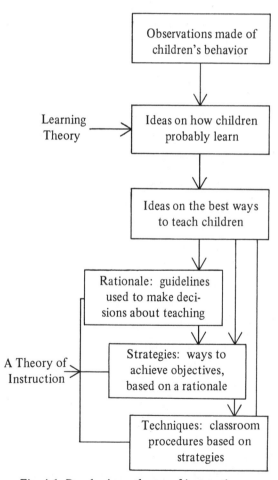

Fig. 4-1 Developing a theory of instruction.

ASSUMPTIONS

The following ideas are extracted from units 1, 2, and 3. They are assumptions on which a rationale may be based.

- Any plans to teach children should be based on what is known about how they learn.

- Knowing developmental stages of children helps adults to know what may be expected of a child.

- Children experience the developmental stages in a fixed order, but the ages at which they reach a stage may differ.

- Particular experiences are critical at certain periods of the young child's life.

- Readiness for any new experience means "having had all the experiences prerequisite to being able to benefit from the new one."

- Children learn best if a task is broken down into several simple steps that build up to the goal task. The steps should be presented in order, simplest to most complex.

- The teacher is responsible for finding ways to motivate each child to learn.

- Children learn many things by discovering them on their own in an environment that is planned by the teacher with discovery in mind.

---

1. Is the child ready for these materials?
2. Are there too many/enough/too few materials?
3. Can the child succeed at this task?
4. Will he think he can succeed?
5. How can he be motivated to try?
6. Is the group the right size for this activity?
7. Is the lesson short enough?
8. Are the children ready to take turns?
9. Is this the next task in developing this skill?
10. Are the children ready for this? In language? conceptually? physically? socially?

Fig. 4-2   In planning a lesson, the teacher must be guided by the answers to these questions.

RATIONALE

When a teacher accepts the assumptions stated above, her rationale may include the following points.

Fig. 4-3   There must be time for each child to choose his own activity.

- It is important to note at which stage of development (physical, social, and intellectual) each child is.

- These observations should be compared with developmental skills charts so the next steps can be planned for each child.

- Every child needs time daily for social-interaction and for independent discovery learning.

- Physical needs must be met before a child can be expected to respond socially and intellectually; a hungry child cannot learn well.

- Gaps in a child's development must be filled before he is expected to progress. If a child's large muscle development is poor, he should not be taught to read or write until he has mastered some gross-motor skills.

- The classroom and materials should be planned so that the child who is self-motivated to learn has many materials for learning independently. This leaves the teacher more time to develop motivational experiences for other children.

- Whenever possible, new concepts should be introduced using three-dimensional objects. Then the concept should be reviewed using two-dimensional-like objects (cutouts). A review of the ideas later using pictures or symbols will thoroughly reinforce the concept in the child's mind (Bruner's theory).

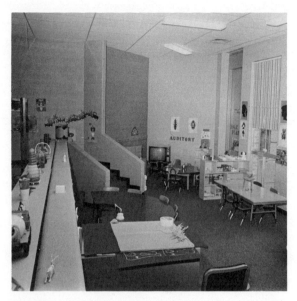

Fig. 4-4 Having a variety of independent activities available helps children to become self-motivated learners.

- Children need to be challenged only a little each time so that they can succeed. The success experience helps a child think well of himself. This motivates him to continue to learn. Too great a challenge results in frustration.

- Parents and teachers are important to the child's development. Involving parents in their child's school experience is necessary for maximum results.

Each teacher will want to add to the above list according to her own knowledge and experience. When she must make a decision about strategies or techniques to use in teaching, she should find guidance in her rationale.

STRATEGIES

Every teacher depends upon numerous ways to reach her goals in the classroom. The following ideas are worthy of every teacher's consideration. When planning strategies, the teacher should

- Know the current conditions and abilities of every child. This should be available in written records.

- Determine for which activities each child is ready.

- Write lesson plans for each week including *behavioral objectives* (what the child is expected

to learn or to do). These should reflect the children's needs and readiness.

- Plan the room so that all the materials in it will be helpful in furthering the development of the children and will meet their current needs.

- Determine the language of instruction for each event if the children and program are not *monolingual* (use one language).

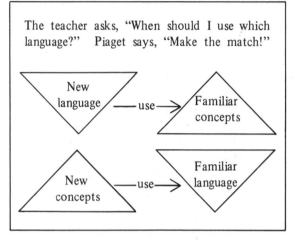

The teacher asks, "When should I use which language?" Piaget says, "Make the match!"

New language —use→ Familiar concepts

New concepts —use→ Familiar language

Fig. 4-5 In a bilingual (use of more than one language) program, the language of instruction can be determined by making a match with either familiar concepts or familiar language according to the purpose of the lesson.

- Implement (put into action) the lesson plans.

- Evaluate the children's progress. If necessary, revise the next day's plans so that the learning experience will match and slightly expand what the children learned today.

The first two weeks at an early childhood education center are vital to the success of the rest of the school year. This time should be spent getting to know each student well — what he can and can not do, what kind of person he is, how well he uses language, how well he gets along with others, and how he can be motivated to learn.

Making the curriculum relevant to each child (adapting it to meet his needs today) is the secret of success for the child and for the teacher. This cannot be overemphasized when developing teaching strategy.

Many teachers prefer to use strategies recommended by educational researchers such as R.M. Gagné, author of *The Conditions of Learning* (1970). According to Gagné, each formal or directly presented lesson requires a set of teaching behaviors to be effective.

- Gaining and controlling attention.

- Telling the child what the teacher expects him to learn to do.

- Helping the child recall some previous learnings he will need.

- Presenting the learning materials.

- Demonstrating and/or interacting with materials.

- Providing feedback.

- Evaluating the results.

- Giving opportunity for generalizing use of the learning or skill.

- Reinforcing activities to insure retaining of the learning (Examples of these activities will be given in a later unit.)

Another type of lesson, the discovery lesson, requires different behaviors. The teacher

- Gives a group of children a set/sets of a selected type of material, for example, inch cubes.

- Gives the children time to manipulate the materials any way they choose.

- Observes their apparent learnings, and talks to the children about them:

  "Why did you put these together?"

  "Tell us about your building."

  "Whose tower is taller?"

  "Which group has more colors?"

- Points out learnings they could have discovered but did not:

  "How can we tell who used more cubes? Let's pair them this way, one-to-one and find out." (No counting ability is needed.)

- Redistributes the materials and repeats the steps listed.

- Evaluates the learning.

- Reapplies the principles using other materials to see if the concepts were learned.

Most lessons designed by the teacher for very young children will be the formally presented or discovery type lessons. However, *incidental* learning occurs in the classroom everyday. This is the unplanned situation in which a child learns something he is ready to learn. When a child unintentionally places the red paint on the blue paint and learns that this makes purple, he excitedly tells about it. The follow-ing strategy may be used for this type of situation. The teacher

- Asks the child to tell what happened.

- Asks if he thinks it could happen again, then gives him materials to verify his findings.

- Finds reinforcement materials to repeat the experience.

- Asks the child to tell others what he did and what he learned. If he is not able to verbalize the learning, he may demonstrate it to other children. (This may take several days.)

The strategies for formally presented lessons, discovery lessons, and incidental learnings are powerful teaching tools that soon become second nature to the teacher who uses them daily.

TECHNIQUES

Each teacher develops her own teaching techniques according to what works for her/him. Hopefully each teacher continues to seek ways to improve her/his techniques. Some "tried and trusted" ideas that are useful for many teachers of young children can be stated. The teacher

- Teaches in small groups of not more than eight children.

- Has lesson materials prepared well in advance and ready for use.

- Presents materials from the child's left to right (to develop eye-sweep needed later for reading and writing).

- Uses a soft, pleasant voice and an appropriate vocabulary level for the child.

- Sits on the same level as the children (so it is easy to maintain eye contact during the lesson).

- Develops a variety of ways to interest children in a lesson:

  Uses an attention signal "Look and tell me." Hides the materials in a surprise box

  Uses puppets

  States the lesson objective, "Today you will learn how to make a two-color pegboard design"

- Gives the child self-evaluation materials when possible, for example, a model sequence/correctly marked worksheet (so he can evaluate his own work).

Objective:	The child will match 24 parquetry blocks (3shapes and 3 colors) to a parquetry design card.

	A sequence for developing the needed skills.

C O L O R	The child is able to 1. discriminate objects, 2 colors, 3-D 2. discriminate objects, 3 colors, 3-D 3. discriminate objects, 3 colors, 3-D and 2-D 4. sort objects, 3 colors, 3-D and 2-D
S H A P E	5. discriminate objects, 2 shapes, 1 color, 3-D 6. discriminate objects, 3 shapes, 3 colors, 3-D 7. discriminate objects, 3 shapes, 3 colors, 2-D 8. sort objects, 3 shapes, 3 colors, 3-D and 2-D
Spatial Relations	9. identify spatial relationships visually, 3-D 10. identify spatial relationships visually, 2-D
Combined Skills	11. match objects, (16 blocks), 2 colors, 2 shapes, 3-D to 3-D 12. match objects, (20 blocks), 3 colors, 2 shapes, 3-D to 2-D 13. match objects, (24 blocks), 3 colors, 3 shapes, 3-D to 2-D

Fig. 4-6 In skill development, each step must be only a little harder than the previous one to insure success and to avoid gaps in learning.

- Tells the child how he is doing.
- Summarizes what has been learned at the end of every lesson: "Today you have been learning how to recognize sounds that are the same and sounds that are not the same."
- Gives the child materials that reinforce the concept learned in the lesson.
- Shows enthusiasm for the activity.
- Demonstrates the correct use of a new material when it is introduced; also, demonstrates how to get it out and put it away; sets a good example.
- Helps children make associations between what they have learned and are learning.
- Keeps a daily written record of observations of children who need help to achieve an objective or develop a skill, and plans accordingly.
- Uses a daily schedule, but stays flexible so that unforeseen things do not become major catastrophes.
- Uses humor when appropriate.
- Provides planned multisensory experiences daily.

- Makes teaching tools that cannot otherwise be acquired.
- Creatively redesigns lesson that must be repeated.
- Alternates physically active experiences with quiet ones.
- Criticizes bad behavior, not the person behaving:

   Do: "That is not the way to do it. I'll show you again."

   Don't: "You did that wrong again. What's the matter with you today?"

- Praises good behavior, not the person behaving:

   Do: "You did that very well, George."

   Don't: "You are a smart boy today, George."

- Has high expectations that the children will do well. Research proves that this is a vital factor in the outcome. The expectations become a self-fulfilling prophecy.
- Provides a variety of materials daily for the children to use creatively.

SUMMARY

Each teacher in an early childhood education situation should develop an individual theory of instruction. This includes a rationale of the ideas she/he considers important in teaching, those in which she/he believes wholeheartedly. Based on the rationale, teaching techniques and strategies are developed. The dedicated teacher continues to learn and to revise and expand a storehouse of ideas as long as she/he teaches. Consistently working within the framework of a personal theory of instruction helps a teacher to mature professionally.

SUGGESTED ACTIVITIES

- Give serious thought to what you have observed and learned so far. Write down at least three ideas (not given in this book) that you want to include in your own rationale for a theory of instruction for the teacher of very young children.
- List one teaching strategy for each of the three new ideas for your rationale. Show the relationship.
- List one teaching technique based on each teaching strategy that you listed.

REVIEW

A. Define each of the following terms and explain the relationships among them: theory of instruction, rationale, teaching strategies, teaching techniques.

B. Select the item in column II which briefly defines each term in column I.

Column I		Column II
1.	Rationale	a. planned unstructured lesson
2.	Developmental stage	b. teacher expectations
3.	Fine-motor skills	c. using a soft, pleasant voice
4.	Relevant curriculum	d. planned structured lesson
5.	Formal learning	e. model design card
6.	Discovery learning	f. reading and writing
7.	Incidental learning	g. educational beliefs
8.	Teaching technique	h. level of skills
9.	Self-evaluation	i. unplanned learning
10.	Self-fulfilling prophecy	j. learnings that meet the child's needs

C. Select three of the rationale statements given earlier in the unit. After each one, list any strategies and/or techniques stated in the book that are based upon the statements selected.

Section II Staffing and Curriculum

unit 5 unit teaching

OBJECTIVES

After studying this unit, the student should be able to

- Explain what is meant by unit teaching in regard to selecting classroom materials and planning curriculum.
- Select and list appropriate unit topics for a year of preschool curriculum in the order in which they would probably be used.
- List criteria for the selection of appropriate materials to use in the curriculum.

When a teacher has developed a theory of instruction with which she/he is comfortable, curriculum may be planned. In some schools for very young children, there is no planned curriculum. Materials are placed in a room and the children are free to learn from them in any way they can.

A similar method is used in other early childhood schools, but the materials are selected according to the developmental needs of the children. As the needs change, the materials are changed. There is very little adult-child interaction.

Each year more schools for very young students plan their curriculum in advance. There is much variation, however. The administrators of a school may dictate which curriculum is to be used or provide a curriculum guide. In many schools the teachers as a group design the curriculum. In others, each teacher teaches whatever she thinks is best for the children in her class.

In designing curriculum, many options must be carefully considered. Where there is a planned curriculum, it is most often composed of units of work, each with a central topic or theme. A unit may include plans for the following:

- Concept development (the topic or theme)
- Activities that expand the topic
- Perceptual skill development
- Related activities, such as field trips
- Other kinds of learnings (language, art, math, science, music, motor skills)

THE CHILD'S INTERESTS

The child learns best when he is naturally interested in a topic or a material. If it appeals to him, he is motivated to learn. Little children are happiest with familiar ideas. Many familiar subjects can be expanded for them: self, family, home, pets, clothing, foods, and toys.

The tremendous curiosity of the very young child makes him naturally a scientist. He explores, observes, concludes, then reexplores in every environment in which he finds himself.

Children like and need a lot of room for large muscle activities. The great outdoors is an appropriate place for much of their learning. Animals, plants, soil, sand, and water provide many concepts and

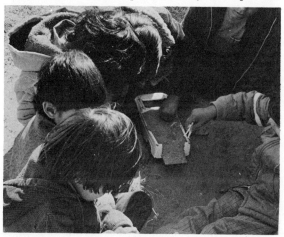

Fig. 5-1   Little children enjoy exploring natural materials.

much fun. The weather and the seasons are popular subjects. The topic of *the natural environment* is inexhaustible.

Since machines are an important part of everyday living, familiar ones, such as the telephone and the family car, lead to interesting studies of communication and transportation on the child's level of understanding. The world of machines includes a variety — from vacuum cleaners and floor polishers in the school to heavy-duty building-construction cranes. The carpenter's power tools and the school's dishwasher are equally fascinating to the very young child.

When the student is ready to enlarge his world, the surrounding community is filled with exciting people who are indirectly a part of the child's life. These are the community helpers: police officer, firefighter, doctor, plumber, librarian, nurse, teacher, and many others. Usually visiting or being visited by as many of these people as possible creates lasting impressions of his community for the child. Career-awareness commercial materials are now available for preschool programs.

Local and national holidays are important. Children's birthdays and suitable folklore traditions deserve attention in the curriculum also.

Fig. 5-2 Simple folk dances are a highly motivating learning experience for the young child.

SELECTING THE UNITS

The scheduling of some of the suggested subjects is dictated by circumstances beyond the control of the teacher. The weather, seasonal changes, and dates of celebrations are among them.

The newness of school life tells the teacher that the most familiar topics are best to help the child adjust to this great change in his life. Even temporary separation from home and family is often traumatic for a very young child. Learning that there are many friendly adults in the school helps him to feel at home there more quickly. He should become familiar with many aspects of the school so that he does not have vague worries and uneasiness from a fear of the unknown.

Some of the themes suggested may not require a whole unit of the curriculum. Learning about the natural environment may be a continuing part of several units (food, toys, community helpers such as the farmer.) The classroom itself should have some living plant or animal in it at all times. It is better to have both, and a variety of them during the year. Planting a small garden at the appropriate time of the year is a good activity regardless of the unit topic being explored.

Special events in a community may help the teacher decide when to use a unit on animals. The annual visit of a circus may be a deciding factor.

There is no one best schedule of topics. Each school's plan should be made to best meet the needs of its children while it makes the best use of the natural scene and local community resources.

In designing curriculum, these ideas should be considered:

Fig. 5-3 Caring for animals also teaches responsibility.

- The first units should be on topics that are familiar to the children.

- Themes related to fixed dates (Thanksgiving, Christmas) must be planned into the schedule first.

- There should be no set time for the length of a unit. Some themes have more factual information on the child's level of understanding than others. Interest in some themes may be greater than in others. Either is a good reason to spend one or more extra days on the subject.

Since scheduling of some field trips and locating special kinds of materials must be done well in advance, it is wise to have the unit topics for the whole school year selected and sequenced before the year begins. It is important, though, to keep the schedule flexible. If a teacher wishes to resequence the topics so she can correlate them with an activity she had not anticipated, this should be possible. Such events as a stock show, ice show, air show, and local holiday celebrations are typical of these events. They are essential in the child's growing awareness of the world about him.

About Self:	About Other People:
I Can Do It	Community Helpers
My Family	Indians
My Home	Eskimos
My Body	Black Americans
What I have Learned	Mexican-Americans
My Vacation Plans	(Fiesta week)
Holiday Celebrations:	About Animals:
Halloween	Pets
Thanksgiving	Forest Animals
Christmas	The Zoo
Valentine's Day	Others:
The Alamo	Seasons
St. Patrick's Day	Transportation
Easter	Communication
Diez y Seis	Gardening

Fig. 5-4   Unit topics used during the school year in a Headstart kindergarten class in southwest Texas.

When a school buys a specific curriculum (commercially produced), such flexibility may not be possible. The skill development and learning goals may be so carefully sequenced that the units must be used in the prescribed order. In these circumstances, the teacher may add a mini-unit of her own between two of the others. This permits her to make use of a special local event not related to the printed curriculum.

SELECTING MATERIALS

The purpose of the curriculum is to help every child achieve all he is capable of in his physical, intellectual, and social-emotional development. Materials to be used should be selected with this purpose in mind.

Unit-Related Materials

Many of the materials used should be related to the theme of the unit. Unit-related materials are needed to

- Present information on the specific topic.

- Reinforce the ideas presented.

- Permit the child to reflect his new learnings.

- Provide creative outlets for the child's feelings about the topic.

A unit topic may be reflected in pictures, fingerplays, stories, the objects themselves (as animals), manipulatives (flannelboard materials), and role-playing accessories (such as "pretend uniforms"). Often some of each of these are available, depending upon the topic. Children need to see, hear, touch, smell and taste unit-related materials to absorb the concepts being presented. Some of these materials and activities are listed for a unit on Autumn.

- Pictures, action songs, fingerplays, and poems about autumn.

- Books about seasonal change, effects on animals.

- Puzzles: boy raking leaves, harvest scene, apple tree.

- Fire extinguisher: review *safety rules* for using heaters/furnaces.
- Practice fire drill.

- Take a nature walk to observe trees in stages of defoliating.

- Draw/paint trees as remembered from nature walk.

- Take nature walk to gather leaves and seeds.

- Sort the gathered items, describe, label, plant some, use some to make a collage mural (10' x 24") on autumn (left end may be a summer scene, right end a fall scene. Backgrounds, scenery, and people's clothing will differ).

- Story of the nature walk or of the collage may be taped or written in children's words and illustrated on an experience chart for some of the children to use to retell the story.

Non-Unit-Related Materials

There should also be available some materials that are not related to any unit. These materials help develop skills. Parquetry design blocks, pegboards, inch cubes, wooden beads for stringing, and puzzles are popular. These provide variety, interest, and change of pace. Other examples are indoor-outdoor motor training equipment, books, and records. A variety of creative materials are needed for drawing, painting, *collage* (pasting art), woodworking, clay molding, and making costumes and puppets.

Criteria for Selecting Materials

It is best to ask some questions in selecting a material or piece of equipment:

- Will it assist in developing the concepts of the unit?
- Will it encourage the non-unit interests of the children?
- Does it add balance to the curriculum? .
- Will it provide a safe outlet for children's feelings?
- Is it worth the cost?
- Is there a suitable substitute that costs less?
- Is it developmentally correct for these children?
- Is it safe and of good quality?
- Is it fun to use?

CAUTION: The teacher is responsible for the safety of her students. Accidents do happen, but often they can be prevented. Be safety-conscious in selecting materials and equipment! Poor quality construction, sharp edges, pointed parts, poor quality paint, and rough boards must be avoided.

Materials for Interest Centers

The short attention span and multiple interests of the very young child call for numerous interest centers in the classroom. Each center has its own set of furnishings. The child is taught to get materials out, to use them appropriately, and to put them away. This develops independence and encourages self-discipline.

Some of the interest centers should be reasonably permanent. This creates an atmosphere of stability for the child. He counts on finding them there. The book, art, construction, and role-playing areas plus manipulatives (pegs, beads, puzzles,) are found in most preschool classrooms. A well furnished classroom will also regularly include math, science, music, and "discovery" areas. The materials in each of these areas should be changed often — weekly or at the end of each unit.

Centers to be set up occasionally might be a carpentry center, sand or water play, sewing center, pouring and measuring materials. Some of these activities may be a part of the "discovery" table. Such a table may be filled with interesting objects for sensory experiences. These may be bought or made by the teacher or children. Some practical examples are listed:

- Sound boxes: pill or match boxes or paper cups with lids; each contains a different material and makes a different sound when shaken; rice, beans, and paper clips may be used.
- Nested objects: three sizes of an object that fit inside one another; bleach bottles, milk cartons, plastic cups, boxes may be used.
- Surprise box: any closed box with a small opening; it contains familiar objects for the child to identify by feeling.
- Carrot tops: top inch of a carrot placed in water sprouts a lovely green plant.
- Color paddles: clear plastic paddles in primary colors; help the child learn how to combine the colors to make secondary colors.
- Texture book: pages contain many textures of cloth, paper, plastic, and other materials for *tactile* (feeling) experiences.

The children spend time each day happily and independently discovering which sounds are the same or different, how to order by size, how to identify by touching, how a plant grows, and how water evaporates. Language development results from all of these. The child loves to use new words such as "crinkly," "slick," "corrugated."

When getting ready to begin a new unit, change some of the materials in the room. For example, if the unit is to be on "pets," the following changes might be made.

- The "Pets" theme may be represented in some of the puzzles, books, and teaching pictures, and recordings.

- Fish or turtle in bowl may be added to science area.

- Discovery table may have small containers of various kinds of pet foods added. Each should have a picture of the pet near it.

- Picture of dog house may be placed near block area.

- Materials to improvise a pet store or veterinarians' office may be placed in role-playing area.

For each unit, the materials related to the unit should be planned for each interest center as well as with the lessons in mind.

Materials for Outdoor Activities

Small motor muscle training takes place when children play with manipulative materials each day. Time for large muscle activities should be included daily also. Outdoor playground equipment is usually stationary. Wheel toys are varied and encourage creativity (a wagon can be innumerable things in the child's play). Playing ball is excellent exercise. The younger the child, the larger and lighter weight the ball should be. A variety of types of balls holds the children's interest.

Fig. 5-5   Playing ball helps develop the large muscles and is fun.

Old car and truck tires have many uses on the playground. They can be swings, ladders, obstacle courses, objects for pushing and pulling, mini-sandboxes, and borders for small gardens.

Children enjoy playing with mud and snow. They are excellent materials for experiments involving the effects of heat and cold.

Fig. 5-6   Children's creative artwork using natural materials—seeds, rocks, shells, feathers, or sticks.

Natural rocks and stones are highly prized preschool materials. Digging, collecting, cleaning, and displaying all contribute toward affective and motor development. Seeds, sticks, seashells, and feathers are other natural materials that are highly motivating toward creativity.

CAUTION: A teacher must supervise the use of natural materials at all times. She must guide the child in the safe use of each one. She must clarify concepts, answer questions and lead in the cleanup activities. She may also have to convince mothers of the educational value of playing in mud!

COORDINATING SKILLS

The child receives the best quality of skill training when it is coordinated into the curriculum. As a unit is being planned, there must be a constant checking to insure that there is a balance among the kinds of skill training planned into the unit. First, the planner must know the needs of her children. Then she must know alternatives to include in the environment that reinforce the concepts taught. She must make tentative choices to meet the children's needs. For example, if the children are weaker on language skills than on motor skills, the teacher may plan to shorten the outdoor play time and spend the time on extra language experiences. She may also plan outdoor language activities. All of these arrangements can be made regardless of the unit theme.

Plan for Coordinating Skills

1. Assess children's individual skill needs.

2. Make tentative unit plans (lessons, activities, interest centers) to meet children's needs.

3. Adjust the plans for a balanced program.

4. Select materials to use with the plan.

5. Divide the tasks among staff members.

Fig. 5-7 The teaching team cooperates in planning, then shares the work.

INDIVIDUALIZATION

It is an accepted fact that young children, just like adult students, have a variety of learning styles. All of them must be accommodated.

- Bill must handle objects, hear teacher tell about them, and see them in books before he is ready to talk about them.

- Bob is very curious and talkative. He asks three questions about an object before the teacher can tell about it.

- Karen is shy but learns quickly. She may be the last in a group to verbalize her ideas, but she may be the first to use new equipment correctly and helps others to do so.

Daily observation of the learning styles of the children helps the teacher meet the unique needs of individuals. It helps her plan the abundance of materials and activities needed in every unit plan.

SUMMARY

The curriculum for very young children is usually composed of units, each with a theme or topic. It is important to begin with topics that are familiar to the child and to expand his concepts of them. Some units, such as celebrating Thanksgiving Day, are fixed on the school calendar. Others may be sequenced as the staff desires.

Many of the classroom materials and activities should reflect the unit theme. Others are needed, however, to encourage other interests of the children. A unit should be planned to meet all the needs of the children — physical, social-emotional, and intellectual.

Children have different learning styles. This means that many options must be given the children if individualization is to become a classroom reality. Coordinating skill development and concept development demands unit planning, and daily reviewing and revising of plans.

SUGGESTED ACTIVITIES

- Make a list of at least twenty unit topics for a school year for a curriculum for five-year-olds. Place them in sequence in which they can probably be used.

- For ten of the units listed, briefly state the kinds of role-playing activities that might be planned. Suggest some appropriate materials for each one.

- For one of the units listed, list four concepts that should be developed. Describe the materials to be placed in the interest centers to help develop the theme.

REVIEW

A. List five areas of learning that may be included in planning a unit of curriculum.

B. List five of the child's natural interests that may be included in planning a year's curriculum.

C. When preparing the classroom to begin a new unit, what are the kinds of materials that can be changed to represent the new theme?

D. What are five of the things a child may independently learn from a "discovery table"?

E. What are six important questions to ask in selecting a material or piece of equipment?

F. Briefly explain a procedure for developing a unit plan that includes ways to meet the needs of all the children.

unit 6 team teaching

OBJECTIVES

After studying this unit, the student should be able to

- List the qualities needed by every member of a teaching team if the team effort is to be successful.
- Briefly discuss the daily responsibilities of the teaching team and the kind of leadership needed.
- State five positive aspects of team teaching.

Team teaching refers to two or more adults working together to provide learning experiences for a group of children. The work includes planning, putting plans into action, and evaluating the results again and again during the year.

THE TEAM

The positions held by the members of a teaching team are

Director: an administrator who also teaches children.

Teacher: the person in charge of classroom lessons and setting; usually has a degree, is certified, or both.

Assistant teacher: teacher with less responsibility for the total program but with many of the same tasks as the teacher; may be certified.

Teacher's aide: an uncertified person who does not teach lessons but assists the team by gathering and preparing materials, doing clerical work and classroom housekeeping.

Volunteer worker: any unpaid worker in the classroom; may work daily or weekly — may sometimes function as an aide, assistant teacher, or teacher.

Any combination of the positions named may form a teaching team. The following kinds of teams are found frequently in classes for very young children:

- A teacher and an assistant teacher for fifteen to twenty-five children (many Head Start groups).
- Two teachers and one teacher's aide for two classes totaling fifty children (many public school kindergartens).
- A teacher and two or more assistant teachers as needed to maintain a one to ten ratio of adults to children (many good child development centers for very young children).
- A teacher and any number of parent volunteers (parent co-op schools, organized and operated by parents).
- A teacher and two to six college student teachers (nonpaid) (early childhood laboratory schools at universities and colleges).
- Director, teacher, and babysitters (commercial day-care centers).

Specific task assignments for the members of a team vary with each situation. However, there are some factors common to any good teaching team for very young children. The members must have

- Mutual respect for one another.
- Mutual high expectations for the children.
- Agreement on what is to be taught.
- Consistency in enforcing the classroom rules.
- Willingness to share in the work of preparation, teaching, and the other tasks vital to the care of the children.

Every team functions best if a leader is named. This responsibility may be a permanent one. In some classrooms it is rotated among the teacher/teachers and assistants. The leader is the coordinator for the team, the one who puts it all together and makes it go. This requires a willingness to assume some extra tasks needed to combine the efforts of individuals into a unified operation. This is needed to provide a harmonious, emotionally warm setting in which children can grow socially and emotionally. Without this kind

A = Teacher B = Assistant Teacher	Assigned
Preparation for Unit _____	
1. Role-playing area: Housekeeping and dress-ups, mirror	A B
2. Books: replace 12 with some on family and homes	B
3. Language Arts: discussion of pictures of boys, girls, both, family members, various kinds of homes; fingerplay	A
4. Visual discrimination: Name tags made in triplicate; child must find the ones that match his.	B
5. Auditory discrimination: three new songs	B
6. Motor: volleyball for throwing and catching	B
7. Creative art: lengths of butcher paper for life size "Me" dolls; markers and crayons, stencils for circles, ovals, and triangles for children to cut to use as facial parts to paste faces; scraps of cloth; precut clothing items. Child will select and glue onto figure drawings (also stenciled).	A B A B A B A

Fig. 6-1   Task assignments for preparing materials for a unit. Daily tasks and lessons will also be assigned.

Teacher/Assistant Teacher Evaluation		
Name: _____ Position: _____		
I Preparedness:		
Room	Materials	Lessons
II Presentation of Curriculum:	Gathering the group Attaining objective	Presenting lesson Transition
III Supervision:	Handling of behavior problems Controlling flow of classroom traffic Interacting with other adults	Playground Snack Lunch
IV Team Member:	Sharing classroom chores Conferring with others Discussing children's needs	Promptness Enthusiasm

Fig. 6-2   This type of evaluation sheet may be designed by a supervisor, director, or principal.

of leadership, a team may be like an otherwise good boat without a rudder — lacking in direction. The team leader must have a long-range view of the goals set for the girls and boys in the class. The goals must be clearly communicated to the other team members so that the objectives can be reached.

If leadership is not felt by the members of the team, they should state this lack and actively seek direction. Each team member should know what is expected of her/him. Each member also needs to know when he is doing his work well and how to improve his job performance.

In some teams, the leadership is dictatorial. Authoritarian attitudes are usually not well accepted. Some good results may be achieved by using only one person's ideas, but often this causes discord and results in a frequent turnover in personnel. More democratic methods of conducting teamwork are desirable.

- They are a better model for the children.

- Most people function and "grow" better when their opinions count.

- "None of us is as smart as all of us."

The quality of the learning in a classroom is better when it is enriched with the ideas of all the members of the teaching team.

DAILY RESPONSIBILITIES

An effective program in any classroom for young students depends upon the successful carrying out of daily responsibilities. A teacher alone in a classroom must attend to everything; the members of a teaching team share the tasks. A minimal list of the tasks includes the following:

- The room must be made ready and inviting before the children arrive.

- Climate conditions must be controlled (light, ventilation, heat).

- Materials and equipment must be ready.

- Teachers and assistant teachers must be prepared to teach.

- Curriculum must be presented and evaluated.

- The learning must be evaluated.

- Children must be listened to individually.

- Administrative requirements must be met (attendance records, forms, curriculum results).

- Plans for the next day must be previewed or revised if necessary.

There are days when many other jobs need to be done. Field trips, parent involvement, coordinating other volunteers, and attending meetings sometimes seem almost daily tasks. Each member of a team should know what is expected of him/her in these extra tasks. In cases of emergency, members should expect extra tasks.

If there is a home-liaison staff member, many time-consuming contacts may be made by her. If there is not such person, then a member of the team must make each of these communications with parents.

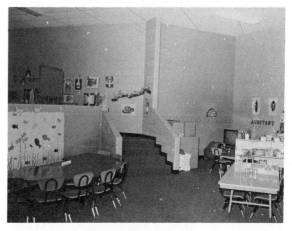

Fig. 6-3   An attractive classroom in an early childhood education center ready for use.

These are sometimes a daily occurence: the child who has had an accident, broken out with chickenpox, been absent three days, did not bring money needed. Also, there should be pleasant positive contacts made with parents so that they learn to think of the school and teachers with pleasure.

ASSIGNING TASKS

When the plans for a unit are made, the tasks must be assigned or assumed by the members of the team. The leader (director/teacher/assistant) may assign tasks according to her best judgment, or she may ask for volunteers. In the ideal situation, an understanding develops so that each person regularly assumes a share of the work and knows that every team member can be counted on to be responsible.

It is important that all agreements or assignments are made at the planning stage. This gives each person the most time possible to prepare. It also makes possible an objective evaluation of the team's work after the unit has been completed.

At the end of each school day, the team reviews the events of the day. This may mean changing the plans that had been made for the next day. For example:

- The classification game scheduled for the next day requires that the children understand the concept of a vehicle, but the children do not seem sure of the concept yet. Change: Postpone the game. Design new activity to reinforce the concept of vehicle (teach the concept again instead of testing it).

- Word is received that Billy's mother is going to bring treats tomorrow for Billy's birthday. The

During Unit # _____	Yes	No	Explain (other)
1. Was prompt daily			
2. Was prepared daily			
3. Taught satisfactorily			
4. Approved the curriculum			
5. Evaluated children's gains			
6. Encouraged creativity			
7. Had good rapport with children			
8. Had no serious discipline problems			
9. Had good rapport with adults			
10. Enjoyed being on a team			

Fig. 6-4   One type of teacher's self-evaluation sheet.

Fig. 6-5   Teachers must review lesson plans and evaluate units of work.

treats were expected next week on his birthday but his mother will be working then. Change: Postpone tomorrow's popping popcorn lesson in the morning. Have the afternoon motor lesson in the morning and Billy's birthday treat in the afternoon.

- Not all of the children reached the lesson objective in auditory discrimination today. Change: Tomorrow some children will have the regularly planned next-harder auditory lesson. Others will repeat a version of today's lesson.

- Mary Lou shows more affection to Paul than he appreciates. Change: See that they are not in the same small groups for lessons tomorrow.

- Raul's mother says she will come to help tomorrow. Change: Plan some activities for her to use with children who are having difficulty with cutting. They must be purposeful, not just cutting up magazines without an objective.

These changes are only a few of those that every team faces in the review at the end of the day.

POSITIVE ASPECTS

There are numerous advantages in team teaching. The experiences of each team member add to the richness of the setting and the quality of the whole program. Also the work load for each person is lighter. This leaves more time for planning and usually leads to a better curriculum.

Staff members are also parents and human beings. This means there are some unavoidable absences due to illness or emergency situations. Where there is no team, the absence of a teacher is often difficult for the children. Even if a substitute is always available, few can duplicate a teacher's way with children even when there are good lesson plans. Children depend on the emotional support they receive from having the same person with them everyday. Having one familiar team member present to see that the routine is the familiar one prevents the children from being upset by the absence of another.

There are times when a person working with children becomes discouraged. On some days, problems can gather more quickly than they can be solved. At these times, the presence of a team member who understands is a great help. Although the teacher who is alone in the classroom probably has a director, coordinator, or principal, their administrative role may prevent the empathy that exists between members of the same teaching team.

Some educators feel that the greatest advantage of team teaching is that it lets the children benefit from each team member's strengths. The teacher who can teach music best can give better musical experiences to the entire group. Some team members avoid even the most basic math concepts because they are ill at ease with math. A team member who likes the subject may help all the children learn to like math.

Fig. 6-6   In an early simple math lesson, the young child may be asked to place the circles by size in the same order as the triangles, then asked to order the rectangles the same way.

This does not mean that one teacher cannot teach everything well. Some teachers do, but most of them will admit to a weakness in one or more areas. Such a problem can often be overcome when there is a great variety of talents in the members of a team. It is safe to say that there are aspects of team teaching that are positive for both the children and the adults in a classroom for very young children.

SPECIAL TEACHER APTITUDES

Working with very young children requires special skills and attitudes:

- An understanding of how children grow and learn.

- A knowledge of good learning experiences and materials suitable for the child in each of the early years.

- Ability to enjoy being with children daily.

- Ability to observe and evaluate the child's readiness for varied learnings.

- A positive attitude toward parents.

- The determination to see that the children develop physically, intellectually, socially, and emotionally.

To be a member of a teaching team requires some additional special aptitudes:

- Willingness to share the credit for what is good: "We did it together."

- Willingness to share the blame if things do not turn out as planned: "We are all at fault."

- Willingness to accept the ideas of others even if they seem no better than ours.

- Ability to admit that other people are just as dedicated to the children.

- Ability to accept constructive criticism for the sake of improving the team effort.

- Flexibility to accommodate changing responsibilities, changing children, and changing team rapport.

Few persons begin team teaching having all the aptitudes listed. A beginner can soon develop a sense of "belonging." Under good leadership, a year of team teaching is an excellent way to grow as a person while working toward the growth of children.

SUMMARY

A teaching team of two or more adults contains a variety of staff roles, but all the members of a team must agree on the curriculum, class rules, and high expectations for the children. They must have mutual respect and willingness to share the work. Leadership must be evident for a team to be effective.

The team members each perform daily responsibilities toward controlling and preparing the learning environment and in implementing curriculum plans. Great flexibility is required because of daily changes that may be necessary.

Some positive aspects of team teaching are

- Greater resources of information

- Lighter workload per person

- More time for planning
- Continuity when one team member is absent
- Utilization of the strong points of each team member's teaching abilities.

SUGGESTED ACTIVITIES

- Observe a teaching team in an early childhood education center in action. Describe the kinds of team member cooperation or interaction you witness.
- From your observations, list any daily responsibilities of the team members that are not stated in this unit.
- Visit a second preschool classroom where there is team teaching. Compare your observations of both classes on the following items:
  a. Qualities every team member should have
  b. Division of the tasks among team members
  c. Daily responsibilities in evidence
  d. Parent involvement and how it was handled
  e. Evidence of the positive aspects of team teaching

REVIEW

A. List the qualities needed in every team member of a teaching team if the team effort is to be successful.

B. Briefly discuss the daily responsibilities of a teaching team and the kind of leadership needed.

C. List five kinds of changes for the next day that may have to be made in an end-of-the-day review by the team.

D. List five positive aspects of team teaching.

E. List at least five special aptitudes a member of a teaching team should have.

unit 7 open classrooms

OBJECTIVES

After studying this unit, the student should be able to

- Describe a preschool open classroom and explain the basic philosophy for it.
- Describe four ways in which a curriculum may be structured.
- Define the following: individualization (in education), unstructured learning, British infant schools, content-oriented curriculum, process-oriented curriculum, affective development curriculum.

The open classroom concept sees the ideal room as a large open area, perhaps twice the usual size of a preschool classroom. Throughout the room, many interest centers or learning stations are in view. Each of these gives the child a chance to learn in a different way or with different materials.

There are usually the same permanent interest centers found in a traditional classroom for very young girls and boys. At the same time there are some of the "occasional" centers of the traditional room. These may be seasonal in theme or they may be uniquely related to the special interests of some of the children in the class.

In such a room there may be twice the number of children usually found in a class of preschool children. The ratio of adults to children may be the

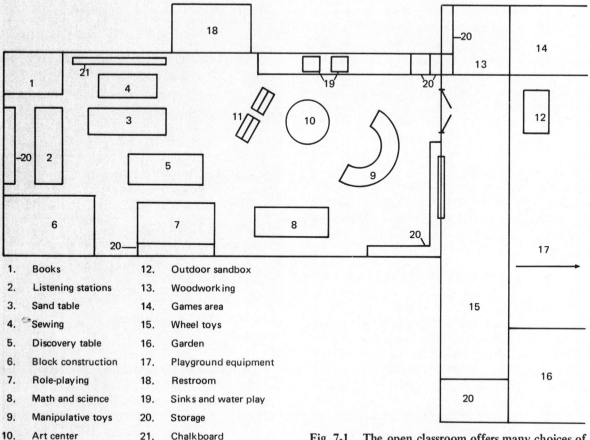

1. Books	12. Outdoor sandbox
2. Listening stations	13. Woodworking
3. Sand table	14. Games area
4. Sewing	15. Wheel toys
5. Discovery table	16. Garden
6. Block construction	17. Playground equipment
7. Role-playing	18. Restroom
8. Math and science	19. Sinks and water play
9. Manipulative toys	20. Storage
10. Art center	21. Chalkboard
11. Easels	

Fig. 7-1 The open classroom offers many choices of both indoor and outdoor activities.

same as in a traditional classroom, however. Each child has many more interest centers to attract him; he must make more choices each day.

BASIC PHILOSOPHY

Today it is agreed that each person is unique. His whole experience before and after birth is different from that of any other person. For this reason, it is now believed that schools have erred in giving many children the same experience in a room. If each child is unique, his needs for school are likely to be different from those of other children. This reasoning is the basis for seeking *individualization* (tailoring curriculum so that it meets the needs of individuals).

Some educators think that learning occurs best when the curriculum is centered on the child's interests as he communicates them to the teacher. Others believe that the child can take much more responsibility for selecting what he is ready to learn and wants to know than the school is willing to give him. People who believe strongly in individualization and in giving children more choices of what and how to learn are excited about the open classroom concept.

The child in an open classroom has a wide variety of work to choose from. Making more decisions can lead to making better decisions. This kind of environment permits each child to use his own learning style. If he wants to learn about shapes from manipulative toys, he may do so. If he prefers to learn about shapes by making them in damp sand, he is permitted to do this. The child who loves the outdoors may build box buildings creatively in a place designed outside for this. At the same time some boys and girls may be designing a block building indoors. Those who believe in the open concept for preschools say that each child learns more by doing it in the way he prefers, using his own learning style.

FORMS

The British infant schools use one form of open classrooms. A head-mistress has nearly the same responsibilities as a school principal in the United States. She has another serious responsibility; she is in charge of curriculum. She may choose what is to be taught in her school. Since the teaching team is always trying to teach through the interests of the children, she works very closely with them to see that the children are learning.

The large room is lined with interest centers. The middle of the room contains more of them. There are classroom doors to the playyard, and the

children are free to learn outdoors when they wish. There are interest centers on the playground as well as traditional outdoor playground equipment.

1. Woodworking equipment	6. Tree house
2. Wheel toys	7. Live animals
3. Sandbox	8. Flower beds
4. Vegetable gardens	9. Outdoor cooking facilities
5. Swings and similar items	10. Construction materials (boxes, tires)

Fig. 7-2   The open classroom extends outdoors. Many interest centers are available for the child who prefers outdoor learning.

The teaching staff is composed of teachers and assistants, but there are more children per adult than in a model school in the United States. British parents are regularly scheduled to serve on volunteer committees. Some help supervise learning. Others assist at meals, make equipment, or give guidance on the playground.

Often children aged four to seven are in the same class. There is much interaction among them.

Fig. 7-3   Children in independent activities: auditory training.

In the United States many preschool classrooms are planned on a modified open concept. A large room (35-50 square feet of play space per child) may be lined with centers for music, art, books, role-playing, construction, and manipulatives. There is often a large open area for language development and indoor motor activities. With the exception of a brief story time, music period, and scheduled outdoor play, the child is free the rest of the day to play and learn as he chooses.

8:30 A.M.	Sing songs; discuss special plans or opportunities for the day.
8:45 A.M.	Self-directed activities in interest centers (Teacher limits the number of children in each center.)
9:45 A.M.	Cleanup time
10:00 A.M.	Snacks (juice, crackers)
10:15 A.M.	Story and discussion time
10:30 A.M.	Self-directed activities, outdoors when weather permits
11:30 A.M.	Cleanup time
11:45 A.M.	Sharing time; children discuss their morning's work, show results
12:00 Noon	Return home

Fig. 7-4 Daily schedule of a modified open classroom typical of many half-day private preschools in the United States.

The most obvious difference between British infant schools and American schools for very young children is in numbers. There are fewer interest centers and fewer children and adults in one room in American preschools. American educational philosophy leans toward a theory that it is easier to individualize if classes and learning groups are smaller. This promotes more adult-child verbal interaction even in the open classroom. Emphasis is placed on the child discovering things by himself or by interacting with peers. Often, though, a teacher joins a group and helps them draw conclusions or gives them appropriate words to use for their discoveries.

In both private and public American early childhood education centers, there is usually a part of the day devoted to curriculum of the school's choice and a larger part for the child's personal interests. In the United States usually all the children in a classroom, self-contained or open concept, are the same age at the opening date of the school year.

Many new elementary schools in the United States are being built with as few support walls as possible. Often grades one through six can be seen in one large auditorium with movable desks and portable equipment. In spite of the many activities taking place at one time, the children concentrate on the immediate task as if others were not there.

Fig. 7-5 Each child finds something he wants to do in one of the interest centers.

It has not yet been proved that the open classroom produces better learning for the very young child. It is being tried for numerous reasons. An important one is that it can help give more children opportunities for learning in spite of the current shortage of teachers who are certified in early childhood education. Where space is adequate, one certified teacher and three assistant teachers are an acceptable team. The same number of children require two teachers and two assistants in self-contained classrooms. Where a number of assistant teachers are on the teaching team, inservice training to develop team unity is an important part of the program.

This type of staffing is also a help in meeting the financial crisis in education today. It reduces the salary item in a school district budget. In commercial day-care centers, staffing patterns usually must conform to state regulations. Only since the 1960s have most of these facilities been having educational programs. Few of them have certified teachers, although some of them do have excellent curricula today.

Every child who is away from his home has a right to the kind of learning experiences that will help him develop in every way. The only difference between the program in half-day school or all-day care should be in the number of hours per day. Both situations should meet all the child's needs as much as possible in the time allowed.

The open classroom concept has possibilities for all programs for very young children, in private and public schools. The successful teaching team in the open classroom can make it succeed if all the members believe in its philosophy and work harmoniously toward its goals for the children.

STRUCTURED AND UNSTRUCTURED LEARNING

In early childhood education, the word *structure* means different things to different people. To many, it means having children sit at a table for long periods while the teacher tells them what she wants them to know. Unstructured curriculum to most people means the type of discovery learning described as "open classrooms." In reality, few schools have such extremes.

Most schools for very young boys and girls have a structure of some type. It may be only the teacher's mental organization of goals set for the children. Into the "outline" idea, she places the parts of the curriculum, the materials, equipment, and activities where they seem to fit best.

Another kind of structure is provided by sequencing the steps needed to develop a skill. Presenting materials in a special order adds structure to the child's learning. A three-year-old is usually given a four-piece inset as his first puzzle. Next he learns to work a four-piece puzzle where each piece is the shape of a whole object. As soon as he learns to work this type, he is given a six-piece puzzle with cuts through the middle of objects. Success at each level means readiness for a more complex puzzle. Gross motor skills are learned in steps, also.

Developing Skills in Sequential Steps
1. Have child draw crayon pictures, standing at the easel.
2. On the floor over newspapers, have child paint using large brush and thick tempera; teach him to rid brush of excess paint.
3. Have child use same technique and materials standing at easel.
4. Have child use same techniques and thinner tempera. Teach him to clean up drips.
5. Teach child to prepare his own paint before proceeding as in step 4.
6. Give child smaller brush when fine muscle control is adequate.

Fig. 7-6 Steps in helping to develop skill in easel painting using tempera paint.

The sequencing of materials and of levels of skill development are stated in a written curriculum as behavioral objectives. A *behavioral objective* states the behavior the child is expected to learn and the conditions under which he is to do it. These kinds of structures are based upon Piaget's learning theory. The child is expected to easily assimilate into his cognitive structures the next level of difficulty after a successful experience.

Behavioral Objective
CONDITIONS:
1. Show the child a model string of nine plastic beads in three colors and three shapes.
2. Give the child an empty string and a duplicate set of beads.
3. Tell him to string his beads to match the model.
BEHAVIOR:
The child will string his beads to match the model string.

Fig. 7-7 A behavioral objective states the behavior the child is expected to learn and the conditions under which he is expected to do it.

Many schools that claim to have unstructured programs, in fact, do have long-range goals for the children and definite plans for achieving the goals. A teacher of four-year-olds may intend to have them learn to classify familiar objects (animals, toys, foods). She includes many discussions of the meanings of these concepts. She brings animals into the room when opportunity presents itself (Mary brings in six-week-old playful kittens). She discusses classroom toys and points out "toys" in pictures and storybooks. She does not have detailed daily behavioral objectives but she does have one form of structure in the curriculum. Such curriculum is called *content-oriented* rather than *process-oriented*. The main goal of this type of program is to enlarge the child's knowledge of his world.

Another type of relatively unstructured learning is found in schools that lean heavily on affective development. These schools have three main goals for the child:

- Learning to get along well with peers.
- Learning to communicate well orally.
- Learning to express emotions in acceptable ways.

These schools usually do not depend on or use step-by-step procedures for results. Understanding, observant teachers are expected to produce observable social skills among all the children regardless of other development that occurs.

Some of the first programs created to meet the needs of economically disadvantaged children are highly structured to make up for the lack of orderliness in their lives. A neat room, consistent placement of materials, and consistency in enforcing rules are good ideas for all children. A good program for any child also gives him opportunities to learn to make choices, to pursue his own interests, and to be creative. Some of the newer programs designed to meet the needs of poor children include all of the above and concentrate on developing each child's positive self-concept while he develops skills. A few of these better innovative programs are both content- and process-oriented.

If a teacher knows how to analyze a child's abilities, he can add to or take away from any printed curriculum whatever is needed to meet the child's needs. A curriculum can be destructured by limiting the time spent each day working toward behavioral objectives. This gives the child more time for interests of his choice or creative endeavors. A curriculum can be made more structured by stating more specific behavioral goals for each child and many ways to achieve them daily.

The program that is too structured is likely to be wrong developmentally for any child under six. It is not compatible with his natural characteristics during these years. Also it may gradually reduce his intrinsic motivation. When extrinsic motivations are used (stars, candy, prizes), the goal is always to gradually develop inner motivation so that the child becomes a self-directed learner. This is one of the best reasons for keeping structure within reasonable limits.

The program that is truly unstructured cannot hope to develop each child to his maximum. Young children need some guidance in opening their eyes to the world of people and things. This is true in the open classroom and in the self-contained classroom.

POSITIVE ASPECTS

The positive aspects of the open classroom are listed:

- All the positive aspects of team teaching can apply.
- The child has a choice of learning styles.
- The child spends a larger portion of his time in activities of his own choosing, both indoors and outdoors.

- The teachers available who have certificates in early childhood education can reach more children in more good programs.

- The open classroom is more economical for school budgets because more assistant teachers than teachers may be used.

In a period when education costs are soaring, administrators of public schools are exploring every possible means to cut costs. (Teaching staff salaries are a large part of a school district's budget.) In private commercially-operated schools, profits are less today because of the increased cost of everything.

Two self-contained preschool classrooms of twenty-five children per room of five-year-olds usually require a staff of two teachers and two assistants. The same amount of floor space in an open classroom accommodates fifty children with one teacher and three assistants. This is another reason why there will probably be more open classrooms in the preschools of the future. These open classrooms can have successful programs for young children if the teaching team members believe in the concept and if the facilities are adequate. The room should be no more crowded than a traditional room for little children.

SPECIAL TEACHER APTITUDES

A teaching team member in an open classroom needs the same qualifications as the one in a self-contained room. Also, she/he must have a strong belief in the need for individualization of learning styles, of content, and of independent activities.

The teaching team in an open classroom must be very flexible if the interest centers are to reflect the choices of the children. All the team members are expected to contribute ideas of how to provide materials to interest and challenge the children and how to reflect the children's ideas.

Evaluating a child's progress in the unstructured learning curriculum is especially difficult. A system must be chosen; training in using the system must be given all the team members. Often each member of the teaching team writes a monthly narrative progress report on each child. Dated samples of a child's work are sometimes kept as evidence of progress. Drawings, paintings, clay shapes, collages, woodworking, and paper construction can be evaluated this way. The staff must write careful observations and devise a variety of means of recording each child's progress.

Perhaps an extra and very essential aptitude is needed by a staff member in an open classroom.

The ability to concentrate in the midst of hubbub is very important. At the same time, there must be an awareness of the many things happening in a very large area.

SUMMARY

The philosophy of the open classroom concept is based on a belief in the need for individualization in education. Because each person is unique, many options should be offered in school so that each student can learn in his own way. To provide this diversity, the open classroom is larger and has more interest centers or learning stations than a self-contained classroom. It also has more staff members and accommodates more students. Each preschool student is able to make more daily choices in this setting because he does not have large group work or lessons. He learns at will from the many choices offered both indoors and outdoors. The curriculum is unstructured. It may be content-oriented or process-oriented according to the child's choices. The students are largely self-directed and are assisted by the teaching staff when help is needed to clarify, expand, or demonstrate equipment.

The teaching staff may have long-range goals for children to achieve but daily behavioral objectives are not used. This makes evaluation of a child's progress difficult. Narrative reports of observations by staff members and dated samples of a child's work are methods of evaluation that are often used.

There is an increasing number of open classrooms in schools. Growing concern about the need for individualization and a shortage of teachers certified in early childhood education are two valid reasons why the open concept is now being tried in many parts of the country. An increasing number of programs to train personnel who do not have baccalaureate degrees can provide the assistant teachers needed for open classrooms. This reduces the salary item in a school's budget and is seen as one way to help reduce the cost of education in public schools. Many people believe that the open classroom concept is in the best interests of the children.

SUGGESTED ACTIVITIES

- Visit a self-contained classroom for five-year-olds in an early childhood education center. Write down all the signs of structure in the curriculum that you observe.

- Visit an open preschool classroom for five-year-olds. Compare the kinds of structure observed in it with those observed in the self-contained classroom.

- Think through and write out your own thoughts on the amount and kinds of structure that are desirable in curriculum for preschool children.

REVIEW

A.   Select all of the correct choices for each of the following statements.

1.   The open preschool classroom

a.   Has more interest centers than a traditional preschool room.

b.   Opens all its windows and doors as often as possible.

c.   Helps to individualize curriculum.

d.   Needs more teachers than the self-contained classrooms for any given number of children.

2.   Structured learning may mean

a.   Having a teacher sit at a table with a group and teach them lessons each day.

b.   Discovery learning.

c.   Helping children reach behavioral objectives daily.

d.   Determining what children will learn by structuring the environment to enable specific kinds of learning to take place.

3.   More public schools are planning open preschool classrooms because

a. Children learn more in the British infant schools (open classrooms).

b. People believe it is a good way for children to learn the most, each in his own way.

c. It is a way to combat the shortage of teachers with early childhood certification or degrees.

d. It is a way to cut the costs of preschool education.

B. Briefly describe an open classroom and state the basic philosophy on which it is based.

C. Briefly define each of the following terms.

1. Individualization (in education)

2. Unstructured learning

3. British infant schools

4. Content-oriented curriculum

5. Process-oriented curriculum

6. Affective-development curriculum

unit 8 planning lessons

OBJECTIVES

After studying this unit, the student should be able to

- Compare the goals of a process-oriented curriculum with those that are content-oriented.

- Explain five factors the teacher must include in planning a lesson to insure that the children achieve the lesson goal (objective).

- Briefly describe how the teacher may organize materials in the classroom.

The long-range educational goals for the very young child are the same whether the learnings are to be structured or unstructured, the room is an open or a self-contained one, or the child is three years old or six years old. Hopefully, the child is to be helped to develop (cognitively, socially, emotionally, and physically) as much as possible during the time he is in school. He is to learn to become a successful member of a group and to be self-fulfilled as an individual.

Daily educational goals in the classroom vary greatly and according to many factors: philosophy of the school, the teacher's understanding of child development, and the child's readiness. In deciding daily goals (planning lessons), an overview of the program objectives is needed.

DECIDING WHAT TO TEACH

The overview of a curriculum provides two major kinds of information: (1) the skills the children are to develop and (2) the content through which the skills are to be developed. The overview helps the teacher decide what to teach.

The Process-Oriented Curriculum

Affective Skills. The affective skills are developmental. Learning to play and work well with others is learned gradually through experience. It is learned faster with guidance. Acquiring an appreciation of others who are different is a major goal. Developing a value system that is durable is vital. Expressing strong emotions in acceptable ways is a "must." An appreciation of beauty develops early in life under proper guidance. These goals tell the teacher some of the things she is to help the child learn.

- To respect the rights of others.

- To play happily with others.
- To accept all children as playmates.
- To respect the values of home and school.
- To express jealousy, fear, and anger in ways that are acceptable at school.
- To be creative.

A method often used for developing social skills in very young children is to place a group of them together and see what happens. If they do not get along, each problem is solved as it occurs. This method is unfair. Every child deserves the right to be able to follow the rules *(positive behavior)*. Before a child can follow the rules, he must have the rules explained to him. It is very important that every child knows the rules. It is equally necessary for the rules to be applied fairly to all the children. Then such values as fairness, justice, and honesty have their beginning in the early years. These values are planned and taught but not necessarily in structured lessons.

An appreciation of beauty is developed best by carefully observing nature. Seeing a brown bulb grow into a vibrant red lily is an exciting experience. A bouquet of beautiful weeds, a collection of shells, leaves, or seeds — all of these stir the emotions of young children.

Preschoolers are not too young to enjoy a lovely piece of man-made art. A genuine Indian necklace or a painting or sculpture of a familiar object increases a child's interest in creative art. Perhaps the best motivation is having many hours to use creative materials in an atmosphere of acceptance. Standards of beauty and perfection must be realistic for the budding young artist. The teacher decides which affective skills are to be developed in everyday interaction and for which ones she is to plan lessons in the curriculum.

Fig. 8-1   A representative drawing by a four-year-old.

1. Objective: When shown six pictures of persons with varying facial expressions, the child will point to the ones that show "not happy."

2. Objective: When asked, the child will state one thing a classmate has done at school that made him feel happy or "good."

3. Objective: When asked, the child will state one thing that happened to him at home or school that made him angry.

4. Objective: When shown a picture of a child who is obviously very angry and asked, the child will state one acceptable way to express anger at school.

Fig. 8-2   Sample behavioral objectives for affective development in four-year-old children show that they are just beginning to learn to talk about their feelings.

Motor Skills.   Learning to safely use stationary playground equipment ranks high on any list of of motor skills.   This includes swings, seesaws, merry-go-rounds, slides, climbers, ladders, tree-houses, and other similar items.

Very young children need to develop body awareness.   They must learn that their legs and arms are used to hop, jump, run, climb, skip, dance, slide, stoop, crawl, kick, throw, wave, push, pull, shake, and wiggle.   They also need to learn about direction: left and right and up and down. A well developed sense of left and right direction is needed before a child can distinguish a letter *p* from the letter *q* or a *d* from a *b*.

Fig. 8-3   A child's experience on a slide teaches him about directions: climb up and slide down.

The infant performs a fine muscle and large muscle feat when he holds his own bottle of milk. Each year he learns to do more fine motor activities. Large blocks and balls prepare the body for using fine beads and pegs in the later preschool years. Many hours of successful manipulative activities prepare the child for the difficult task of controlling a pencil on paper (writing) in first grade. If a preschooler is ready, he will try to print his name. He should not be forced to do this.

Using a ball, scissors, large paintbrush, simple tools (hammer and saw) are skills that the preschool child can develop under supervision. Puzzles, blocks, beads, inch cubes, pegs, and flannel board cutouts all help develop small arm and hand muscles and motor skills.   The teacher decides which motor skills must be planned as lessons.

Cognitive Skills. Acquiring cognitive skills or developing intelligence is happening all the time. It is not separate from affective and psychomotor development. A child must remember rules for expressing emotions in acceptable ways. He learns that larger blocks must be placed at the bottom or his tower will fall. However, there are some skills that are predominantly mental activities based on perceptual experience.

Cognitive skills help the child deal intelligently with his environment. He classifies the information he receives from his five senses so that he can easily recall it when he wishes. He learns to focus on what is relevant around him and to mentally eliminate what he cannot use. Thus it is said that a child learns to classify, categorize, order, remember, associate, solve problems, and develop visual and auditory discrimination. A good curriculum for very young children includes plans to teach all these cognitive skills. Of course, at all times the level of the skill must be appropriate for the child's stage of readiness.

Language Development. Some children enter early childhood education classes able to communicate their needs in oral language. Many others are not yet highly verbal. Some reasons for this are listed:

- Lack of opportunity.
- Lack of experiences to talk about.
- Lack of a highly verbal model in the home.
- Lack of motivation.
- Physical problems (hearing or sight).

In planning the language activities for a specific child, the cause of his nonverbal state should be determined. Then a procedure may be developed to fit the child's situation. His physical condition should be checked first. If there is no physical problem, a look at the other possible causes helps the teacher decide what is best for the child.

Later, the child learns that the printed word is "talk written down." The more "talk" he has experi-

enced, the easier it is for him to transfer to "written talk" (learn to read). Being unable to express his thoughts in words can prevent a child from learning to read. This puts a heavy responsibility on the preschool teacher to develop the child's oral language skills. These skills include sentence structure, vocabulary, and concept development. A child needs ideas, words to express them, and patterns for conveying them accurately to others.

Television, radio, recordings, tapes, audio-cassettes, videotapes, and "language machines" are used for language experience in preschool curriculum. But prior to benefiting from these, the child needs experiences to discuss. He needs to see and hear many people, places, and things. The greater the variety of "real life" experiences a child has, the faster his vocabulary and concepts grow. This assumes that there are always preparation, adult interaction and follow-up activities for each experience.

Reading an appropriate book to a group of children means reading one that is not too long for their attention span, is of interest to them, and has a vocabulary equal to their *receptive language level* (the level they can understand but do not yet speak).

Fig. 8-5   This library is just for four-year-olds. They love it.

Fig. 8-4   A child's ability to express thoughts verbally is directly related to the ease with which he later learns symbols (numbers, letters, written words).

Books and stories supply children with many vicarious experiences in place of actual experiences they cannot have in person. Discussing stories adds other values to this experience.

It helps to keep the emotional atmosphere in the room friendly when children learn to verbalize their feelings. It is equally important for every adult to learn to accept these orally expressed emotions.

A child should not be made to feel guilty for having them. A teacher who consistently acknowledges the feelings a child expresses verbally before she corrects the problem, encourages this important kind of language skill and affective development.

Fig. 8-6 Daily group interaction helps language development.

In the bilingual classroom, language development flourishes best when all the adults are bilingual. Instant interaction between a child and an adult encourages speech. Using an interpreter discourages speech. If a child is non-English speaking, small amounts of standard English structures may be given daily. The content must be limited to objects and ideas that are familiar to the child (so that there will be a "match"!). There are several systems for teaching English as a second language. Each school usually adopts one system and trains all its teachers to use the system.

The development of cognitive skills should proceed in the child's familiar language so that learning is not at a standstill while the child learns to speak English. Vocabulary acquired through the English lessons can be used wherever appropriate in social situations, but it is usually considered confusing to the child to use both languages in one lesson.

Black dialect is recognized as a valid form of verbal communication. The child should be permitted to use it in social interaction, but there should always be present in the classroom an adult model who speaks standard English well.

A role-playing center is the scene of rich verbal social interaction. The setting must be relevant to the children's lives or it must reflect vicarious experiences the children have had in the classroom.

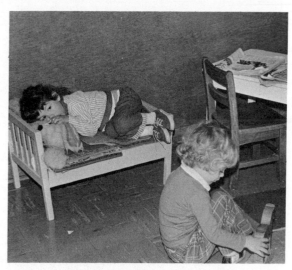

Fig. 8-7 Children imitate family members in the role-playing center.

Puppets are popular with children. The shy child frequently becomes less shy using puppets. It is the puppet who is bold and talkative. Using puppets is a good way for five-year-olds to dramatize familiar stories, such as *The Three Little Pigs*.

Singing and choral activities are found in all preschool programs. They offer pleasure and contribute skill-building to the language development of the children.

Every classroom activity that involves two or more persons contributes to oral language growth. The quality of the results for each child depends upon the level of skill the child brings to school, his opportunities for practice, the models he hears at school, his experiences, and the teacher's expectations. A teacher who believes that the children will become very talkative usually plans the kind of program that develops the oral language skills of the children.

Getting along, appreciating, valuing, using muscles, classifying, problem solving, and speaking are all *processes*. When the lessons are planned to teach these processes, the curriculum is said to be a *process-oriented* curriculum.

Content-Oriented Curriculum

Preschool curriculum is viewed in three ways: as skill building (process-oriented) which was just previously discussed; through unit themes (unit 5), and by elementary school subject matter. Many lesson plans are organized according to language, social studies, math, science, art, and music. Usually the subjects are taught within the framework of a unit.

Date: Sept. 10-14	Unit: Health, Cleanliness, Growing					
M O N D A Y	Songs	Language Arts	Science/ Math	Social Studies	Related Art	Evaluation
	"I'm Growing"	Discuss category of food. Have C's name favorite foods	Compare foods in raw and cooked forms: carrots, popcorn, potatoes. Pop corn in class.	Discuss food processing at home and commercially: canning and freezing.	Have children cut out magazine pictures. Make a favorite foods book for the class.	Very interested in food processing. Expand on this. Language development very good. Cook in class soon.

Fig. 8-8   **Sample daily lesson plan for kindergarten in a content-oriented curriculum.**

If the unit topic is "The Zoo," animal stories, poems, and discussions about zoo pictures are the language section. Of course, a trip to the zoo is planned if possible. It is ideal social studies material. Math and science activities evolve around the animals' habitats, amounts of foods needed, number of kinds of animals seen, which one is largest.

If the curriculum is also process-oriented, visual skills include recognizing an animal's characteristics and differences between kinds of animals. Auditory skill includes recognizing sounds unique to various animals. Motor skills may include imitating the movements of the animals. Cognitive skills can mean remembering the order in which the animals were visited, classifying types of animals, and understanding behaviors typical of some types.

The unstructured curriculum in the open classroom is set up so that the child who prefers a subject matter approach through music has alternatives from which he can also select content or skills.

Although schools emphasize different approaches, it is difficult to visualize a preschool curriculum which does not in fact contain generous amounts of all three: (1) developmental skill building, (2) themes of interest, and (3) subject matter content. There are variations in the amount of time spent each day in a particular way. Other factors that create differences are the equipment and materials available and the philosophy of the school. Differences in teachers is a factor that matters. Teachers are unique human beings. Deciding wisely what to teach in any curriculum can result in a good program using any of the approaches described thus far.

DECIDING HOW TO TEACH

When the curriculum overview of content and skills is ready, the teacher still needs to make decisions about how to teach. Questions about the following must be answered:

- Which supplementary materials to use.
- Grouping for each activity.
- The daily schedule.
- How to teach specific skills and concepts.

Supplementary materials are those that reinforce the learnings from the lessons. In most schools each teacher selects these for his/her students. Frequently, the creative teacher designs and makes games to give the children practice in their new skills.

Fig. 8-9   **Speaking skills and listening skills develop during conversation.**

Group sizes are determined by the nature of the activity, the amount of available material, the nature of the children, and by the room arrangement. Singing may be a successful experience with a group of fifteen. Teaching children a memory task may be difficult with a group of eight. Conversation groups are best when there are very few children so that each child has more turns to talk.

The daily schedule must be adjusted according to the snack, breakfast, and lunch schedules, playground schedule, and "cleanup and prepare to go home" schedule. These vary even in public school settings. Each teacher must remain flexible and be able to cope with a school's rules wherever she works. If the rules are not in the best interests of the children, however, the teacher is responsible for bringing this to the attention of the school administrator and suggesting changes.

Each teacher develops her own style of teaching lessons. There are some factors that are known to influence the children's success in attaining behavioral objectives:

- The setting must be appropriate. An auditory training lesson must be given in a relatively quiet area (away from the block building area).

- There must be enough lesson materials so that a child does not become tired or bored while waiting for his turn.

- The child must have readiness for the skill or concept.

- The setting must be prepared in advance.

- The teaching strategies must be appropriate for the children and for the lesson objective.

The following are some examples of appropriate teaching procedures:

- Discovery lesson
  1. Introduce new material.
  2. Have children examine and discuss possible ways to use it.
  3. Have each child use some of the materials any way he chooses.
  4. Call attention to the processes or products of each child.
  5. Have children relate their thoughts and feelings about the material.
  6. Evaluate the results.

- Skill development lesson (visual)
  1. Get attention by explaining the behavioral objective: "Today you will be learning to . . ."
  2. Show the materials; have the children identify them.
  3. Demonstrate the procedure, step by step.
  4. Give each child or pairs of children a set of materials.
  5. Have each child duplicate the model: place four cutouts in order by size.
  6. Evaluate each child's work: help a child make corrections if needed.
  7. Provide a second similar activity for practice or transfer.
  8. Evaluate each child's performance and record on a progress chart. See page 54 for example.

- Language lesson
  1. Show a teaching picture (18" x 24") portraying familiar and unfamiliar objects.
  2. Have the children discuss what they see, identifying as many objects as they can.
  3. Identify for them and discuss with them the unnamed objects.
  4. Have the children repeat each new name, point to the object in the picture, and explain its relationship to the whole picture.
  5. On the next day, show this picture, name objects, have children identify them.
  6. Help the children create a story about the picture. One child begins, makes two or three statements, then other children add to the story until every child has contributed.
  7. Note language development achieved by each child and record this.
  8. Plan to have small group discussion with the children who mastered the new words to further expand their understanding and vocabulary.

- Second (foreign) language lesson
  1. Show three familiar objects; have the children name them in their first language.
  2. Give the children the same word each time in the new language: "gato-cat."

PROGRESS CHART Unit 7 Theme: Animals' Homes																								
SKILLS	**Visual Skills**					**Auditory Skills**					**Motor Skills**					**Thinking Skills**					**Language Skills**			
LESSON	1	2	3	4		1	2	3	4		1	2	3	4		1	2	3	4		1	2	3	4
1. Mary C.																								
2. Rudy D.																								
3.																								
4.																								
5.																								
6.																								
.																								
.																								
.																								
.																								
15. Tom W.																								

X	Child reached objective during lesson.	/X	Child reached objective when lesson was repeated.
/	Child did not reach objective during repeated lesson.		

Fig. 8-10 Keeping an accurate record of a child's progress helps the teacher to individualize according to each child's needs.

3. Using the statement "This is a _____.", review the English name of each one. Have the children repeat the sentence each time.

4. Have one child close his eyes while another child moves the objects — changing their positions.

5. The child with his eyes closed puts out his hand and touches one object.

6. He opens his eyes and names the object in English. If he is correct, it is his turn to reposition the objects.

7. Note which children achieve the objective. Plan a second lesson using the same objects for those who do not learn the new words.

• Review lesson

Design a review lesson that requires having knowledge of several concepts previously taught. Games are excellent for this. For example, after learning the concepts of color, shape, size, same, and not the same, the child plays an attribute game. He is given a collection of objects in different colors, sizes, and shapes. He is told to find all the objects having a specified attribute. Later he is asked to find an object having two specified attributes ("large red").

Teaching strategies must include many ways to get and keep the attention of the children. When a group of children is selected, although each one is cognitively ready for the new skill level, they may vary in language development. A teacher individualizes by phrasing questions so that each child may respond according to his own level of verbal skill.

Some tasks are learned by watching a demonstration, then practicing. Teaching some fine motor skills, such as copying designs on pegboards, requires little talking for some children. If some of the children have a good vocabulary for spatial relationships, however, they can be asked to explain the positions of the pegs: "Where is the next red one on the model . . . ?" "It is beside the row of blue ones." Thus all

1. Make frequent eye contact with each child.

2. Use new attractive materials.

3. Address each child by name; touch the children sometimes.

4. Do not call on children in a fixed order; keep them alert.

5. Keep the lessons brief, 10-15 minutes.

6. Make each objective a little harder than the previous one on the same skill or concept.

7. Use a soft, conversational tone of voice.

8. When possible, give every child material and keep all of them involved in the activity.

9. Be well prepared and in advance; do not prepare while the children sit there.

10. If the children become loudvoiced, lower your voice so they must become quiet to hear you.

Fig. 8-11 The teacher needs a variety of techniques to get and hold the attention of children.

1. Level of response: nonverbal

   The teacher says, "point to the one that is the vehicle." (Child points.)

2. Level of response: yes/no

   The teacher asks, "Is this one the vehicle?" (Child: "Yes.")

3. Level of response: labels

   The teacher says, "Name the kind of object I point to." (Child: "A vehicle.")

4. Level of response: phrases

   The teacher says, "Tell me about this object." (Child: "Blue car.")

5. Level of response: simple sentence

   The teacher says, "Name the kind of objects in this picture." (Child: "They are vehicles.")

Fig. 8-12 Children on one cognitive level may vary greatly in language skills. The above are examples of ways the teacher may individualize.

children may participate and no one feels inferior about his language level. The secret lies in the teacher knowing the abilities of each child. Then when she plans a pleasing variety of methods and effective strategies, her lessons are likely to provide good learning experiences for the children.

ORGANIZING MATERIALS

Every teacher is responsible for organizing the materials to be used. Many steps and minutes are saved by planning and preparing materials in advance of curriculum needs. The following ideas are often useful for the classroom teacher.

- If there are not adequate storage spaces in the room, the teacher may make some of packing boxes painted an attractive color.

- Classroom materials are to be stored in the storage spaces nearest the place where they are to be used.

- Only materials needed currently are to remain in view. Others are to be stored out of sight.

- Classroom materials belong in designated places. Children are taught to return them to those places after using them.

- Interest centers should be organized so that there is a smooth flow of traffic in the room.

- The number of children playing in any one center at one time should be limited to avoid crowding.

- The materials to be used the next day should be prepared and gathered before the teachers leave at the end of the day.

- Each evening the room should be left looking clean, neat, and ready for the next day.

- Each child should have a place to keep his belongings, even if it is just a large paper bag with his name on it. These bags may be attached with clothespins to a heavy cord. All the children's personal belongings except coats may be kept in lockers.

- The teacher should build up a supply of teaching pictures. They may be kept in a large cardboard box in folders. Each folder may hold pictures in one category (clothing, buildings, vehicles). The folders should be labeled and kept in alphabetical order for convenience.

- An envelope file of favorite poems may be organized in the same way as the teaching pictures.

- Lesson plans, reports, progress charts, and school records of all kinds should be kept in separate folders, alphabetized and kept in the teacher's desk or closet.

- A personal record file is kept for each child, with pertinent data, anecdotal records, and dated samples of the child's work.

In general, there are three kinds of materials that must be organized daily: those needed to teach the lessons, those that create the learning environment (interest centers), and record files. Each teacher finds her own way to organize these materials so that there is maximum learning and efficiency with minimum effort.

SUMMARY

In deciding what to teach, the teacher considers the long-range goals for each child and his readiness for the development of language and of affective, psychomotor, and cognitive skills. If the curriculum is process-oriented, the teacher concentrates on the processes. If the curriculum is content-oriented, she/he considers the processes but focuses on unit topics and/ or such subjects as language, music, and social studies. In any curriculum, lessons are planned to have the children meet specific behavioral objectives. The teacher may also plan some specific goals for the children that are achieved without structured learning (for example, learning to share materials), according to the needs of the children.

When the content has been determined, teaching strategies and techniques are selected. A daily schedule, grouping for activities, and teaching procedures must be planned. How to individualize according to language levels and other aspects of readiness is a daily problem for the teacher to solve. She must plan which kinds of lesson are needed each time: discovery, skill development, language, second language, or review. The teacher plans a variety of lesson procedures and techniques for gaining and holding the child's attention.

Long range and daily organization of materials — such as those used in lessons, in creating the learning environment, and in keeping records — creates efficiency and facilitates learning. Such organization should be planned along with the curriculum.

SUGGESTED ACTIVITIES

- Visit a classroom in an early childhood education center. Write your observations of activities where good planning is evident. If a lack of planning is evident, describe the situation and make constructive criticisms.

- If possible, visit a preschool curriculum planning meeting. Take notes and prepare an evaluation of the planning and of the meeting procedure.

- Visit a kindergarten classroom. Describe the kinds of organization you observe. Add suggestions to improve the organization of materials if this is needed.

REVIEW

A. Briefly compare the goals of a process-oriented curriculum with those of a content-oriented curriculum.

B. Besides lesson planning, there are other kinds of planning the teacher must do. List four of these.

C. List five factors that influence children's success in attaining behavioral objectives.

D. Select all the phrases that correctly complete each of the following statements.

1. The teacher can plan to individualize in her lessons by

   a. Writing a different behavioral objective for a child who is less ready than other children for new material.

   b. Structuring the learning environment to meet the individual needs of every child (such as in choice of supplementary materials).

    c.   Knowing the degree of readiness or developmental levels of every child.

    d.   Varying a question so that the level of verbal response required of each child is appropriate for him.

2.   The following affective goals are appropriate for preschool children

    a.   To learn to express anger in ways that are acceptable at school.

    b.   To tell about one's dreams and why one likes or dislikes them.

    c.   To learn to respect the rights of others.

    d.   To describe one's feelings when looking at a famous painting.

3.   The teacher who carefully organizes her materials will

    a.   Look for lesson materials as soon as she gets to school each morning.

    b.   Keep the paint, brushes and paper near the easel.

    c.   Write notes about a child's progress on the morning of a conference with the child's parents.

    d.   Carefully stack the role-playing accessories from yesterday on the floor near her desk.

unit 9 behavioral objectives

OBJECTIVES

After studying this unit, the student should be able to

- Define and state four important uses of behavioral objectives.
- Explain five advantages of mastery learning (using behavioral objectives).
- Recognize good behavioral objectives.

The first steps in developing curriculum for very young children involve discovering the developmental levels of the children, determining the type of curriculum, and finding themes of interest to the children. Then the teacher or planning group is ready to make daily lesson plans.

Learning is sequential. A skill is developed best from the easiest part to the hardest part, one step at a time. The teacher must know when a child masters each step so that she knows when he is ready for the next step. An evaluation tool such as a behavioral objective is needed.

THE IMPORTANCE OF A BEHAVIORAL OBJECTIVE

A *behavioral objective* is a statement of the behavior expected of a student at the end of a specific learning experience. Such a statement has these characteristics:

- The objective is stated in terms of the child's behavior, not in terms of the teaching process.
- The conditions for learning are stated in specific terms.
- The behavior must be observable (not "appreciating" or "thinking").
- The amount or extent of the expected behavior is stated ("all," "three of four times," and similar conditions).

In each area of learning the preschool teacher has some broad general learning outcomes for her children. Some examples for a class of three-year-olds are listed:

- Cognitive: The child will learn some classifying skills.
- Affective: The child will learn to get along with other children in group games.

Fig. 9-1   **During the third and fourth years, the child gives up parallel play in favor of small group activities**

- Psychomotor: The child will learn to control a large ball.

To achieve each of these outcomes, the teacher develops a sequence of steps that leads to that goal. Each step is written as a behavioral objective. Each objective is the goal of a lesson.

Behavioral objectives are important because they help the teacher evaluate daily the progress of each child. If a child does not reach an objective, he is not ready for the next harder one. Special help is given to him individually or in a small group with others who need help. Only after mastering each objective is a child ready for the next harder one of that skill. This is called *mastery learning*. Only after a child masters step A is he encouraged to try step B. The following are some of the advantages in mastery learning:

- The slower learner can reach the same goals as other children, but at his own rate of learning.

- The less apt child reaches the same goal as the the more apt child. It just takes longer.

- Every student feels successful.

- No gaps in learning are likely to occur. A better foundation for future learning is built.

- It simplifies evaluating a child's progress.

- It is a democratic way of giving all children the opportunity to achieve in school.

WRITING OBJECTIVES

The end-of-the-year goals for a group of children may be thought of in terms of several shorter range goals. These may be sequenced according to complexity, developmental characteristics, and the children's needs. The affective goal — to get along with others in a group activity — has several shorter range goals for a three-year-old. The child

- Will share one kind of outdoor stationary equipment with another child.

- Will share one kind of indoor material with another child. ·

- Will return materials to the appropriate storage space when through using them.

- Will play harmoniously with a group of children in a small group activity.

These goals are stated in the order in which the three-year-old is most likely to master them. Each can be broken into several simpler objectives. Each objective must state the conditions of learning and the behavioral outcome expected of the child. As an example, the third goal (the ultimate desired behavior is to return materials to their proper storage places) may be divided this way:

- When asked to find three kinds of specified classroom toys or materials, the child will select each of the three from its storage place.

- When shown any four kinds of classroom equipment, and asked to return each one to its storage place, the child will place at least three of them in their appropriate storage spaces.

- Having used a toy or material of his own choosing, the child will return the item to the correct storage place without being reminded.

Fig. 9-2 Three-year-olds learn to put toys away.

Each objective states the conditions of learning:

- When asked . . . . .

- When shown . . . . .

- Having used . . . . .

Each objective is stated as an observable behavior:

- The child will select . . . . .

- The child will place . . . . .

- The child will return . . . . .

Such objectives are easy to evaluate:

- Were the specified conditions met?

- Was the stated behavior observed?

If the answers are "yes," the child is ready for the objective that is one step harder.

In writing behavioral objectives, the conditions of the learning must be stated in detail. An objective may involve having a child reproduce a parquetry design. The objective must state

- Large or small parquetry blocks.

- How many blocks.

- How many colors of blocks.

- Which kind of model design: block or design card; if a design card, whether it is on the table or standing up.

It may state "a five block design in two colors from a model design card, lying on the table." If the details are not stated, a child may be given a harder task before an easier one, or he may be tested on a harder task than the one he learned in the lesson experience.

Fig. 9-3 Puzzles of increasing difficulty (with more pieces) are examples of materials used in "mastery learning."

Another problem is in remembering to state the scoring procedure exactly. Sometimes a child is expected to completely fulfill a stated behavior: "Will reproduce a large parquetry design using five blocks in two colors from a three-dimensional block model." At other times, it is better to expect the child to partially fulfill a possible behavior. Some examples of this type of scoring are listed:

- Shown six photos of faces showing strong feelings, the child will correctly identify four of the emotions shown.

- Throwing four beanbags at a target container (18-inch diameter) four feet away, the child will throw at least three of the beanbags into the target container.

- Shown a collection of ten pictures (five foods and five nonfoods), when asked to select the pictures that are not of foods, the child will select at least four correctly.

Stating conditions of learning and behavioral outcomes in fine detail makes it easy to evaluate a child's behavior, his progress, and his readiness and to develop sequences of learning tasks of increasing complexity.

USING BEHAVIORAL OBJECTIVES

A series of behavioral objectives such as those stated previously need not be used on successive days.

Many days may be needed to teach a child the names and storage places of toys and materials in the classroom. When a series of tasks is carefully sequenced and ready, then whenever a child masters one, the next one is there so he can progress. The time to use a new objective is whenever the child has mastered the previous one in the series.

Daily lesson plans show a variety of objectives being mastered on any one day. They may be in several skill and content areas. The teacher must keep in mind that all the objectives for one child must be within the limits of his developmental levels and his readiness for the tasks. The child who is absent may need special help before he joins a group who progressed during his absence. He is to complete each task in sequence just as the others did. Student helpers, volunteers, or parents may help him master the objectives he missed.

Fig. 9-4 One-to-one work helps a child master objectives achieved by others during her absence.

If results for each child are recorded daily on a progress chart, a glance at the end of the day tells the teacher how to group for the next day. If one or two children from each small group do not reach the objective, they may make one group the next day to review the skill or concept. Those who reached the objective go on to the next harder task. This is an important way to individualize instruction.

It helps to know whether a child can work a puzzle with six or ten pieces. It insures continued challenge and growth for every child. Carefully sequenced behavioral objectives make this possible when conditions and behaviors are stated in specific terms.

Using objectives insures teaching with a purpose. It is a systematic way to help every child progress as much as he can during his school experience. It also gives the teacher facts to use in talking with a child's parents. Parents appreciate knowing the goals accomplished by the child *(objective information)* as well as the teacher's opinion of his work *(subjective information)*.

Carefully kept records are very useful to physicians and specialists of many kinds. If a child has or develops problems, the facts of his progress or lack of it are sometimes useful indicators that help in analyzing the problem.

SUMMARY

A final step in designing curriculum is the writing of behavioral objectives for the lessons. A behavioral objective is a statement of the behavior expected of a child after a specific learning experience. Cognitive, affective, and psychomotor learnings may be stated in behavioral terms. Each objective represents one step in a sequence designed to help the child reach a long-range goal in one area of learning.

Mastery learning means that a student masters each objective in a series before he is given the next more complex objective. The advantages of mastery learning are (1) a student may learn at his own rate, (2) there are likely to be fewer gaps in the child's learning, (3) the less apt child can learn as well as the child with greater aptitude, (4) children develop a feeling of competence, (5) a teacher can easily evaluate a student's progress, and (6) it is a democratic approach to academic achievement in school.

In writing behavioral objectives, it is necessary to state the details of the conditions under which a child is expected to learn and the extent to which he is expected to behave in a stated way. Behavioral objectives are used to break down a complex task into simple tasks, to determine the abilities and progress of a child, and to insure giving each child continuous challenge in school. Records of a child's achievement of behavioral objectives provide facts to use with a child's parents or physician concerning the child's progress in school.

SUGGESTED ACTIVITIES

- Locate a curriculum that has behavioral objectives used with three-, four- or five-year-old children. List the kinds of specific conditions for learning stated in ten lesson objectives. List the observable behaviors stated in the ten lessons.

- Observe a teacher who is giving a small group lesson to five-year-olds. From your observations, write the behavioral objective used.

- Select an affective goal for a three-, four-, or five-year-old child (Be specific as to the age.) Write behavioral objectives for at least three subskills for the goal. Sequence the objectives, easiest to hardest.

REVIEW

A. Define and briefly state the characteristics of a behavioral objective.

B. Define and briefly state five advantages of mastery learning.

C. Carefully read the following. Decide whether each statement is a good behavioral objective. If the statement is not adequate, state its weakness. (you may assume they are developmentally appropriate.)

1. Shown some pictures on a flannel board, the child will select all those that are of animals.

2. Given a volleyball, the child will throw it a distance of at least five feet.

3. Shown a picture of a five-year-old boy looking very angry and when asked to do so, the child will state one thing that makes him feel like the boy appears to feel in the picture.

4. After hearing the story *The Three Pigs,* the child will feel sorry for the little pigs whose houses were blown down.

Section III Teacher Effectiveness

unit 10 qualifications

OBJECTIVES

After studying this unit, the student should be able to

- List at least five aptitudes needed for teaching very young children in school.
- List and briefly explain five desirable attitudes for teachers in early childhood education.
- Briefly discuss how a person with aptitudes and the correct attitudes may continue to grow professionally and become better qualified as an early childhood teacher.

There are many meanings attached to the term *qualified teacher* in early childhood education. In discussing the term, the specific meaning intended must be defined. Here, *qualified teacher* refers to a person who has the potential to become an effective teacher of very young boys and girls. This differs from the term *certified,* which refers to having earned academic credits for a college degree or for a certificate for teaching.

Head Start and similar programs hire persons living in the school community to assist a Lead Teacher in the classroom. These persons are qualified; that is, they demonstrate certain aptitudes and attitudes as well as a knowledge of or interest in little children. They usually do not have college degrees or teaching certificates. Much of the success of Head Start is due to the efforts of these qualified assistant teachers. Thus a closer look at teacher qualifications is needed.

APTITUDES

The aptitudes for teaching very young children are the talents and characteristics needed in addition to the studying, training, and practicing required. Aptitudes are the results of a person's inherent qualites and his life experience. They include health, stamina, and character.

Certainly, many years of living or working with preschool children helps in developing an instant rapport with them. This aptitude is important to a teacher. It is only a beginning when a teacher gets acquainted with a child, however; all the rest of the school experience is still to come. It is necessary for a teacher to sustain a good relationship on a day-to-

day basis through bad days as well as good ones. This precludes a sensitivity on the part of the teacher to the emotional ups and downs of the girls and boys. It also means a knowledge of self on the part of the teacher. Being able to change plans when teacher or children are not up to them requires flexibility — a quality needed by every successful teacher.

Fig. 10-1 To become an effective teacher of very young children, a person must have special aptitudes and attitudes.

To keep a group situation from deteriorating may mean relying on one's sense of humor. No list of qualities needed for success is complete without this one. On those days when the weather, parents, school administration, and chickenpox all conspire against the teacher, a bit of the pixie near the surface helps her to survive.

In spite of having all the aptitudes just mentioned, there are days when every teacher feels that she/he does not "have all the answers." A person who is qualified to teach in early childhood education continues actively to seek the answers to the riddles of working with very young boys and girls. She seeks further knowledge all during her career.

All the characteristics of a good teacher combine to produce a person who is consciously aware of her role in the learning experience of the child. She dedicates her daily efforts to helping each child to be and do his best. A qualified teacher assumes responsibility for her students.

ATTITUDES

The teacher who has the aptitudes just outlined also needs specific attitudes to guide her in making decisions. Motivation reveals a person's attitudes toward his work. A reason for wanting to teach little children often explains a teacher's other attitudes as well. Only when concern for the children is the primary reason are decisions made in their best interests. Child-centered motivation is essential for effective teaching.

I like to take care of kids.

I need a job; this I can do.

People say I'm good with kids.

I want to help disadvantaged children.

I didn't like teaching older children.

It ought to be the easiest to learn.

I believe early childhood education can mean successful lives for the children.

It's easy work for pretty good pay.

Fig. 10-2   These reasons are often stated for teaching very young children. Some are child-centered; others are self-centered.

Each teacher entering early childhood education today should be made aware of recent changes in it. It is no longer a professional babysitting service even for the youngest infant. There are valuable appropriate learning experiences to be planned for every child. An attitude of wanting to learn what is best for every child is essential on the part of all persons working with very young children. Teaching skills and knowledge can be learned if the right attitude exists.

Another important attitude for teachers is the one which influences all of their interpersonal relationships. How they get along with children and with adults depends upon the degree to which they believe "I'm OK, You're OK". Personal prejudices are contagious. Children are not born prejudiced. They learn prejudice from the adults in their lives, including teachers. The fewer prejudices a person has, the better he is qualified as a model for children. Tolerance of others as persons affects the teacher's relationships with children, other staff members, parents, administrators, and the public at large. It also means a happier home life and thus freedom to concentrate on teaching responsibilities when at school.

This acceptance of the personhood of others does not include acceptance of behavior that is substandard, illegal, or immoral. Loving a child means caring enough about him to see that he stays within the acceptable limits of behavior.

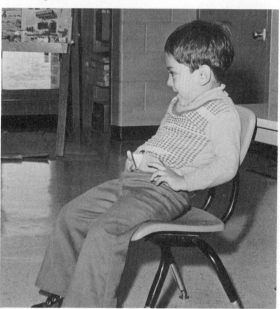

Fig. 10-3   A very few minutes of "time-out" is adequate discipline in many situations.

Educational research has proved that a teacher's behavior is influenced by her high expectations for the behavior and school achievements of her students. The high expectations cause her to act in ways that bring about the high achievements. Believing her students are going to do well in school is a critical attitude for a teacher to have.

A teacher must believe in the importance of her work in order to give it the priorities needed of her time, her thinking, her constant awareness of her environment.   Teaching very young children today may well be one of the answers to the dropout problem of tomorrow. The preschool years are now believed to be a critical period for developing the intelligence of the child and for developing positive attitudes toward learning. Though the formal education of the future may differ greatly from that of today, the need for continual learning grows greater as changes occur faster in the world each day. The good preschool teacher shows a positive attitude toward whetting the child's natural appetite for learning. She sees herself as a facilitator of learning, as one who is responsible and makes it possible. She accepts the responsibility because she is dedicated to early childhood education.

Fig. 10-4   One who works successfully with young children has a positive attitude toward early childhood education.

KNOWLEDGE OF CHILDREN AND OF HOW THEY LEARN

Persons who have most of the aptitudes and attitudes just described are never content with their present knowledge of children and of how they learn. They find ways to continue learning. One of these is through inservice training where they are employed. Inservice training may include a wide variety of topics. Well-planned inservice training considers the needs of the participants.

Many good early childhood professional magazines are now available. Many schools subscribe to several of these so that their teaching personnel may benefit from them. Many other education magazines now regularly have sections devoted to early child-

hood. Early childhood book clubs exist. Full length books are available on many aspects of working with very young children.

One of the oldest and still one of the best ways to learn more about teaching is to observe a very good teacher. Discussing the observations with the teacher observed or with another experienced teacher can help the observer benefit even more.

Willingness to cooperate with a good supervisor can quickly improve teaching techniques. A good supervisor criticizes constructively and makes positive suggestions for changes.

The technique of comparing one's observations of children with information on norms in child development books soon helps a teacher to accept the uniqueness of every child. This knowledge can be applied to her knowledge of how children learn or of how intelligence develops as Piaget explains it. Some college courses are helpful even if taken without credit.

Child Care Assistant

Creative Dramatics for Young Children

Children's Literature

Kindergarten Curriculum

Child Growth and Development

Introduction to Child Psychology

Nursery and Day-Care Centers

Behavioral Psychology

Music for Young Children

English as a Second Language

The Bilingual Child

Fig. 10-5   The listed junior college, college, and university courses are often useful to the beginning early childhood teacher.   Most do not require prerequisite courses.

A teacher who has desirable aptitudes and attitudes seeks opportunities to improve her knowledge by reading, studying, observing, discussing, comparing, and cooperating with the supervisory person. She seeks further training in the areas in which she needs help. A person who is a qualified teacher may not be engaged in many of these activities at first, but she accepts the opportunities to broaden her outlook on early childhood education when they are presented to her.

SUMMARY

To qualify as a teacher of very young boys and girls, a teacher is expected to have aptitudes for the work. A teacher is expected to be able to get along well with children, to be sensitive to their feelings, and to understand herself as well. She must be flexible, have a good sense of humor, and be humbly aware of her role in the life of the child. She must be a knowledge-seeker.

A person qualified to teach preschool children must be motivated out of concern for the well-being of children. This coincides with an attitude of wanting to learn more about children and about how they learn. An attitude of acceptance toward all persons is a basic attribute for effective teaching. A good teacher has sincere high expectations for students. She/he is dedicated to the cause of early childhood education.

Such dedication to their students and to their work causes qualified teachers to continue learning by reading, observing, studying, seeking training, and cooperating with their supervisors. Thus those without degrees and uncertified persons can qualify to become effective teachers. Improved training programs are being developed throughout the United States so that qualified persons who are eager to perform well in the role of "teacher" can be properly trained and rewarded for their efforts.

SUGGESTED ACTIVITIES

- Think of an early childhood teacher whom you consider "a very good teacher." Of the qualified teacher's characteristics listed in this unit, evaluate her on each one. List any other major characteristics that she possesses. Compare your evaluation with that of another student. What did you both learn?

- Evaluate yourself on the aptitudes listed in this unit. What areas of weakness do you detect? Write some suggestions for you to use in overcoming these.

- Make an honest appraisal of your personal motivation in entering the field of early childhood education. Discuss your appraisal with your instructor.

REVIEW

A. List at least five aptitudes needed for teaching very young children.

B. List and briefly explain five attitudes a person should have to become an effective teacher in early childhood education.

C. Briefly discuss how a person with necessary aptitudes and correct attitudes may continue to grow professionally and become better qualified as an early childhood teacher.

D. Select the choices that correctly complete each of the following statements.

1. A person who is qualified to teach very young children

a. Must be keenly aware of changes in a child's emotions.

b. Need not understand herself very well as long as she understands children.

c. Accepts a responsibility to see that her pupils learn and develop.

d. Tolerates everything about her students.

e. Realizes immediately that some of her children will not learn in school.

f. Looks at the humorous side of a situation (if there is one).

2. A qualified teacher of very young children needs to continue her education by

   a. Attending college until she has an academic degree (B.A. or B.S.).

   b. Reading about children and early childhood education in various kinds of publications.

   c. Observing the nearest teacher for help with teaching techniques.

   d. Studying what is known about how children learn.

   e. Learning from discussions with other more experienced teachers or with a supervisor.

   f. Not wasting time on inservice training that might be boring.

unit 11 communication techniques

OBJECTIVES

After studying this unit, the student should be able to

- List eight verbal communication techniques by which a teacher reflects appropriate attitudes toward children.

- List eight behavioral communication techniques by which a teacher reflects appropriate attitudes toward children.

- Briefly discuss good attitudes toward parents and how to communicate these attitudes.

Communication is a two-way event: a message is sent, received, and responded to. Wherever people are interacting, there is communication. Where there is communication, there is also the possibility of a communication problem. Often this happens in schools. Teachers need to be aware of good communication techniques to use with children and with adults. Using appropriate communication techniques helps prevent communication problems at school.

Modes of communication are the same between adults and children and between adults and other adults. Staff-child and staff-parent communications are all made by words that are spoken or not spoken and by deeds that are done and not done. Things that people say and do as well as the things they fail to say and do send messages to others, and are responded to accordingly.

STAFF-CHILD COMMUNICATION

Adults in a classroom need to send many kinds of "telling" messages to the children (instructions for lessons, activities, rules, praise, correction). They also need to convey "asking" messages: "I need to know . . ," (who? what? why? which? how?)

The teacher who wholeheartedly believes "I'm OK, you're OK" shows this to children in her verbal messages, both telling and asking, by these techniques:

- Using a soft, well-modulated voice and speaking clearly.

- Using words the listener understands in brief sentences.

- Phrasing messages so that they reflect a friendly, positive, and nonprejudiced attitude.

- Using good manners respectfully.

- Providing a good language model for others.

- Accepting the language the very young child brings to school while teaching him another language form.

- Praising the child's acts frequently and sincerely,

Say:	Do not say:
1. I know thunder is very scary to children. Do you want to hold my hand tightly or sit in my lap?	1. A great big boy like you is afraid of thunder?
2. Let's talk to Maria. If it was an accident, she will want to tell you she is sorry.	2. Why cry about a little thing like that? You know it was an accident.
3. Let's wash it and get a "Bandaid®" for it.	3. Don't be a crybaby. When you stop crying, we'll fix it.

Fig. 11-1 **A teacher's statements to a child should show a friendly positive attitude.
They should not embarrass or belittle the child.**

- Correcting a child in a way that is not belittling or embarrassing.

Behavior of staff members that says "I'm OK, you're OK" to children includes listening daily to each child and responding to each individual. It means making allowances for each child who has special needs (is not feeling well, just returned from an absence, has a new baby in the home, is handicapped in any way). The teacher who has realistic expectations for a child shows an understanding of child growth and development as well as of the uniqueness of every child.

Sometimes it is hard for an adult not to show favoritism, but it is absolutely necessary. Helping each child to think well of himself requires that every child believes he rates as highly as any other child with the teacher. It is easy to overlook the very quiet child who gives no trouble, but he must be given personal attention even though he does not seem to require it.

Getting down to a child's level when speaking to him is an action that makes him feel important — not dwarfed by the teacher's height as well as by her authority. Placing the children's artwork at their eye level shows a respect for the limitations of their height.

Fig. 11-2 So that children can enjoy and appreciate each other's artwork, it must be displayed at children's eye level.

An attractive, orderly room tells the child that the teacher cares enough to have an attractive well-equipped place for him.

A child notices a teacher's attitude toward his parents when they come to the school. He becomes aware if they are welcome. Showing an interest in the members of a child's family further communicates to him that he is a very important person.

Reflecting the children's interests in the curriculum motivates interest in learning. This is especially important when there are several ethnic groups represented in the class. Elements of each child's culture deserve a place in the learning experiences of the group: dress, foods, music, customs. The world is shrinking. Multiculturalism is the norm today in many places. When today's children are adults, most of them will live in multicultural settings.

Fig. 11-3 Elements of each child's family culture should be shown in the classroom.

There are many words and deeds by which the teaching staff communicates to the children love, concern, respect, admiration, and enjoyment. Failure to speak these words or do the deeds tells the children very clearly that there is a lack of these feelings. In such a climate, a child does not do or become his best. When a teacher does not listen and does not show affection for each child, the children soon become disinterested in school. When members of the staff are aware of good verbal and nonverbal communication techniques and use them — the school experience becomes a rewarding one for both the staff and the children.

STAFF-PARENT COMMUNICATION

For many years, communication between teachers and parents was limited to report cards, parent-teacher meetings, and a phone call if Johnny was a naughty boy. Educators now know that parents and schools must cooperate as a team in the education of children. Preschool programs have pioneered large-scale parent-involvement programs.

Many of the newer kinds of schools during the sixties initiated programs that send teachers into the homes of infants and toddlers to teach the mothers how to play with their children in ways that help the children develop. Programs for economically disadvantaged children are more effective when parents are active in helping the school. Parents often change their negative attitudes toward schools when they are made to feel welcome as partners in the education of their children.

Schools are learning to be helpful to parents as persons. Special kinds of school meetings to fill the needs of parents are not unusual. The success of all kinds of parent involvement includes many factors. Among them are the communication techniques used by the staff in communicating with the parents.

The attitude or thought that precedes any action is often visible. It is important that teachers maintain these positive attitudes in working with parents:

- Most parents are very concerned about their children.

- Each parent is a person, not just a member of the category *parents.*

- Parents appreciate hearing good things about their child, not just the bad things.

- Parents will help teachers in many ways if given the opportunity.

- Helping a parent learn to teach his child at home can give a long-lasting boost to the child's learning.

A teacher who has these attitudes reflects them in her oral and written communications with parents. She is careful not to offend them. She communicates with them often. She responds readily to communication that is initiated by a parent. (It is not "communication" until she answers.) Each teacher develops her own techniques to some degree, but a few general rules can be helpful. The teacher should

- Greet a parent by name, not as "Johnny's Mother."

- Speak in a friendly way, not as the voice of authority.

- Speak person-to-person if problem behavior of the child must be discussed; this kind of message should not be sent home in a note.

- Speak the parent's language and use vocabulary he can understand.

- Speak objectively and do not place blame. (Criticize only the child's behavior.)

1. Conversation in the room before or after school.
2. Phone call.
3. Handwritten note.
4. Conference by appointment at home or school.
5. Parent-teacher meetings, for class or school.
6. Volunteer training sessions/workshops.
7. School open house.

Fig. 11-4 Staff-parent communication has many forms in addition to the usual typed notice of school activities.

Nonverbal communication techniques include those that are needed for good interpersonal relationships anywhere:

- Be a good listener.

- Make any meetings as convenient for parents as you can.

- Be a patient teacher — with parents as well as with children.

- Try to be unhurried with parents; be friendly even when you are in a hurry.

- Try to find ways for each parent to become actively involved in his child's educational experience.

The mother of a preschool child is reluctant to relinquish her role of taking care of her child. This natural dread of the separation when the child goes to school makes it easier to develop parent volunteers at this time than when the child is older. When a teacher is willing to take the time needed to plan how her volunteer mothers can be helpful in the classroom, the experience often becomes worthwhile for everyone. Of course, this means getting acquainted with mothers and discovering their abilities and their limitations. It is usually easy to find helpful tasks, but it is not always easy to match the persons with the activities.

Early childhood education programs are noted for their lack of male personnel, although the number of male teachers is steadily increasing. Volunteer fathers find many ways to serve schools when they are made to feel they are wanted, needed, and very

Fig. 11-5   More male teachers are needed in early childhood education.

important to the school. Just having a male image available is helpful for some children. It is the teacher who must communicate this to fathers. Special lists of tasks for volunteer fathers should be available. Fathers and mothers should be consulted about their ideas of how they would like to become active at the school.

---

1. Read stories.
2. Supervise woodworking/playground.
3. Make and repair equipment.
4. Paint/decorate equipment.
5. Provide transportation/assist on field trips. (To his place of work for example).
6. Demonstrate an art or craft.

Fig. 11-6   Examples of tasks in which a volunteer father may be actively involved.

It is desirable for each child to have a teacher visit in his home. A first visit is usually a matter of getting needed information about the child — his social and physical history. Later visits may help ferret out the special ways in which the parent and school can work together. All home visits should be made by appointment so the parents will be prepared.

Showing concern for parents has resulted in numerous training centers for them. Specific kinds of information to meet their needs are available there. The teacher can help discover those needs of the parents that can be met by the school. Tactfulness, respect, and a knowledge of the language

and culture of the parents enable a teacher to communicate her sincere desire to be helpful.

---

1. Providing information on subjects as requested: child discipline, consumer economics, voting, politics in education, saving money, insurance, birth control, legal aid.
2. Providing training as requested: on teaching children at home or at school, academic or literacy classes, paraprofessional teacher training, preparing nutritious meals.
3. Providing a referral service with information on agencies whose services are available to parents.
4. Providing a place where parents can get together to discuss mutual problems.

Fig. 11-7   The above are examples of ways some schools are meeting the needs of parents.

The teacher can visit a child's home, telephone the parents, write brief messages to attach to a child's work, hold parent conferences, and attend parent-teacher meetings. She may train parents to be volunteers at school. Early in the year she sees that parents learn about the school program: in a handbook for parents, through a discussion at a meeting, when the child is brought to school. Appropriate teacher attitudes and an atmosphere of "welcome" are most important and lead to frequent and effective staff-parent communications of every kind.

SUMMARY

Communication is always a two-way event. A message is sent, received, and responded to in a communication. Teachers communicate with children and with parents in various ways: words that are spoken or not spoken and actions that occur or do not occur. Failure to speak or act when it is needed is responded to just as a verbal or a behavioral message is.

When a teacher believes, "I'm OK, you're OK," all her messages reflect this. Her manner of speaking, disciplining, and teaching children is a pleasant, considerate, well-mannered one. Her messages to parents are friendly and cooperative. A teacher who wants to be helpful to parents is likely to get more parent involvement than a teacher who thinks of parents only as those who are responsible to her in some way. Communication techniques with parents are the same as with any adults: appropriate use of language, respect, positive expectations, and recognition of the individuality of persons.

Fathers as well as mothers often make significant contributions to school programs if teachers communicate to them that they are needed and wanted. An awareness of the modes and techniques of communication and of the need for suitable attitudes results in good staff-child and staff-parent two-way communication.

SUGGESTED ACTIVITIES

- Observe a teacher giving a small group lesson to five-year-olds. Evaluate the presentation using the eight criteria given for verbal staff-child communication.

- With another student, role-play the following situation: a teacher is visiting the the mother of a four-year-old girl in the family home. The child is completely lacking in self-discipline after four weeks of school. The purpose of the visit is to enlist the mother's cooperation in teaching the child self-discipline. After role-playing the situation, exchange roles and replay it. How does this affect your attitudes toward each role?

- Examine your personal attitudes toward the parents of children you may teach. Write an honest statement about your attitudes. Discuss this with your instructor.

REVIEW

A. List eight verbal communication techniques by which a teacher reflects appropriate attitudes toward children.

B. List eight behavioral communication techniques by which a teacher reflects appropriate attitudes toward children.

C. Select the endings that correctly complete each of the following statements.

1. Good ways to get better acquainted with a parent are

   a. Make a surprise visit to the home.

   b. Ask her/him to attend a meeting with all the other parents.

   c. Invite her/him to have coffee at a time convenient for both of you.

   d. Wait until you have a complaint to make about the child before arranging a conference.

   e. Make an appointment by phone to make a home visit when it is convenient for both of you.

2. It is desirable to have fathers involved in the school program because

   a. They can give invaluable assistance that mothers cannot give (male image for boys to identify with).

   b. They, too, are concerned about their child's education.

   c. They can handle naughty boys better than female teachers.

   d. When both parents are active in helping the school, lasting good attitudes toward school are instilled in the child.

   e. It helps a child's self-image to have his/her dad welcome and participating in the school's affairs.

3. A teacher can communicate a desire to help parents by

   a. Telling them how they are failing to teach their children how to behave.

   b. Getting to know them well enough to discover some of their needs.

   c. By making herself available when parents express a desire to talk to her.

   d. Telling them she wishes to be helpful, and asking how she may do this.

   e. Giving special training to any parents who volunteer their services in the classroom.

unit 12 observable behaviors

OBJECTIVES

After studying this unit, the student should be able to

- List ten observable behaviors that indicate the teacher's effectiveness with children.
- List ten observable behaviors reflecting the teacher's effectiveness with parents.
- Briefly discuss a teacher's behaviors that indicate her effectiveness with adults at school other than parents.

The qualified teacher of very young children has been described in terms of her essentially human characteristics. She is expected to have certain aptitudes, attitudes, and teaching abilities. Some persons who have the desired qualities when listed on paper are not considered "good teachers" by those who observe them. This phenomenon deserves consideration.

The rapidly increasing need for preschool teachers discloses a critical shortage of certified early childhood education personnel. Therefore, other qualified persons are being encouraged to enter the field. One problem encountered is that of finding an appropriate way to determine who is qualified.

The Child Development Consortium, Inc. (C.D. A.) in Washington, D.C. is currently conducting research projects in many parts of the United States to create ways of testing the performance of teachers in early childhood programs. The concern of C.D.A. is

to find those observable behaviors that can serve as the criteria for evaluating the teacher. These behaviors may be the result of schooling, inservice training, family experience, or natural human endowment. The source is not a concern. It is the actions that can be observed that are qualifying teachers to fill many of the teaching positions available. The C.D.A. projects were still incomplete as of January 1974.

There are some basic observable behaviors that set the effective preschool teacher apart from others, however. People who have observed many teachers over a period of years sometimes distinguish certain ones with the comment, "There is a good teacher."

EFFECTIVENESS WITH CHILDREN

To be effective with children, the teacher in a day-care or a private or public school situation for young children assumes two roles. She is the transition

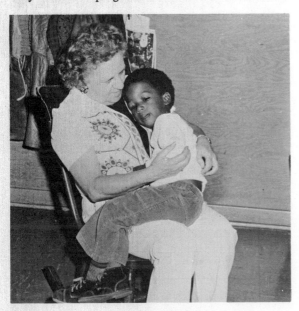

Fig. 12-1   A teacher of very young children "mothers" as well as teaches.

between the loving, cuddling mother of the infant and the much more objective elementary school teacher. Sometimes she must wear one hat, and at other times she must wear the other. There are even moments when she wears both hats. The needs of the children determine which it is. A skilled teaching technician must also be able to love, share the feelings of, and hold closely the dirty, crying, frightened four-year-old with a skinned knee. Mothering when it is needed is an observable behavior of a good teacher of little boys and girls.

The "mothering" teacher with good intentions may have a group of six children for a lesson in *visual discrimination* (finding the pictures that are the same). Two children may not meet the lesson objective. The teacher must analyze the children's responses, then restructure the lesson so that the steps are simpler. She must fill in the gaps of understanding. If she does not understand how to do this, she can not meet the children's needs for cognitive development. Being able to "reach" each child consistently is an observable behavior of an effective teacher.

A consistently pleasant personality attracts both children and adults. A warm personal greeting by name, holding a small hand as she walks through a hall, a smile — these are obvious behaviors but nonetheless important.

Flexibility shows in the teacher's spontaneous reaction to crises of daily living with preschoolers.

Fig. 12-2   Being able to hold teacher's hand for a moment brings a feeling of security to a young child.

If she remains calm, soft-voiced, sympathetic, yet reacts practically and quickly in finding a solution, she has demonstrated effectively a desirable behavior.

A teacher's ability to organize the room into learning centers appropriately equipped and inviting is easily observed. (Hopefully, she also changes the materials frequently to retain interest.)

If the children who are not having lessons are very busy pursuing independent interests and seem happy, one observes the teacher's ability to develop the children's autonomy and decision-making skills. Of course, even the best of teachers has "one of those days" occasionally.

When children warmly share their surprises, treats, and artwork with the teacher, it is because she consistently demonstrates her appreciation. Her frequent sincere praise of something the child has done further demonstrates her awareness of children's emotional needs. The acts of appreciation — a pat, hug, smile, and/or verbal praise — are observable.

When lessons are appropriate in theme, materials, and procedures, it is because the teacher analyzes children's needs and plans to meet them. When suitable lessons are prepared, children are interested during the lessons and reach the objective. This can be easily observed.

Discipline should be administered with an air of teaching, not punishing. There is no need for corporal punishment in the classroom. With some children who have known only spanking as discipline before entering school, it may be more difficult to find other effective means, but it is possible and desirable. The teacher's method of disciplining is as important as the results.

Discipline for the Very Young Child

1. Set behavioral limits; enforce the rules consistently.

2. Remind the child of the rule he has forgotten.

3. Seek the inner causes of a child's frequent misbehavior; do not just treat the symptoms.

4. Ignore minor occasional misbehavior if it does not disturb another child or destroy property.

5. When possible, let two children settle their own quarrel.

6. If two children always disagree, keep them in separate groups for a few days and then

plan activities so they can have a good experience together.

7. Accept normal curiosity about the human body. To forbid exploration is to make this an attention-getting device.

8. Avoid overstimulating situations; some children become destructive when too excited.

9. Praise good behavior; the child will want to earn more praise and will do more good things.

10. Isolate the disturber/disruptive child from the group. Give him something interesting to do.

11. The five-year-old may benefit from a discussion of his poor behavior; a younger child requires action, not words. Substitute a positive action immediately.

12. When the child expresses deep negative feelings, always repeat his statement in your own words; let him know you understand.

Fig. 12-3 Appropriate methods of discipline develop the child's self-discipline; punishment does not.

Perhaps the difference between the teacher who is effective with children and the one who is not, is that the "good teacher" cares enough about each child as an individual to find ways to help him develop to his greatest potential at the time. A lesser motivation results in lesser effectiveness.

EFFECTIVENESS WITH ADULTS

Two-way home-school cooperation can develop into a partnership that provides the best possible guidance and development for the child. The teacher establishes this bond by the manner in which she communicates with parents. If her interaction with parents is always friendly and never authoritarian or coldly businesslike, she is more effective in securing their cooperation and their involvement with the school.

It was suggested earlier that parents are to be welcomed in the classroom. Getting to know a parent personally (not at school) can be a pleasure. The meeting may be brief but beneficial. The teacher who finds ways to involve each parent in some school activities is effective with parents. She communicates with them. She shows that she understands that they

and all members of the school staff are on the same team.

In a successful program, parents are given all the information they need to understand the teacher's goals for their child. They are kept informed of his progress. Their help is asked when it is needed.

A teacher is not employed to be a social worker, but if she knows a resource or solution for any problems of the parents, she should be as helpful as possible. She wants to help them understand their child better. She is willing to teach them how to help the child learn more at home.

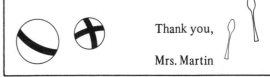

Dear Parents:

Maria is learning about sizes. She is learning to recognize an object that is *larger than* another object.

Please show her pairs of objects in her home each day. Ask her which object is "larger than" the other in each pair.

Thank you,

Mrs. Martin

Fig. 12-4 This letter is a typical request for a parent to help a child at home with a concept that is difficult for the child.

Visiting in a child's home (after making an appointment), gives the teacher insights into the child's behavior. Most parents are honored when a teacher visits them. The teacher puts them at ease, does not pry, is not critical in her conversation with them.

Parents who serve the school in any way are given some kind of recognition. It may be a handwritten "thank you" note from the teacher. It may be recognition at a parent meeting or a certificate for a specified number of hours of help in the classroom. The teacher assumes the responsibility of communicating appreciation in a way that is pleasing to the parents.

The teacher who is effective with parents can be seen warmly greeting and responding to them at every opportunity, planned and incidental. She sees that there are many formal and informal messages between school and home. A teacher who finds ways for the school to cooperate with each home is likely to be effective in developing parents who desire to cooperate with the school.

Fig. 12-5   When a parent feels welcome in the class-room, she wants to help the teacher and the children.

Fig. 12-6   The teacher appreciates the importance of those who prepare food at school.

An effective teacher reflects the culture of each family in the classroom. She makes sure that her room reflects the community's values.

A teacher has other interpersonal relationships at school besides those with parents. There are other teachers, nonparent volunteers, the school administrator and/or supervisor, specialists or consultants, evaluators, cafeteria workers or cooks, and custodians. The necessary "I'm OK, you're OK" thinking is reflected in the teacher's interactions with all these other adults. She finds time for them but does not neglect the children to do so. The effective teacher also helps children learn to appreciate the large number of adults who help to make school a good place to be.

A good relationship with the supervisor, evaluator, and principal involves professional efficiency and friendly communications. A teacher who works well with children must also work consistently to perform well in her other job duties. She is cooperative with various levels of administration.

A teacher who sincerely respects the importance of school food workers and maintenance personnel is likely to

- Show this in her manner of speaking to them.

- Point out their importance to the children so that they develop appropriate attitudes of appreciation.

- Be considerate in the ways she cooperates with them.

The behavior of the teacher when she interacts with those adults who are outside the school system (volunteers, consultants, specialists, observers) may result in greater help for the children, or it may alienate these possible sources of help. She welcomes their contributions if she wants "the most and the best" for her students.

The difference between a teacher who is rated "excellent" and one who is not may lie in the frequency in which these behaviors are observed. One who knows how to do well but fails to persist under difficult circumstances or tires before results are seen, does not achieve the same goals as a stronger, more determined person. Daily consistency in showing the behaviors desirable for the teacher results in greater effectiveness with both children and adults.

SUMMARY

A national shortage of certified early childhood personnel is making it necessary to find other qualified persons to staff early childhood programs. This is being done by choosing observable behaviors seen in effective teachers to be used as evaluation criteria. Other persons who behave these same ways are considered effective teachers and may qualify for the positions. The room, the independent learning behavior of the children, their responses to her direct teaching activities, and the general emotional climate of the classroom reveal how effective a teacher is with children.

Effectiveness with parents is observed in the types and frequency of teacher-parent communications. The quantity and quality of parent involvement for a group is another indicator of effectiveness. When the family cultures of children are visible in the classroom, it shows appropriate attitudes of appreciation of the home as an important part of the child's education.

The teacher's interaction with members of the school administration must reveal an acceptance of the importance of their roles and a willingness to cooperate in the best interest of the children. Helping children learn to appreciate the help of subordinate school personnel, such as cafeteria workers and custodians, adds to the good teacher-adult relationships at school. The daily performance of these desirable behaviors is part of the uniqueness of the teacher who is effective with children and with adults.

SUGGESTED ACTIVITIES

- Observe for a whole morning in the classroom of a preschool teacher who is rated "excellent" by her supervisor/principal. List the desirable behaviors you observe that were mentioned in this unit.

- Compare the behaviors of two teachers during the lunch period as they interact with cafeteria or maintenance personnel. List any differences of attitudes that are observed. State how you determined this.

- Observe a team of teachers (two or more) in a preschool classroom for one hour each morning on three successive days. List each of the desirable teacher behaviors observed each day. Determine the consistency. If there is a lack of it, take notes on this and explain why you think this happened.

REVIEW

A.   List ten observable behaviors of the teacher who is effective with children.

B.   List ten observable behaviors of the teacher who is effective with parents.

C.   Briefly discuss the kinds of observable behaviors that can indicate a teacher's effectiveness in school with adults other than parents.

D.   Select the correct choices to complete each of the following statements.

1.   Billy has just kicked down a tower of blocks that Tom was building. The teacher should

   a.   Tell Billy he is a mean child and cannot play with blocks anymore.

   b.   Remind Billy of the rules, remove him from the scene for a three-minute time-out on a chair in a different part of the room.

   c.   Insist that Billy apologize and rebuild the tower for Tom.

   d.   Find out why Billy behaved this way and seek to remove the cause of Billy's problem, if possible.

2.   The teacher has noticed that the janitor has not thoroughly cleaned her floor the last few weeks. She should

   a.   Discuss the problem with the janitor, asking him if there is something else she can do to cooperate.

   b.   Discuss the problem with the janitor, telling him she will report it to the principal/director if it is not cleaned thoroughly the next time.

    c.   Report it to the principal/director and ask to have the janitor clean it now.

    d.   Mop the floor or remove marks herself, then show the custodian how she expects it to be the next time.

3.   The teaching supervisor has pointed out to the teacher that the arrangement of the interest centers is creating a traffic problem in the room. The teacher should

    a.   Try to observe the problem as the supervisor stated it, then figure out a tentative rearrangement to discuss with the supervisor.

    b.   Tell the supervisor it is the best she can do with what she has.

    c.   Ask the supervisor's advice on how to eliminate the problem.

    d.   Tell the supervisor that she and the children are happy with it, and she does not see any need to change it.

Section IV Evaluation

unit 13 testing for placement

OBJECTIVES

After studying this unit, the student should be able to

- Briefly compare formal and informal testing of preschool children.
- List four criteria for selecting a test to be used with very young children.
- List at least seven "dos" and seven "don'ts" for testing the very young child.

Since time is so precious to everyone, it is an obvious waste to spend time teaching a child things that he already knows. One-year-olds show great differences in their abilities and stages of development. Some have a few teeth; others more. Some are walking; some are not. Some have a speaking vocabulary of fifty understandable words. Many use fewer words; some use more. Some are toilet-trained; most are not. If these differences can occur within one year of birth, it is not surprising that there is so much variation in the children of any other one-age level.

At present, most schools for very young boys and girls still group by age. However, mixed-age grouping is increasing now in open concept learning programs and in nongraded elementary schools. In any event, the rule of thumb for the teacher in any kind of grouping is for her to design or implement curriculum that meets the needs of every child. To do this, she must evaluate each child's needs by formal, informal, or both, kinds of testing procedures.

FORMAL AND INFORMAL TESTING

Formal testing implies that commercially produced tests are used in which every child is given the same test or tests for the purpose for which each is designed. It may be a general intelligence test to reveal child's IQ *(intelligence quotient)*. The scoring in these tests is stated in the number of months of credit received (not a percentage). The score is called the child's mental age (MA). The IQ is found by dividing mental age by chronological age (CA) (in months). The result is then multiplied by 100.

$$\boxed{\frac{MA}{CA} \cdot 100 = IQ}$$

Thus, if a child's score on an IQ test is 60 and he is 5 years old (60 months), his IQ is 100, which is considered average. Such a test is usually regarded as an indication of the child's potential for learning.

Some of these tests are designed with small objects that the child uses in a specified way or with pictures on blocks or on paper. These tests are meant to measure the child's ability to think. For some tests, he is required to understand oral directions. For others, a behavior is demonstrated using certain materials without verbal instructions or comments. Then the child is given similar materials to use in the same way. The nonverbal test is more likely to give assessments that are more nearly fair to children who have any kind of language problems.

Fig. 13-1 A formal test given to determine conceptual development may require a child to point out the objects that are "furniture."

Usually each child is given the same test or tests in the first few weeks of school. Sometimes the children are then grouped according to test scores. (This is unfair to some children who may not have been at their best on the testing day.)

If the same test is again given to each child at the end of the school year, the earlier test is called a pretest; the other is called a posttest. A child's pretest score is subtracted from his posttest score to determine how many points the child's IQ has been raised during the school year.

Other formal tests are given to determine a child's conceptual development. He may be shown two pictures and asked which one shows a specified concept (for example, something that is cold).

Formal language tests are given more frequently where children speak little or no English. Many of these use pictures to have the child (1) name in his predominant language the object/role/season shown, (2) state the names in both languages if possible, (3) test the child's sentence structures and ability to grasp the ideas in a picture. Scoring is done according to rules used with every child.

The "draw-a-man" test is sometimes used to determine a child's maturity. Points are given for each facial and body part drawn in the correct position.

Fig. 13-2   The child's drawing of a man is sometimes used as a test of his social awareness and maturity.

Formal tests are used for various purposes:

- To determine eligibility to enter a school.

- To guide the teacher in designing curriculum.

- To help complete the teacher's knowledge of the whole child.

- To detect learning disabilities or other handicaps.

- To evaluate for grouping.

- To evaluate curriculum effectiveness.

Proper uses of testing justify the increasing use of formal testing with little children. However, abuses of test scores do occur. Scores must never be used to praise or threaten either the child's parents or his teacher. Also, test scores are a poor basis for grouping in the classroom. Perhaps the greatest abuse occurs when the scores of two or more children are made available to individuals who are likely to draw incorrect conclusions from them.

A teacher must see that test results are used properly to benefit children. Formal tests may be given by a teacher but more often are administered by specially trained persons or psychologists. The cost of formal testing often makes it impractical.

Many preschools do not use formal testing. Instead they rely on informal testing usually done by the teacher. Informal testing varies from casual observations made and recorded by the teacher to the use of finely detailed checklists for each kind of development. Often the checklists are compared with developmental skills charts to determine the stages of each kind of development and what to teach next.

Many teachers develop their own checklists. When a teacher plans to develop specific skills in the children, she/he lists the concepts and subskills needed. The children are tested when they enroll to see which of the needed ideas and subskills they lack. Then the teacher develops behavioral objectives and teaches the chosen concepts and subskills.

Teachers learn to test children in a play situation so that tension is avoided for the child. Many points on a motor checklist can be observed without setting up a test at a specified time. Watching the child at play reveals some of his motor skills and limitations.

Language, also, can be tested informally. Some social skills may be tested in a natural or contrived play setting as well as during lessons. Checklists help the teacher make more thorough observations.

1. The child talks with the teacher
2. The child talks with other children
3. The child responds to questions.
4. The child identifies pictures in books.
5. The child retells a story to another child.

Fig. 13-3 Many informal language activities enable the teacher to informally evaluate the child's skills.

CRITERIA FOR TESTING

In public school systems, traditionally the teacher has little input in designing the testing program. Administrators and testing specialists decide how the children are to be evaluated. Many districts have federally funded programs for children with various kinds of handicaps: economic, language, physical, and mental. These programs include financing for thorough testing so that the effectiveness of a program may be measured. Children's needs are carefully analyzed because meeting special needs is the reason for the existence of the program.

Private schools have much more freedom in testing. Teachers often have influence about the kinds of testing that are used.

Teachers need to be aware of criteria for selecting tests or for designing new ones:

• Is the test necessary?

If unusual opportunities are available for children with specific handicaps, it is necessary to test the children for placement and eligibility. There are other kinds of situations when pretesting and posttesting is needed. This is sometimes done to show cognitive gains in testing newly developed curriculum. In other schools careful emphasis is placed on "the whole child." Such a school may feel it needs all the information available on every child. Both tests and checklists may be used for this. But if there is no special need for a test, none should be given.

• What kind of information is needed?

IQ tests have some valid uses, but they are not helpful to a teacher who needs to know the math concepts the children have so that she can write challenging behavioral objectives. The kind of information needed must be determined; then, the best way to get it must be considered.

1. Social history — birth to present; family data
2. Medical history — birth to present; immunizations
3. Entry interview evaluation
4. Records of each kind of testing, formal and informal
5. Anecdotal records — stories of incidents at school
6. Duplicates of special communications sent to parents
7. Parents' responses to communications from school
8. Dated samples of the child's work to show progress

Fig. 13-4 A "Picture" of the whole child requires many written records in his file.

• Is the test a *valid* one?

Does the selected test really test for the information needed? Commercially prepared tests provide information on validity and how it was determined. Teacher-made tests are not as reliable on this point. They must be checked very carefully for thoroughness, developmental accuracy, and relevance to needs.

• Is the selected test appropriate for the children being tested?

After a test is found necessary and informational needs are determined, the test selected must be not only a valid one but one that is appropriate for the children being tested. The pictures used in many tests are *regionally oriented*. It is unfair to show a picture of a snowball fight to a preschool child in south Texas and expect him to identify it as representative of "cold" or "winter." Clothing pictures are sometimes outdated or unfamiliar to children from varying ethnic backgrounds.

If an English language test is given to children, very careful use must be made of the scores if some of the children are *monolingual* (one language) English speakers and others are fluent in Spanish but know very little English. Such scores are useless except for determining the level of English language lessons to give each child.

In many situations informal testing by teacher observations and by using checklists is preferable. A new teacher should use developmental checklists (such as shown in unit 3) or those designed at her school to find out the stages of readiness of the children.

A teacher may also use as tests the behavioral objectives of lessons she plans to teach. Each objective tests the child's readiness for the next objective. This assumes that the objectives are in order from the easiest to the hardest developmentally.

---

1. Shown four photos, two of happy children and two that look unhappy, the child will select the two that are unhappy when asked to find them.

2. When shown three photos of persons expressing "happy," "angry," "afraid," the child will identify the feelings expressed by each of the faces in the photos.

3. When shown a picture of a smiling child, the child will tell one thing that makes him feel that way (happy).

4. When asked to tell one thing that makes him unhappy/angry at school, the child will do so.

Fig. 13-5   For affective development, this sequence of objectives may be used with four-year-olds.

The informal teacher observation is the most widely used form of evaluation for preschool children. When a child enters school, the teacher helps him adjust to the strange new situation. He/she explains rules, demonstrates equipment, and plans activities for the child to particiapte in and enjoy. The teacher observes the child's behavior during all of this and jots down notes daily on his strengths and his weaknesses until enough information is acquired to make plans for the child's development.

In comparing the folders of observed facts on the children, the teacher decides how many need help with a particular social problem, such as sharing. Then she/he designs activities and lesson objectives to help the children learn to share toys. Songs, stories, having children work in pairs with clay/blocks, and small group discussions on sharing at home and at school are included. She makes a point of carefully observing these children so that she can praise their deeds any time that they voluntarily share. This

positively reinforces behavior that the teacher wants to see continued or repeated. This is the way teacher observations are used as testing information for designing curriculum.

Date	Comments
10-3-74	Daryl persists in refusing to share. He would not share blocks, truck, and swings today. I must find stories, filmstrips, poems on *sharing*.
10-6-74	Daryl responded when given a too-large ball of clay. He shared it with Mary next to him. He was glad to get rid of the extra because he could not work with it. I will try some similar strategies each day. He liked the song and filmstrip.

Fig. 13-6   Anecdotal records often tell the story of the child's development later in the year.

DOs AND DON'Ts IN TESTING

The teacher must be aware of some *DOs* and *DON'Ts* in testing so that tests are used profitably and no kind of testing is abused. These are some of the DOs in testing very young children:

- Have parental permission for the tests to be used — except in a public school situation.

- Be sure the test is needed, valid, and appropriate for the children being tested.

- Be sure the person giving the test is qualified and has good rapport with the child.

- Know in advance what uses are to be made of test scores. (Object if they are inappropriate.)

- Test a child's intelligence only if he seems in normal good health, in good spirits, and is not tired.

- Test a child for suspected disabilities when he is at his best (rested, well-fed, at ease).

- Allow adequate time for testing; the child should never be hurried through a test.

- Make the testing as game-like as possible to keep the child free of tension.

- Test in a private place free of disturbance.

- Date all tests and observations so that they are of help in making an accurate record of attainment or of the course of a problem.

For every list of *DOs* there is a comparable list of *DON'Ts* such as the following:

- Don't give any test unless you feel qualified. Practice if necessary to perfect techniques.

- Don't make up your own rules for giving a prepared test.

- Don't discuss test scores with parents (if this is possible).

- Don't attach too much importance to a child's score on any one test.

- Don't interpret a child's needs on the basis of test scores alone. (Be alert to other needs that are revealed in other ways.)

- Don't tell the child how well he did or did not do on a test. (Never compare the scores of two children: "Mary, you did not do as well as Lucy on this.")

- Don't trust your memory in observing children; write the observation on paper.

- Don't draw conclusions from a single day's observations when using checklists. Observe the child several times before recording a yes or no.

- Don't test if you feel out of sorts or pressured. It can affect the results.

- Don't be too quick to make placement decisions on a basis of a test. Consider the whole child.

- Don't resent the time that testing takes. It usually is well worth the time. The information from any kind of test can be used in some way to better the education of that child.

SUMMARY

Formal and informal testing is needed to give the teacher information for designing learning situations to meet the needs of the children. Tests for intelligence, language, and concepts are frequently used with very young boys and girls. Nonverbal tests are more fair for preschoolers — except when testing language skills, of course. Pretesting and posttesting with the same test is sometimes used to judge the effectiveness of curriculum. Tests are used to reveal readiness, to determine eligibility to enter a class or school, to add to the picture of the whole child, and to determine grouping.

Informal testing using teacher-made tests and checklists of developmental skills is used more commonly in preschools. Informal testing is sometimes just teacher-observing in a gamelike activity. The observations should be written and dated to be most useful later.

In selecting a test, some questions should be asked: (1) Is the test necessary? (2) What kind of information is needed? (3) Is the test valid? (4) Is it appropriate for the children to be tested?

There are conditions of the person giving the test and of the child being tested that are needed for a test score to be useful. It is necessary to know the DOs and DON'Ts of testing to obtain useful scores. A teacher must know how to use, not abuse, test scores.

SUGGESTED ACTIVITIES

- Compare two intelligence tests designed to be used with children five or younger. List ways the tests are the same and ways that they are different.

- Observe a three-year-old in a nursery school program. Make written observations on the child's highest level of social, motor, and cognitive skills.

- Design three successive behavioral objectives (on one skill) that may be used as part of a checklist for a five-year-old entering kindergarten.

REVIEW

A. Briefly compare formal and informal testing of preschool children.

B. List four criteria for selecting a test to be used with very young children.

C. List at least seven DOs and seven DON'Ts for testing the very young child.

D.   Select the correct choices to complete each of the following statements.

1.   A teacher has motor skills checklists for children two, three, and four years of age. She has a new class of twelve three-year-olds on the playground and an assistant teacher to help her. She wishes to inventory the children's motor skills. The teacher should

   a.   Take the three-year-olds' checklist and a pen to the playground.

   b.   Leave the lists indoors and ask the assistant to help observe the children's play carefully to see what they can do.

   c.   Take all three lists and a pen to the playground and inform the assistant what is to be done so that she, too, can help with the observations.

   d.   Leave the lists indoors and leave the playground occasionally to mark the observations on the checklists.

2.   A school has given a teacher a conceptual development test to use with the children. Later the information is to be used in designing lessons for them. The teacher should

   a.   Give the test as it is to every child.

   b.   Check the pictures to make sure they are appropriate for the students.

   c.   Remove inappropriate pictures. Find appropriate substitute pictures if possible.

   d.   Use the test as it is but make notes on each child's score to explain the use of inappropriate pictures.

3.   A non-Spanish-speaking teacher has been trained to give a formal intelligence test to five-year-olds. The test is nonverbal for the child, but verbal directions on procedure must precede the test. Some of the pupils are Spanish-speaking and know very little English. The teacher should

   a.   Have someone write the directions in Spanish so she can learn to pronounce them in Spanish.

   b.   Ask a bilingual child in the class to repeat the directions in Spanish.

   c.   Have an interpreter there to repeat each of the directions in Spanish.

   d.   Have a qualified bilingual person give the test.

unit 14 keeping records

OBJECTIVES

After studying this unit, the student should be able to

- Briefly explain the following terms: registration form, medical history, PRC, progress chart, permission slip, anecdotal record, pretest, posttest, behavioral objective.
- List ten kinds of records a teacher may be expected to keep.
- Briefly explain three ways to keep a record of a child's progress throughout the year.

Keeping records is a time-consuming part of a teacher's responsibility which cannot be avoided. Every teacher must keep some kinds of records. The kinds and amount vary according to schools. Where there are assistant teachers, some of the clerical work is delegated to them. Teachers seldom have choices as to the types of records to be kept. In the public school systems, district administrators, the state government, and the federal government all require records. The taxpayers want to know what they are financing. In public facilities outside of the schools, the same accountability is found. Every teacher participates by providing data on the children.

Some private schools are nonprofit institutions but they, too, must keep records to prove they are nonprofit. Commercially operated day-care, kindergarten, and child development centers are businesses, with an additional business income accountability to the Internal Revenue Service.

How much record keeping is done by teachers varies in a wide range. A willingness to fulfill record keeping responsibilities, whatever they are, is a good trait for a teacher to have. Student teachers should learn to keep records.

SCHOOL REQUIREMENTS

Although states vary in their requirements regarding school records, there are some kinds that are common to nearly all public schools. These include registration form, medical history, and permanent record card (PRC) for each child.

The *registration form* is filled out when the child first enters a school district. (It may be transferred to other schools within a school district.) It contains pertinent current facts about the child's life, some family information, and possibly information needed to qualify the child for a special program in the district, such as bilingual, Headstart, and handicap programs.

A *medical history* may include only a record of immunizations. More often it also includes a record of early childhood illnesses, any known condition requiring medication, and developmental history. It

Evaluation of Aptitudes								
Placement at time of evaluation								
Initiative								
Leadership								
Sense of Humor								
Self-Control								
Soc. Acceptability								
Service to School								

Fig. 14-1A   These charts are taken from a permanent record card (PRC).

Evaluation of Adjustments								
Placement at time of evaluation								
Self-confidence								
Work Habits								
Punctuality								
Effort in Studies								
Social Adjustments								
To Peers								
To Adults								
To Authority								

Fig. 14-1B   These charts are taken from a permanent record card (PRC).

HEALTH INFORMATION AND EMERGENCY CARE AUTHORIZATION

Pupil's Name _____ Teacher _____ Room ___
         Last   First

Address _____ Home Phone _____

Dear Parent: In order to provide better service to your child, the school needs the
              following information on file:

_____
Family Doctor's Name   Address   Phone

_____
Alternate adult (if parent   Address   Phone
cannot be reached at home)

The school does not assume any financial responsibility, but does wish to provide
the best service possible in an emergency. By signing this card you are giving us
authority to call a physician or to transport your child to the County Hospital
if neither you nor the listed alternate adult can be reached immediately.

Parent's or Guardian's Signature   Date   Phone

_____
Father's place of employment   Address   Phone

_____
Mother's place of employment   Address   Phone

Fig. 14-2   Most schools for very young children use forms similar to this one for emergency information.

may include when the child first talked and walked, any allergies he may have, and other information of this kind.

The PRC (permanent record card) is a large form intended to be used for a child from preschool through high school. It goes with him wherever he transfers. It contains family information on parents and siblings (sisters and brothers). The language spoken in the child's home is noted. A record of attendance by school terms is on the PRC. The child's academic record, as well as his teachers' names and dates of all the schools he has attended are kept on this important form. Part of it includes a medical history and behavioral picture recorded by teachers. There may be space for evaluations of aptitudes, adjustments, and test data not directly relating to curriculum.

Many types of records other than these may be found: the kinds of information needed to qualify for federal assistance to schools, such as Free Lunch Program, Bilingual Education, Education for the Handicapped, the Exceptional Child, Headstart, and others. Emergency information cards on where to reach parents, alternate adults, family physician, and clinic are required in most early childhood schools. *Progress charts* to inform parents are sometimes used but the current trend is away from this practice.

A parent conference is more helpful to both parent and teacher. There must be interaction to achieve cooperation.

Daily written records include attendance, lunch count, school emergencies. Periodical records include the PRC, progress reports if used, quarterly or mid-term school reports and evaluations. "One time" reports are the registration form, social history, emergency forms, and medical record before entering school.

A class register is kept by each teacher for the use of her school office. In private schools, additional financial records are required about tuition, donations, books, and similar items. Large schools may have a finance office for keeping these records. In small schools, the teacher keeps them. A principal or school head is usually responsible to higher administration for turning in all records on a schedule set by the administration (Board of Education, Trustees, Owner, Superintendent). Permission slips of several kinds may be needed. Many schools encourage parents to sign blanket *permission slips* for medical emergencies and for field trips.

A good teacher develops the habit of keeping all records up to date daily. A few minutes a day spent in record keeping saves many hours later.

PERMISSION SLIP

I give my permission for _____ to have all necessary medical tests, medical examinations, immunizations, laboratory tests, and treatments from the physicians, dentists, and other health personnel of the preschool and school health program and to be transported by school personnel for these services if I cannot take the child myself.

_____
Parent's Signature

PERMISSION TO GO ON FIELD TRIPS

I give my child _____ permission to attend any and all field trips sponsored by the EARLY CHILDHOOD PROGRAM during the school year. .

_____
Parent's Signature

INSURANCE: Medicaid or other _____

Fig. 14-3   Some schools ask parents to sign permission slips like this one to cover many events during the school year.

ANECDOTAL RECORDS

Anecdotal records are very brief *anecdotes* (stories) of an event or situation involving a child. If a teacher thinks that an incident involving the child is important or very unusual, she jots down her observation on a note card or in a notebook and dates it. An individual folder is kept for each child. Several cards in the child's folder may be about one kind of behavior, indicating the kind of problem he has. As was mentioned in the unit on testing, these records can be very helpful for a doctor or specialist if one is needed.

Looking back, the stories (anecdotes) can be a record of social progress, affective development, and improvement of self-discipline. They can also help a teacher in self-evaluation if they reflect consistent effectiveness, or lack of it.

Only a very unusual act, a problem, or suspicion of a problem merits the teacher's time in writing anecdotal records. If there is a need, however, this very simple measure serves the purpose in many cases.

PRETESTING AND POSTTESTING

A school that has specific goals in mind for its children is often justified in testing them at the beginning of the year and again at the end of the school year using the same test/tests both times. By comparing a child's scores on one particular test, his progress may be determined in the area tested. This may be his IQ, his language, conceptual or motor development. By comparing his pretest and posttest scores on a whole battery of tests, school personnel are likely to form a clearer picture of the child's development.

Many variables affect test scores: the conditions under which the testing takes place, the condition of the person testing and of the child, and the appropriateness of the test. Where it is deemed necessary to test for the effectiveness of new curriculum, only random sampling is used. This means children are selected at random. (It may be that every tenth name on the list is chosen.) Teachers are not given the privilege of selecting students to be tested for this purpose. It would be too tempting for a teacher to select the best students and this would not suit the purpose of the testing. At least ten percent of a group is tested before the results can be meaningful. The same children who are pretested must be the ones who are posttested.

If several of the children in a class are pretested,

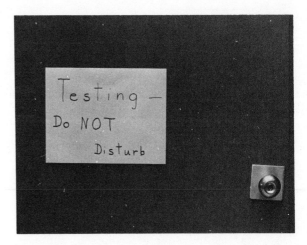

Fig. 14-4   Testing must be done in a place that is free from distractions.

they must not be given any special treatment during the year by the teacher. To give them attention not received by the other children would nullify the validity of any gains that are shown. In a minimal way, consistent high gains made by children of one teacher are a reflection of successful teaching, too. No written curriculum is teacher-proof. It is the teacher who makes any curriculum effective or not effective.

BEHAVIORAL OBJECTIVES

A behavioral objective states the performance (behavior) that is expected of the student at the end of a period of instruction (lesson). It describes the conditions under which the behavior is expected to occur. It does not describe the process or procedure for learning. It states the goal or objective that should result.

A series of behavioral objectives may be developed leading to a high level of skill (for a four-year-old). The objectives may be placed sequentially in the lesson plan twice a week, weekly, biweekly, or any chosen time. The child must reach objective A before he is ready to try objective B; he must perform the behavior stated in objective B before he is ready for objective C.

Records are kept for each child. By looking at the child's name on a class progress chart where the objectives are enumerated, the teacher has a record of the child's achievement in the designated skill. The records are used to design lessons for him for sectional or monthly tests, and for parent conferences. Since the child masters each objective before he is given a harder one, he retains his self-confidence. There is no

Specific Conditions	Specific Behaviors
1. After listening to a tape of the story,	the child will correctly answer two questions about the story events.
2. When shown an illustration from a familiar story,	the child will tell the story incident illustrated by the picture.
3. Given a volley ball and standing five feet away,	the child will bounce the ball to the teacher so that she need not step to catch it.
4. Given 6 inch-cubes (3 red, 3 blue) and a design card for 5 cubes (3 red, 2 blue),	the child will reproduce the model design with 5 of the inch cubes.

Fig. 14-5 Carefully stated behavioral objectives make it easy to evaluate the level of the child's skill if each success is recorded on a progress chart.

failure. There are only differences in time between successes for different children. Keeping a daily record of objectives mastered by each child is a crucial form of record keeping. It means a steady progression of development for the child when the progress charts are used wisely by a teacher.

PROGRESS CHARTS

There are many varieties of progress charts in use for very young children. Progress may be measured in every kind of development: motor, cognitive, and affective. Where each of these is a planned part of the curriculum, some record of each child's success is needed for two reasons: (1) to know what each child is ready to learn next and (2) to make changes in the curriculum when the children's needs are not being met.

When behavioral objectives are used to state instructional outcomes, a simple chart listing children's names at the side and numbered or lettered objectives across the top gives information at a quick glance. This helps the teacher to group children according to learning needs. It also tells her which objectives each child is ready for the next day.

If behavioral objectives are not used, other kinds of record keeping must be considered. If general instructional goals are listed, individual record sheets may contain a list of the goals. As the child reaches a goal, it is checked and dated.

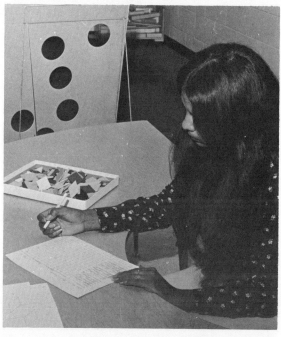

Fig. 14-6 At the end of each lesson, the results should be marked on a daily progress chart.

If developmental skills charts are used to test children when they enter school, these tests may be given again periodically to record progress. If the teacher-written observations are used to determine the readiness of the children, then time should be set aside at least twice more during the school year for making careful written observations. These may then be compared with any earlier ones to determine changes the child is showing.

Some schools design their own methods of keeping records. The source of the record keeping is not as vital as the consistency with which it is done. Thorough record keeping is helpful to children in many ways. A teacher never knows when a child may show signs of a serious problem of some nature. Usually this means finding out by all possible means everything that is known about the child. Records of every kind can be important to an accurate, swift analysis of the problem.

SUMMARY

All schools require every teacher to keep several kinds of records. Public school requirements include records of the children's progress for the teacher's use, class records of attendance and lunch or other money brought by the child for school purposes, and other records for school district administration. All programs not financed by the general budget of the school district require special forms of record keeping. Private schools have similar records and additional kinds of bookkeeping for business income for tax purposes.

Three important kinds of records that the teacher can use are progress charts, anecdotal records, and behavioral objectives. Using these can result in curriculum that better meets each child's needs.

SUGGESTED ACTIVITIES

- Design a progress chart that would be helpful to you in evaluating a five-year-old's progress in motor development. Compare yours with those of other students.

- Write an imaginary series of five anecdotal note cards on a three-year-old child who bites her classmates.

- Select an age level: three, four, or five. Write a series of four to six behavioral objectives to be used one per week in developing one cognitive skill (any you wish). Show how to keep a group's record of achievement in developing the skill.

REVIEW

A. Briefly explain the following terms: registration form, medical history, PRC, progress chart, permission slip, anecdotal record, pretest, posttest, behavioral objective.

B. List ten kinds of records a teacher may be expected to keep.

C. Briefly explain three ways to record a child's progress throughout the year.

unit 15 evaluation of teachers

OBJECTIVES

After studying this unit, the student should be able to

- Briefly describe and compare self-evaluation, supervisory evaluation, and parent evaluation of teachers.
- Compare formal and informal teacher evaluations.
- Explain the importance of parent evaluations of teachers.

In a good program, curriculum is constantly evaluated, then improved according to needs shown by the evaluations. But any curriculum is only as effective as the teacher who uses it. So it is essential that teachers, too, be more effective. To be fair, a picture of "the whole teacher" is needed just as a picture of "the whole child" is needed in an evaluation. In early childhood education this includes self-evaluation on the part of the teacher and evaluations of the teacher by a supervisor and by parents. Each kind can be helpful to the teacher if the reports are largely objective (based on facts, not on opinions), honest, and thorough.

SELF-EVALUATION

A teacher who wants each child to have maximum benefits from his school days is constantly making changes to meet the child's needs. This teacher is a pragmatist, one who says: "Plan A was not successful, so I'll try Plan B. If it does not work, I'll try other plans until I find one that does work."

Each change is preceded by a self-evaluation. The teacher admits the fact that her efforts are sometimes ineffective. Then she seeks better ways to do things. This indirect self-evaluation is highly motivating to improving teacher effectiveness.

On all levels of education today, the uses of more direct forms of self-evaluation are on the increase. In some schools, new teachers are given a checklist of teacher behaviors that are considered important in that particular school. The list may be for the teacher's private use only. In other schools, at the beginning of the school year, the teacher is given a self-evaluation sheet to be reviewed periodically with the head of the school (principal/director). Usually the teacher's strengths and weaknesses are discussed by both persons in a conference. Suggestions for im-

provement are to be based on the teacher's self-evaluation. She should be given help in areas where she needs and requests it.

Fig. 15-1 A teacher reviews her self-evaluation checklist with her director.

A typical self-evaluation form for teachers usually contains some items that are subjective, such as good grooming and health habits. Today the trend is toward greater objectivity based on teaching performance. However, because of the nature of the teacher's role in early childhood education—being a model for young children in every way—items that ask for *subjective information* (personal opinion) must not be completely eliminated. It has been previously established that a preschool teacher's effectiveness depends somewhat on the kind of person she is. If the teacher thinks of herself as a model for the children on the items that call for opinion, she is more likely to be objective in her responses.

Judging personal traits of a teacher can easily result in differences of opinion in two persons. For

---

Teacher's Self Evaluation Checklist

1.   Am I prepared for the lessons every day? _____

2.   Do I use the curriculum guide accurately? _____

3.   Do I provide additional relevant materials? _____

4.   Do I individualize instruction if needed? _____

5.   Am I fair to every child? _____

6.   Am I warm-natured with every child? _____

7.   Am I consistently well-groomed and appropriately dressed? _____

8.   Am I consciously helping every child develop a positive self-concept? _____

9.   Do I admit my errors? _____

10. Do I persist until I reach every child? _____

11. Do I keep my records accurately and up to date? _____

12. Am I trying to involve all the parents in their child's educational experience? _____

13. Do I contact parents as often as I should? _____

14. Do I actively seek help when I need it? _____

15. Have I a good personal relationship with the children and with adults at school? _____

S=satisfactory   S+=outstanding   I=improvement needed

Fig. 15-2   The teacher must think of herself as a model for the children as she uses this kind of self-evaluation chart.

---

this reason, open exchange of ideas and verbal interaction is vital to reaching an understanding on areas where improvement is needed.

Experienced teachers in some schools have an interview with the head of the school soon after school begins. At this time the teacher is asked to evaluate her past performance and to set specific behaviorally stated goals for the new year. At midyear in a conference, the teacher reevaluates her performance according to the goals she has set for herself. If necessary, new goals may be stated for the rest of the year.

In public schools, if a teacher and principal do not agree on the teacher's evaluation of herself, she may ask for a hearing by the school board or by a higher level person in the district. In some few cases, other staff in the same school may be asked for their observations although peer evaluation is not popular. Usually one teacher has not had enough free time to carefully observe another teacher.

If a school does not have a self-evaluation chart for the teacher, she may write her own goals and use

1.   I will individualize instruction to see that every child meets every objective in each sequence.

2.   I will devote at least three hours weekly to communicating with parents by phone or in person.

3.   I will give every child time for creativity each week, (daily when possible).

4.   I will accentuate the positive and eliminate the negative in the room, as much as I can.

5.   I will read to the children and listen to them daily.

Fig. 15-3   A preschool teacher wrote these behaviorally stated goals for her own self-evaluation checklist.

them as a checklist for evaluating herself. She may ask others to make observations to help her. Using a videotaping machine is the best way for a teacher to evaluate herself. If a school principal does little classroom observing, he may gladly do more if asked. He may feel happy that the teacher wishes to improve and that he is welcome in the classroom.

There are many forms of self-evaluation for the teacher. All or any of them can improve teaching and increase total effectiveness as a teacher.

SUPERVISORY EVALUATION

The role and title of the teaching supervisor varies greatly from school to school. The variety of titles includes teaching supervisor, head teacher, lead teacher, consultant, principal, assistant principal, director, assistant director, instructional leader, and others.

The role of "supervisor" in public schools is gradually changing from that of a teacher and teaching-evaluator to that of a resource person for the teacher. This person is one to whom the teacher turns for advice, help, and materials. However, in all good schools, some one (regardless of title) is responsible for the quality of the program. This person has a need to evaluate teaching in order to improve the quality of the instructional program. It is the evaluating done by this person that is to be discussed in this section.

Children behave best when limits and goals are set for them and made known to them at the beginning of the school year. This is also true of teachers. A teacher has a right to know the criteria on which she is to be evaluated later.

The evaluation form should be shown before the school year starts. This gives the teacher a frame of reference (limits) within which she can operate. It helps her to set her own goals and to more efficiently evaluate herself. If the evaluator has other criteria to add, this, too, should be made known before mistakes are made.

Many kinds of evaluation forms are used. For teachers of very young children the following major headings are found in most of them: (1) preparation, (2) teaching, (3) classroom, (4) discipline, (5) interpersonal relationships.

To receive a favorable report, a teacher must give evidence of planning and preparedness for daily activities. Room appearance, convenience of needed materials, and handling of emergencies are included.

The teaching procedures used may or may not be evaluated in great detail. Where teachers have

been trained in teaching techniques and strategies, they are evaluated on those.

The classroom should appear attractive, be arranged for children's convenience, and be stocked with appropriate furnishings, including furniture of an appropriate size.

Discipline is to be apparent in the self-discipline of the children rather than by punishment for breaking rules. When rules are broken, teaching the rules is appropriate discipline.

The teacher's rapport with the children and warmth and pleasantness in interaction with others in the room (especially parents) are criteria for evaluating her interpersonal relationships in the classroom. The teacher's attitude toward observation and evaluation is also considered.

In a private moment, the supervisor discusses her evaluation with the teacher. Usually a teacher is asked to sign the evaluation, saying that she has been informed of it. If she does not agree, or feels that the supervisor is unfair, she may tell the evaluator, then request a hearing from a higher level of administration.

The most important part of a supervisory evaluation is the follow-up. Based on the evaluation, needs that are revealed are to be met by the teacher. Help is to be found for her if she is unable to solve the problem herself. After a reasonable, agreed-on time, another evaluation is held to determine if the teacher has acted upon the information and deserves a better evaluation.

Small private schools often do not use formal evaluation procedures. Daily informal observations may be reflected in casual conversation. Where a supervisory evaluator is located daily at the school site, in a small school, occasional suggestions can be given to help improve a teaching situation. This is informal supervisory evaluation. The size and type of school usually determines which kind is better: formal, written, detailed evaluations or informal, conversational praise, suggestion, and correction.

PARENT EVALUATION

Parent involvement in schools is now recognized as a necessity. Cooperation between school and home can prevent many of the problems the schools are having today. Parents of very young children have set a good example for parents of older children in this matter. As a child grows less dependent on his parents, the parents tend to reduce their involvement with the school to signing report cards, discussing

---

Teacher Evaluation

Teacher:	Date:
Evaluator:	Time:
<u>Kind of Lesson:</u>	<u>Age Level or Grade:</u>

1.   Preparation (room and lessons) _____

2.   Transitions _____

3.   Discipline _____

4.   Individualized instruction _____

5.   Use of teaching media _____

6.   Self-directed activities _____

7.   Relationships with adults in room _____

8.   Punctuality (attendance and clerical work) _____

9.   Evidence of creativity _____

10.   Appearance and enthusiasm _____

Fig. 15-4   This chart is typical of many used for supervisory evaluations of teachers.

poor grades with the teacher, and attending a monthly meeting of the Parent-Teacher Association (the **PTA).**

Schools for special causes and federally financed school programs have experimented, hoping to find how to have maximum parent involvement. Parents are now part of policy-making groups for some schools. This has proved beneficial where schools previously seemed indifferent to the needs of the students. In other places, parents are part of the evaluation team.

Many problems can be foreseen in having a formal evaluation of teaching by parents, however.

- Employment schedules prevent some parents from observing in the classroom.

Guide for Evaluating Lesson Presentation		
		Superior — Weak
Objectives	1. Clear, understood by learners	(1) 5 4 3 2 1
	2. Appropriate for learners	(2) 5 4 3 2 1
Planning	3. Organization of learning experiences, content	(3) 5 4 3 2 1
	4. Instructional procedures and materials prearranged	(4) 5 4 3 2 1
Performance	5. Appropriateness of instructional procedures	(5) 5 4 3 2 1
	6. Involvement of learners	(6) 5 4 3 2 1
	7. Questions asked by teacher: designed to encourage creative and independent thinking	(7) 5 4 3 2 1
	8. Evidence of the right amount of teacher direction	(8) 5 4 3 2 1
	9. Learner interest and attention	(9) 5 4 3 2 1
	10. Teacher-pupil rapport	(10) 5 4 3 2 1
Follow-up and Evaluation	11. Appropriate for objectives designed to reinforce concepts of skills presented in lesson	(11) 5 4 3 2 1
	12. Appropriate for learners, not too difficult	(12) 5 4 3 2 1
Total Presentation	13. General evaluation of this teacher and of this presentation	(13) 5 4 3 2 1

Highest Possible Score 65. This is
Teacher's Score _____

_____

Lesson Taught: (Visual Discrimination/Auditory Discrimination)

Teacher _____

Observer _____

Length of time observed _____   Date _____

Fig. 15-5   Detailed evaluation of teaching strategies is helpful in improving teaching effectiveness.

- Some classrooms are so small and crowded that visitors and students are uncomfortable if observers are squeezed in.

- Some parents cannot be objective.

- Some parents are unable to understand the purposes and criteria for evaluation.

- It has not been determined how much importance the parent evaluations should be given compared to that of the supervisor.

In spite of these difficulties, where parent's evaluative input is sought, improvements are being made. The form of the evaluation must vary according to the

Fig. 15-6 Classroom furnishings of the correct size show the teacher's understanding of children's needs.

parents. Minimally it should include asking each parent to state any changes he would like to see in his child's classroom and his approval or disapproval of his child's learning experiences at school. The parent's evaluations—written, whenever possible—must not be considered more important than the professional educator's observations. They can, however, be considered a part of the picture of "the whole teacher". When enough importance is placed on parents' evaluations, it will be easier to keep parents interested in cooperating with schools as their children grow older.

Since the affective development of the child is crucial in the preschool years, parent evaluation of preschool teachers is essential. Possibly it is also more reliable than their evaluations of teachers of older

children. A child's moods, appreciations, personality growth, ability to get along with others, and self-discipline are more obvious in the home than is his cognitive development.

Another encouraging aspect of parent evaluations is that it implies that schools will inform parents of program content, goals for students, and of evaluation procedures used. In turn, parents make a greater effort to learn more about what does go on in their child's classroom. Parent evaluation of teaching can lead to much improved home-school communications. This leads to the greater cooperative team effort for home and school that is a major goal in education today.

SUMMARY

The primary purpose of the evaluation of teachers is to help teachers become more effective as persons and as teachers.

Self-evaluation by a teacher may be self-initiated or part of a school program for professional growth. A teacher may list her own goals, then frequently check her list. She may use checklists given her by the school for her own use or for a conference later. The administrator or instructional leader may help her redefine her goals when reviewing her list with her.

Supervisory criteria for evaluation should be given a teacher at the beginning of the school year. The trend is toward using performance-based observations and away from using the evaluator's opinions. A teacher who does not agree with an evaluation may request a hearing from a higher level of administration. Most forms require observations on the teacher's preparedness, teaching procedures, and interpersonal relationships. They also require information

<table>
<tr><td colspan="3" align="center">**Orientation for Parents**</td></tr>
<tr><td colspan="3" align="center">**Table of Contents**</td></tr>
<tr><td>1.</td><td>Our Philosophy of Education . . . .</td><td>p. 1</td></tr>
<tr><td>2.</td><td>Our Goals for Your Child . . . .</td><td>p. 4</td></tr>
<tr><td>3.</td><td>The Curriculum . . . .</td><td>p. 7</td></tr>
<tr><td>4.</td><td>How We Can Help You . . . .</td><td>p. 12</td></tr>
<tr><td>5.</td><td>How You Can Help Us . . . .</td><td>p. 15</td></tr>
</table>

Fig. 15-7 A booklet given to parents at the beginning of the school year can motivate cooperation between the school and the home.

on the appearance and management of the classroom as well as discipline of the children in the room.

Necessary follow-up procedure includes a later conference to evaluate the changes made by teacher as a result of the earlier conference. This is essential.

Small private schools often use informal supervisory methods such as casual conversation to relay needs observed and ideas for handling them.

Parent evaluation of teaching is proving to be a viable extension of parental involvement in schools. While parents need help to become objective evaluators, giving them this help improves home-school cooperation. The affective development of the child is of utmost importance in the early years. It is also the easiest form to observe in the home. Parents can learn to carefully evaluate this part of their child's development. This provides assistance for the teacher who wants to improve her program.

SUGGESTED ACTIVITIES

- Create a teacher self-evaluation checklist that you think will be helpful to you. Compare it with those created by other students and make changes if you wish.

- Find a supervisory teacher evaluation checklist currently in use. Using the list, evaluate any preschool teacher you have observed three or more times. Base your report on teacher behaviors and not on personal opinion. Discuss the report with your instructor.

- Obtain a parent's written evaluation of one of his preschool child's teachers. No names need be used. After reading the evaluation, write a summary of how you think this evaluation may or may not be useful.

REVIEW

A. Briefly define each of the following: self-evaluation, supervisory evaluation, parent evaluation, formal evaluation, informal evaluation, "the whole teacher", pragmatist, subjective information, objective information, and resource person.

B. Name and briefly define the five areas of evaluation that are common to nearly all teacher evaluation checklists.

C. Select the choices that correctly complete each of the following statements.

1. A pragmatic kindergarten teacher has made phone calls and home visits and has sent home typewritten notes for three months, but the parents of her students do not come to the PTA meetings.

    She will probably

    a. Ask other teachers to help her find ideas to interest the parents.

    b. Say she has done more than most teachers and resign herself to having parents who will not come.

    c. Find out from some of the parents the reasons why they do not come, then develop plans to counteract the reasons.

    d. Go right on telephoning, visiting, and sending notes to the parents and hope they will start coming.

2. At a conference, a school principal has shown a very good teacher of four-year-olds the evaluation sheet he has made out about her teaching performances. She disagrees with his evaluation of her room discipline. He has rated her ineffective because of the noise level and movement in her room. She thinks the principal does not understand four-year-old children. She considers the very active learning activities and increasing verbalization appropriate.

    She will probably

a. Sign the evaluation sheet and try to restrict the children more.

b. Explain to the principal the developmental differences between fours and fives so that he can understand her reasons for having the room as he observed it.

c. Sign the sheet and immediately write a letter of protest to the personnel office.

d. Agree to sincerely try to understand his position and to observe carefully the children's behavior as well as to invite him to visit the classroom at a time when she is free to explain the purpose and needs for the kinds of things he observed.

3. Twelve pairs of parents of children in a nursery school class of three-year-olds have turned in to the director some forms that are used to evaluate the teacher. All the evaluations but one are highly positive. One set of parents are complaining that the teacher is not teaching their child anything.

The director will probably

a. Give the teacher an excellent rating in her personnel file and ignore the one negative report.

b. Inform the teacher that she needs to spend more time teaching the one child whose parents complained.

c. Give the teacher an excellent rating in her personnel file, but arrange a conference with the teacher and parents to find out in what ways the school can do more for the child.

d. Write a letter to the parents explaining that every child learns from his environment and inviting them to come and observe their child as he learns.

Section V Interstaff Relationships

unit 16 teacher and assistant teacher

OBJECTIVES

After studying this unit, the student should be able to

- Briefly discuss the kinds of objectives that should be mutual to the members of a teaching team.
- Briefly discuss ways to handle points of disagreement between the members of a teaching team.
- List six kinds of behavior found in job descriptions for both teacher and assistant teacher and two behaviors unlikely to be found in that of the assistant teacher.

The teaching team composed of a teacher and one or more assistant teachers operates best if each team member believes that "two heads are better than one". There are still a few experienced and less flexible teachers who prefer to work independently without an assistant. The teacher who is concerned about each child knows that every group of very young children needs an extra pair of eyes, ears, hands, and legs — on some days if not on all days. Realizing this need, most early childhood teachers truly appreciate assistants. They find it worth the time and effort needed to develop democratic teamwork of the finest kind.

MUTUAL OBJECTIVES

The teacher and assistant teacher must agree on long-range objectives for the children so that both will be striving toward the same goals and learning outcomes. A mutual understanding of the developmental characteristics of each child enables the team to agree on short-range objectives. The more specific goals may then be in terms of levels of visual, motor, auditory, language, and social skills and of concept development.

Finally, the team members are ready to write behavioral objectives for daily lessons. As a planning team, they should agree on the activities for each day and the behavioral goals for the children.

If a prepared curriculum is given to the staff, it should be carefully reviewed for its appropriateness for the children. The teaching team should agree on

any changes needed to meet the specific circumstances. For instance, if the curriculum is for children just learning the English language, the language of instruction recommended in a commercial curriculum guide may not be desirable for some of the children. The language to be used should be agreed upon by the staff members, all of whom are aware of the levels of the children's language development.

Long-range learning outcomes, goals for skill development in the children, and behavioral objectives for working toward each skill are the three kinds of mutual objectives that the members of a teaching team must share if their work is to be effective. If one member of a teaching team does not agree with the goals of another, there is behavioral evidence of the disagreement. Soon the children notice and are quick to take advantage of the situation.

Mrs. A considers it important that children learn to put away their toys and materials. Mrs. B thinks they will have the rest of their lives for that and that "they're only little once". The children will soon leave out all the toys and materials (even those children who are required to pick them up at home). They hope that Mrs. B puts them away before Mrs. A notices. Mrs. A has little chance to teach what is important to her as long as Mrs. B puts away the children's things.

If Mrs. A is the teacher and Mrs. B the assistant, Mrs. A has the right to require Mrs. B to see that the children observe the classroom rule. If Mrs. B is the

	Mrs. Lopez Teacher	Mrs. Jones Assistant	Independent Activities
8:30-9:00 A.M.	Greet and circulate	Greet and circulate	
9:00-9:15 A.M.	Group A Visual	Group B Auditory	Group C
9:15-9:30 A.M.	Group B Visual	Group C Auditory	Group A
9:30-9:45 A.M.	Group C Visual	Group A Auditory	Group B
9:45-10:00 A.M.	Snack for all groups		
10:00-10:45 A.M.	Group A Concepts Group B Concepts Group C Concepts	Group B Motor Group C Motor Group A Motor	Group C Group A Group B
10:45-11:00 A.M.	Group A Language	Group B Magic Circle	Group C
11:00-11:15 A.M.	Group B Language	Group C Magic Circle	Group A
11:15-11:30 A.M.	Group C Language	Group A Magic Circle	Group B
11:30-11:50 A.M.	Playground for all		
11:50-12 Noon	Clean up and set tables		
12:00-12:30 P.M.	Lunch for all		
12:30-1:15 P.M.	Rest for all		(each adult takes a 15 minute break)
1:15-1:30 P.M.	Music for all		
1:30-2:00 P.M.	Creative Art for all		

Fig. 16-1 This planning chart shows which lessons are to be taught by the teacher and which ones by the assistant.

Fig. 16-2   Unless all the members of the teaching team agree that it is important, the children may not learn to put away the toys.

Teacher:	Alice, you seem very unhappy th morning, and I'm concerned. Could we talk about it while the children rest after lunch?
Assistant:	Yes, I am unhappy. I'm sorry if it showed, though. I don't want to upset the children, but there were some things I didn't like this morning.
Teacher:	I sense that I may be responsible. If so, I'm sorry. I'd like to discuss it.
Assistant:	So would I. I'll feel better. Yes, let's talk about it when the children rest.

Fig. 16-3   When a staff member is unhappy about the actions of another staff member, the matter should be discussed promptly.

teacher and Mrs. A the assistant, Mrs. A may not be able to teach the children what is important to her because she will not receive support from Mrs. B who has the authority to refuse.

In a democratic atmosphere, such disagreements are talked over. If there are more than two members on the team and the matter is an arbitrary one, a decision may be voted on, and a majority vote rules. Often a compromise can be worked out: if the children may receive help in putting away small manipulatives and art materials but are required to put away wheel toys, blocks, and role-playing materials, both adults may have enough satisfaction that friction will not be apparent to the children. The teachers' behaviors reflect mutual objectives in a compromise.

PERSONALITIES

Effective teachers and assistant teachers may be found with a wide range of personalities. It is not important that labels be given to the types of personalities found in a teaching team. It is very important, however, that the personalities complement each other to produce harmony. Personality differences may mean that each person is an outstanding model for the team in one aspect of personality. All members of a teaching team must be good models for the children. Each member can also be an excellent model for the adults in the room.

Miss Mary's personality is at its best in greeting each child, making him feel welcome, and seeing that he is engaged in an interest of his choice. Miss Sylvia is shy but becomes more open and warm later in the

day. It is she from whom the children receive a gentle push to complete what has been started in late-in-the-day projects. When a child is overly tired, he turns to Miss Sylvia for a moment of quiet warmth. Miss Mary and Miss Sylvia work well together in meeting all the children's needs.

Frequently one member of a team is a superior model for language development. The others should take advantage of the opportunity to work with this person and actively seek to imitate the better language model—for their own sakes and for the children's benefit. In these and other ways, teaching team members can benefit from one another. When their goals are mutually accepted, personality enrichment can result for the adults as well as the children.

In spite of good intentions and mutual objectives, occasionally a personality conflict occurs. There should be opportunities for two staff members to frankly, but privately, discuss the behaviors which are upsetting to them. (Dissatisfaction is usually com-

Mary Ruben

Fig. 16-4   All members of the teaching team should be good models for the children in every way. The child's name on his papers should be in good manuscript form even though he has not yet begun to write: staff members should practice, if necessary.

mon to both team members.) If both members intend to be cooperative, each will explain and each will listen to the other. Frequently, hearing an explanation for an annoying behavior places it in a different perspective. If there is no apparent need or reason for the behavior to continue, it may be ended once the guilty but considerate person realizes that the action is annoying the other person. Sometimes a teacher's or an assistant teacher's personality seems to blossom once she is a member of a teaching team dedicated to the well-being of the adults as well as to the best interests of the children.

Fig. 16-5 It is helpful to discuss dissatisfactions before they grow.

JOB DESCRIPTIONS

A job description is a list of duties and behaviors that describes the work expected of a person holding the job. The duties of early childhood teachers vary greatly. Many of those common to all have been discussed in previous units:

- Analyzing children's levels of development.
- Designing and implementing curriculum to meet the children's needs.
- Communicating effectively with staff, children, and parents.
- Testing.
- Keeping records.
- Self-evaluation.

The detailed form of each of these tasks varies from school to school.

Assistant teachers were once held responsible only for carrying out the plans of teachers. This is no longer true in many schools—public, nonprofit private, and commercial. To develop the assistant teacher's skills, inservice training is scheduled regularly during working hours. In some schools, the teachers and assistants are trained together so that they can operate from a single base of information.

Position: Assistant teacher for a class of three-year-olds. Male or female is expected to perform the following:

a. Learn to teach lessons as prescribed by the certified teacher.

b. Become involved in the parental involvement program.

c. Establish good rapport with the children.

d. Be a reasonably good model for the children in grooming, cleanliness, and use of language.

e. Help the teacher plan and implement the curriculum.

f. Attend regularly the inservice training sessions held during working hours.

g. Assist teacher with clerical work and other duties in the classroom.

h. Help supervise outdoor activities and field trips.

Fig. 16-6 Job descriptions for assistant teachers are usually brief and contain generalized statements.

In some instances, the official school district rules require the certified teacher to fill out specified official forms and records. Usually clerical work is shared by the team members wherever this is permitted.

Consistently, two differences are found between the job description of the teacher and that of the assistant teacher. In most schools the teacher must accept ultimate responsibility for the learning environment, the emotional climate in the classroom, and the education of the children assigned to her during school hours. Also, the teacher is responsible for the accuracy of the required record keeping regardless of who performs the clerical tasks.

The teacher in charge is responsible to parents and to administrators. Therefore, in cases where a

teacher and an assistant cannot agree or compromise, the final decision must rest with the teacher. It is easier for an assistant teacher to understand when a decision is made contrary to her ideas if she thinks about how it would be if she were the one held responsible. This empathy on her part usually helps her to be gracious under the circumstances.

Both the teacher and the assistant teacher can take pride and pleasure in their daily routines as they realize that both of them are engaged in shaping the future lives of the children. To do this always in a cooperative manner elevates their teamwork to a high level of professional achievement.

For the reasons stated, job descriptions for teachers and assistant teachers are often not specified in detail. Public school teachers have contracts with the local Board of Education. The Board assumes that a teacher who has a state teaching certificate can fulfill any teaching job description that might be required of her until or unless she proves that this is not so. Schools employing certified teachers are state accredited schools. Others do not always give contracts. In some schools, they are optional or lacking entirely. The press for higher standards in early childhood education is resulting in more schools offering contracts in order to hold their better qualified staff members.

It is hoped that eventually there will be a state recognized certification for assistant teachers. Behaviorally based qualifications are being researched today. These are to be used in evaluating the assistant teach-er's performance on the job in lieu of academic performance at college. In this way, many qualified assistant teachers may receive recognition they deserve and a pay scale suited to their skills.

SUMMARY

The very nature of very young children (including their great dependency on adults) makes the assistant teacher a necessity if every child is to receive maximum benefits from his preschool experience. Harmony among the members of the teaching team requires that they have mutual long-range, short-range, and daily goals for the children, compatible personalities, and a thorough understanding of their roles.

When differences arise between team members, discussing the problem and arriving at a decision that is acceptable to both is expected. If this is not possible, the final decision must rest with the teacher because it is she who is accountable to parents and administrators.

Teachers' positions are filled from certification requirements in state accredited schools. Their job descriptions are not usually written with fine details. In nonaccredited schools, a job description may be written but usually it is in general terms. Assistant teachers presently do not have state certification available to them. They may or may not have written job descriptions. Hopefully the present movement toward performance-based evaluation of any member of a teaching team is leading to a public and economic recognition of the assistant teacher's work.

SUGGESTED ACTIVITIES

- Observe a two-member team with a class of five-year-olds in a day-care center. List all the kinds of behavior that are common to both adults during the morning; for example, both teach lessons.

- With another student, role play a meeting to resolve a personality conflict between a teacher and an assistant teacher. List the steps you used and the results. Reverse roles and then compare these results with the others.

- Observe a harmonious teaching team with a class of four-year-olds. Describe how the personalities of the team members complement one another.

REVIEW

A.   Briefly discuss the kinds of objectives that should be mutual to the members of a teaching team.

B.   Briefly discuss ways to handle points of disagreement between the members of a teaching team.

C.   1.   List six kinds of behaviors that might be found in the job descriptions of both the early childhood teacher and her assistant teacher.

     2.   List two kinds of behaviors that would probably be found in a teacher's job description that are not likely to be found in that of the assistant teacher.

unit 17 professional and non professional staff

OBJECTIVES

After studying this unit, the student should be able to

- Briefly compare the meaning of the terms "professional staff" and "nonprofessional staff" in a classroom.

- Briefly discuss three desirable attitudes for members of the teaching team: role acceptance, harmony, and supportiveness.

- List ten brief rules for the members of a teaching team to use in achieving cooperation.

There are two separate unrelated sets of meanings for the terms *professional* and *nonprofessional.* Professional athletes are those who accept salary for their athletic performances. Nonprofessional athletes are those who do not receive money for their athletic performances. They are called amateur athletes.

In education, however, professional teaching staff members are those who are academically qualified to hold the position of teacher and are paid a salary to perform in this role. Nonprofessional staff members are those who perform many of the same duties as a professional teacher and are paid a salary to do this. (Sometimes these persons are called *paraprofessionals*–those who work with the professional in charge.) However, they are not usually educationally qualified to fulfill the role of teacher. In any one school, the nonprofessional staff members receive less pay than the professional staff members because (a) they have not yet met the educational qualification requirements and (b) they are given lesser responsibilities. In schools which are not accredited, teachers often lack state certificates for teaching, but they are usually better prepared academically to teach than the nonprofessional staff. The quality of the interpersonal relationships between the two kinds of school staff affects the quality of the total school program.

ATTITUDES

Specific attitudes are necessary for a team to function well in the classroom. A student entering the field of early childhood education should know what is expected of her/him.

Role Acceptance

The nonprofessional staff is hired through a school district personnel office or through a school owner or director, just as the teacher is hired. Positions most frequently found are assistant teacher and teacher's aide. If a room has one or the other, that person usually assists the teacher with some of the teaching, assumes some responsibility for the children's behavior, and shares in all of the physical work required to operate the classroom. This may include getting and storing equipment, rearranging the room, minor cleanup tasks. The paraprofessional may help the teacher with keeping the records (attendance, lunch count, materials purchased). The assistant does not have total responsibility for the records, the environment, and the children's learning.

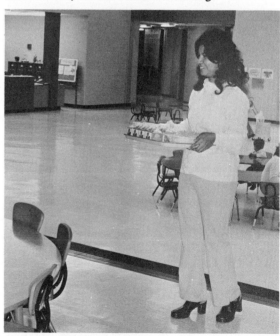

Fig. 17-1 Team members share the housekeeping tasks in the classroom.

When both an assistant teacher and a teacher's aide are members of a teaching team, there is usually a difference in their job descriptions. The role described above is that of the assistant teacher. The aide is often not asked to teach lessons. She may read stories to the children and play records for them. She may escort them to the playground and gather art materials. She works closely under the teacher's direction. She is not required to show great initiative. The willingness of the assistant teacher and the teacher's aide to accept their roles contributes to their success and to that of the team.

Fig. 17-2 The paraprofessional teacher often prepares lesson materials.

The role of the professional teacher includes a high degree of accountability. He/she answers for the total product both to parents and to administrators. If printed curriculum is not available, the professional must decide on or design what is to be used. She is responsible for what happens to the children. To be able to succeed in all of this requires *professionalism,* which may be defined as having those attitudes and behaviors that reflect dedication to the best interests of the children, the staff, the school, and its adminis-

tration. Teacher performance is based on thorough academic knowledge and practical understanding of all that is required to succeed in the job. Being "a professional" includes having the attitudes that produce interpersonal relationships that make the teaching team the best possible work arrangement for its members. Accepting the responsibilities of professionalism is expected of the teacher.

Harmony

Reaching the goal of an ideal classroom is possible only if the attitudes of the nonprofessionals agree with those of the teacher. Mutual respect for one another as persons is needed. The assistant and/or aide must also have respect for the knowledge and teaching ability of the teacher. Daily problems must be viewed by all team members on a basis of what is best for the children.

It is essential that all team members start the year by assuming that each one has appropriate attitudes toward one another and toward the work. High expectations of one another leads to high achievement by the team. Wanting to learn is a "must" characteristic for all team members. No one has all the answers to the everyday problems in a school for little girls and boys.

Fig. 17-3 The assistants learn new teaching techniques by role-playing a lesson with the teacher.

Openness to constructive criticism is an attitude that helps any team function smoothly. Willingness to make needed helpful criticism should accompany the openmindedness although this is hard to do for most people.

Supportiveness

All team members should support the philosophy that the home and school must cooperate in the education of the child. The need for direct involvement on the part of "moms and dads" should be seen by the whole team. A team member who finds parents "in the way" can hurt the program. The staff is expected to support parents in the development of their children.

Loyalty to one's teaching team and to the school produces workers who do their best to make the room and the school places of which to be proud. It means keeping problems within team discussions and not carrying tales outside of school.

Seeing children in the right way is of prime importance. They are human beings who want to learn and who will learn if given opportunity and guidance. Loving concern for the children dictates much of the behavior of teaching team members.

ACHIEVING COOPERATION

Each member of the teaching team bears some responsibility for cooperation with all the other members of the team. Each one can achieve cooperation from the others by observing some simple rules.

- Be prompt; it is a virtue. Being on time when arriving at school, fulfilling commitments, preparing materials, and observing the school schedule prevents the annoyance produced by being late.

- Be polite. Good manners encourage a positive cooperative response. "Please" and "Thank you" are magic words for grown-ups, too.

- Observe rules that are agreed on. Do not expect exceptions to be made for you. (The larger the teaching team, the more important this rule is.)

- Try to see the viewpoints of others. Then they are more likely to see yours when it differs from theirs.

- Carry your share of the load. Everyone should go home a little tired; not one person exhausted, and others not tired at all.

- Air grievances while they are small. In a friendly mature discussion, slight differences can be eliminated. If allowed to grow, they sometimes cannot be overcome.

- Communicate often and well. Each member of a team must keep the others informed of his thoughts on matters pertaining to the children. Communication is "two-way". It also means to listen well and respond to others.

- Never neglect the children. Sometimes adults socialize while they are on duty at school, on the playground, for example. This is failure to cooperate with others who are also responsible for the safety of the children.

Fig. 17-4   On the playground, the staff must be alert to prevent accidents.

Playground Schedule		
9:30-9:50 A.M.	Threes	(Mrs. White and Miss Salazar)
9:50-10:15 A.M.	Fours	(Miss Martin and Mrs. Miller)
10:15-10:40 A.M.	Fours	(Mrs. Martinez and Miss Lee)
10:40-11:10 A.M.	Fives	(Mrs. Schramm and Mrs. Hart)
11:10-11:30 A.M.	Threes	(Mrs. White and Miss Salazar)

Fig. 17-5   Limited space means scheduling the use of the playground for half-day preschool. Promptness is required in fairness to the children.

- Let others help you. The too-independent staff member says "I don't need you" by his behavior. Later if he really does need help, he is not likely to achieve cooperation.

- Treat others as you would like to be treated. The Golden Rule still works!

The rules for achieving cooperation are intended for all staff members. No distinction is being made between professional and nonprofessional staff. The same rules apply in all situations where members of a group are working together with a single purpose.

The success of interpersonal relationships is basic to teamwork of any kind. A selflessness of attitudes and behaviors usually achieves cooperation even from a reluctant one in any group. When a team cooperates well, the nonprofessional staff is closer to achieving the professional commitment required to progress upward on the ladder of success.

SUMMARY

The difference in the terms *professional* and *nonprofessional* school staff is one of academic achievement by the former. State certified teachers and nonaccredited teachers who are hired in the role of "teacher" are considered professionals. Assistant teachers and aides are paraprofessional staff. The major differences in job descriptions between professional and nonprofessional staff lie in the amount of accountability placed on the roles. Accepting greater responsibility earns a higher salary for the professional teacher on the team.

A teaching team is more successful if all the members have the same good attitudes. Accepting one's role is important for all staff members. An attitude of professionalism is required of the teacher and admirable in others. Assuming that others want to do what is best for children prevents misunderstandings. Wanting to learn and openness to constructive criticism are vital to a team's success and continued improvement.

Accepting parents as a highly desirable part of the classroom program is required of each team member. Loyalty to the team and the school unites the persons involved. Loving concern for all children is prerequisite to success in teaching.

Interpersonal relationships in any group depend on simple rules which apply to all lives. How to get along well with others in a classroom is based on the same rules used for getting along well in any group. The rules are the same for all members of the team. Cooperation can be best achieved if it is freely given to others.

SUGGESTED ACTIVITIES

- Observe a preschool teaching team. List the staff interactions observed that express some positive and some negative attitudes; identify the attitudes.

- Discuss steps that might have prevented or possibly will eliminate the negative attitudes observed in the preceding activity.

- Talk to the professional teacher of a successful teaching team. Ask her how she achieves cooperation from her team members. Add her ideas to the list given in this unit.

REVIEW

A. Briefly define the following: professional teaching staff member, paraprofessional teaching staff, role acceptance, teacher's accountability, professionalism.

B. List seven desirable attitudes for the members of a teaching team.

C. List ten simple rules for achieving cooperation from the other members of a teaching team.

unit 18 full-time and part-time staff

OBJECTIVES

After studying this unit, the student should be able to

- Describe part-time staffing patterns.
- Explain the need for flexibility and foresight in starting a program of part-time staff, teacher's aides, and/or volunteers.
- Briefly explain the process of becoming a parent or community volunteer in a school.

Much has been said about the recent trend toward using paraprofessional staff members in early childhood programs. Another increasingly popular trend in staffing is the use of part-time staff in addition to full-time staff members. This too, originated in the day-care centers.

Most day-care schools are open from six or seven a.m. until six or seven p.m. This is because they must accommodate the children whose mothers are full-time workers where they are employed. Some start their day at seven a.m., others at nine a.m. Thus, there is a long day for the day-care centers. (Some large factories maintain day-care facilities for children of employees around the clock when the factory operates three shifts daily.) To keep the day-care employee's day a normal eight-hour length, part-time

Fig. 18-1 Most children are left at the day-care center by a parent on the way to work.

workers are hired. Teachers and assistants open the school and teach the children until nap or rest period after lunch. Then a part-time staff relieves them and sees that the children are cared for until the parents come for them at the end of the day.

An administrator (director, owner, or lead teacher) is responsible for the entire staff. She may appoint an assistant to supervise while she is not there, or she may work a split schedule. She may come early to get the day off to a good start at the school, then leave for a few hours in the middle of the day. She may return to see that the part-time workers have the children ready for their parents and leave the school in condition for opening in the morning.

Public school schedules are never as lengthy as those of day-care facilities. These schools are finding that there is a place for a part-time staff, however.

FLEXIBILITY

Some public school systems are approaching the use of a paraprofessional staff warily. Others who would like to give each teacher an assistant or an aide cannot afford to do so. The answer to both situations is the part-time staff.

Where teachers have never had a helper, are reluctant to change, and are not trained in the use of a helper in the classroom, an aide is sometimes furnished on a half-day basis. Hopefully, the teacher finds enough tasks for the aide so that she benefits from the help for a part of each day. In some cases, the aide is in fact a full-time employee who works for one teacher half of the day and for a second teacher, the second half of the day. In other schools, a full-time aide is part-time staff in two rooms by working full time in one room for a week and in the second room full time the next week.

School districts that have many special programs have other part-time staff: medical personnel, social workers, family services staff, home liaison workers, consultants. All of these may have some contact with the children.

One of the most essential elements of a successful part-time staff program is outstanding flexibility on the part of the staff members involved. Even experienced teachers cannot be expected to make the adjustment unless they are prepared by inservice training. Careful explanation of the role of each part-time worker helps the full-time staff understand and accept their new help. (If there seems to be a problem in adjusting, the criteria recommended earlier ⦙lies. It should be considered in the light of what ⦙ for the children or of what can become best ⦙hildren.)

⦙full-time staff have been negative in their ⦙ the grounds that it requires too much ⦙ the children. Experience has shown ⦙are invariably more flexible than the ⦙rt-time staff is a new part of the

⦙ adjustment to the idea of extra ⦙on a regular basis, the task of ⦙details remains. Some of the ⦙ooth transitions of author-⦙dinating the exchange of ⦙ble both full-time and ⦙to handle all situa-⦙rs this is especially ⦙home before the

parents pick up the children.), (3) acquainting parents with the part-time staff members who will be working with the children, (4) coordinating the parent involvement program and the part-time staff program (When part-time staffing begins, parent volunteers may misunderstand and feel rejected. They may want to stop volunteering.), (5) adjusting the schedule to achieve maximum satisfaction for everyone (deciding who has help in the morning and who can use the help better in the afternoon, for example). Most of the areas of concern can be satisfactorily dealt with if everyone makes the effort to be flexible. The need for this quality cannot be overemphasized. The pragmatic approach for teachers which was discussed in an earlier unit applies to the efficient use of a part-time staff. Several readjustments may be needed, but nearly always a better program for the children results.

SCHEDULING VOLUNTEERS

Parents are the heart of the school volunteer program. Additional help may be recruited in the neighborhood of the school. Word of mouth is the best but not the only good form of advertising a volunteer program. Signs placed strategically in neighborhood businesses or on the school property are helpful. School representatives may spread the word at their churches, clubs, or parties. The public mass media may be used. When a staff works consistently to enlarge the volunteer program, the results show.

When parents volunteer their services in the classroom, it is the teacher who arranges the work to

⦙RNOON STAFF, PLEASE NOTE:

⦙ion for her son Bobby to go home with Mrs. Teaque

⦙.m. Doctor's instructions are with the Rx in the ⦙ file.

⦙older brother today. Have the brother call ⦙ere.

⦙might make her late. If she is late, she ⦙stays with Alicia.

⦙t 4 p.m.: slight fever appeared in the ⦙Mother needs info for doctor.

⦙of vital information between the full-time and ⦙er.

Fig. 18-3   Posters in the schoolyard and the community often help recruit volunteers to assist in the classrooms and with many other tasks.

be done. She must find out the capabilities and limitations of each parent. Then she decides how the skills of each can be used to benefit the program. She discusses the classroom needs with the parent and the parent informs the teacher when he/she is available and what he/she would like to do. If a parent does not know what she can do well, the teacher assigns her a simple task, observes, then evaluates. She may increase the difficulty of the task if it seems warranted.

When persons other than parents volunteer, some one in the school (administrator, volunteer coordinator, administrative assistant) accepts the same responsibility that the teacher has with parents, that of getting enough information from the volunteers and from the teachers to be able to place the new helpers wisely.

Some volunteers may be counted on regularly, one day a week perhaps. Others may be available for one specialized kind of help, such as demonstrating a musical instrument and performing prior to field trips that are musical in nature. When volunteer recruitment is good, a regular volunteer coordinator can be kept busy, getting and exchanging information between the volunteers and the teaching staff.

one special service intended for a spe
acquainting him with the premises, the
and equipment needed, a careful plar
and the preparations the school
be arranged in person, if possibl
teer may be desirable. Carefi
mended.

In the case of paren
should be refused, but eac
or permitted to do only t
is appropriate. This
with all the childre
things any parent

Initiating a
inservice trainin
standing of a
possibilities
tions to th
aides ne
too, v
contr
the
t

FORESIGHT

More part-time staff programs (salaried and volunteer) have failed for lack of foresight than for any other reason. The time spent carefully obtaining all the necessary information from volunteers is valuable. Without it, volunteers may be improperly placed and therefore not appreciated. Telephone calls are not enough. The volunteer must be asked to come to the school for an interview. Even if he is offering

Fig. 18-4 By observing in the classroom, a parent learns good ways to interact with her child.

Having the foresight to see the affective development possible for the child and his parent can motivate the teaching staff to be interested in developing a closer working relationship with as many parents of the students as possible.

Many schools have begun their parent volunteer system by offering recognition for a specified number of hours of volunteer service. Certificates may be offered for ten hours of service, small plaques for twenty hours of service, and other awards for still greater amounts of volunteering. Records must

be kept accurately. At a meeting near the end of the term, the parents may be given public recognition and their official rewards.

Whether this incentive system succeeds depends on the foresight of those who design the incentive schedule and the rewards. The schedule must be realistic, and enough but not too much service must be required if parents are to accept it. The incentives must be desirable to the parents. If not, they will not motivate them to volunteer. Having the foresight to research both of these elements can mean having a more successful parent-volunteer program.

It is always better to prevent problems than to have to solve them after the fact. Foreseeing the difficulties that may arise in having a part-time paraprofessional staff usually results in planning ways to prevent the problems. Teachers usually receive an orientation of some kind when they join a school staff. This answers many of their questions, explains some of the rules of the operation, and expresses a guiding philosophy of some sort.

Part-time staff, salaried and volunteer, need a similar orientation. After a mother has applied inappropriate disciplinary measures to a child, it is too late to undo the harm. It is embarassing to explain at that time a situation which should have been prevented. Out of foresight, a simple list of rules for volunteers should be ready from the beginning of the year. It should be explained verbally by the

---

September 11

Dear Parents:

This is to let you know how very important you are to our school. Many of you have volunteered many hours of your service to us in the past. We hope more of you will this year. We think our volunteers should be honored for all that they do to help us — so we are going to do just that.

Please meet here at the school at 7 p.m. next Friday, September 15th. We will explain to you how you may earn a school award this year. The more hours of volunteer work, the greater the award you will receive. All our volunteers will be recognized at our December meeting.

See you Friday,

Mrs. Fern Malson,
Principal

Fig. 18-5 An incentive awards system may be used to motivate parents to volunteer their time to help the school.

teacher to each volunteer before her service begins. This kind of preparedness prevents unpleasant situations from developing.

SUMMARY

The long working day of day-care centers, the financial limitations of public schools, and the wariness of some teachers have created the need for part-time staff members to assist the full-time staff in improving their programs for children. Introducing a part-time staffing pattern requires the greatest possible flexibility on the part of each person involved. Arrangements may have to be changed several times until a workable solution is found.

Volunteer parents who are a nonpaid part of the daily staffing pattern must be considered in the same way that the paid part-time workers are viewed. Their tasks are assigned and scheduled by the teacher.

Volunteers other than parents should be interviewed, screened, and scheduled by an administrator or a volunteer coordinator. Getting a volunteer program started must be a cooperative effort. Word of mouth, mass media, and signs may be used to recruit volunteers from the community. Teachers are expected to encourage the parents of their students to participate. Careful screening of volunteers is important to the successful operation of the volunteer program.

Without foresight on the part of professional full-time staff, a part-time staff (paid or volunteer) giving assistance to teachers may not be productive. Much time must be spent preparing to have the program. Much information is needed in advance. Full-time staff must be given preparation. Part-time staff must be provided with an orientation period to become adequately informed about the program and procedures in order to prevent problems. Specialists for unique events should be interviewed and all arrangements made in person when possible. Staff who foresee the great benefits to a child and his parent when the parent voluntarily serves as a helper are likely to encourage all parents to participate.

Sometimes an incentive system of inexpensive kinds of recognition for volunteer service helps to get the program underway. The schedule of incentives must be realistic and the awards desirable to the participants if the system is to motivate volunteers.

The interpersonal relationships described earlier between the full-time staff and the part-time paid staff and volunteers should be of the same high quality as those described as ideal for the members of the teaching team. For in a very real sense, all of them are members of one very large teaching team. Every member of the staff affects the lives of the children. Therefore, building positive interstaff relations is a necessary and very worthy endeavor. It can be achieved when each person cooperates.

SUGGESTED ACTIVITIES

- List kinds of information that might need to be exchanged between the full-time staff in a day-care center and the part-time workers who come just before the others leave.

- Pretend you are a kindergarten teacher (all day, one class) and have just been told you will soon have an aide daily from 12 noon to 3 p.m. You have fifteen children and no assistant teacher. Write a tentative daily schedule 9 a.m. - 3 p.m., showing your duties and the duties of the aide for the 12 noon - 3 p.m. period. (Compare your schedule with those of other students.)

- Role-play a scene with another student. Pretend you are teachers. Each of you has been told you will soon share a teacher's aide. You are discussing the prospect. She is displeased, and you are trying to convince her it is a wonderful opportunity.

REVIEW

A. Briefly describe some part-time staffing patterns.

B. Explain why great flexibility is needed when a program of part-time staffing begins.

C. List five steps to insure success that must be done before a part-time staffing program begins.

D. List six kinds of foresight that will facilitate a successful part-time (paid and/or volunteer) program.

Section VI Parent Involvement

unit 19 kinds of parent involvement

OBJECTIVES

After studying this unit, the student should be able to

- Briefly explain how present parent involvement programs came into being.

- Briefly explain how parents of the very young child can be of service at their child's school.

- Briefly explain some ways the parents of a child in an early childhood education center may be involved with the school but not at the school.

When parents are actively participating in the affairs of their children's school, the parents, the children, and the school usually benefit from it. Many years ago parent-teacher organizations were formed because schools recognized this as one way to achieve better support from parents and to receive more help from them. Parents accept the idea because it means not only a way to help the school but also a way to express their thoughts and feelings about the school. Membership in the PTA or another parent-teacher group is a recognized avenue for dialogue between the home and the school. Home situations are not the same today as they were fifty years ago; unfortuately, very many PTA meetings are still held in the afternoon during school hours. This makes attendance impossible for a large portion of today's parents. Very slowly the concept of home-school interactions is being modernized. Today the PTA provides only one of many opportunities for parents and teachers to work together.

Since World War II there has been an ever increasing need for places to care for children of working mothers. Commercial day-care centers, church-related schools, state-supported community nurseries, and private homes were the answer until the federally financed antipoverty programs of the sixties. In these, in return for free educational day care for their children, parents were required to become actively involved in the affairs of the school. These school activities usually included providing help for the parents in many needed areas: child development, discipline, nutrition, legal services, job training.

It also meant that parents were required to give some kinds of personal service to the school in their non-working hours. To accommodate the varying schedules of working parents, many kinds of parent involvement were created.

In the fast expansion of public school programs for children under six, the same kinds of home-parent interactions plus new ones of their own are being used. Each teacher should know of the many options there are for the moms and dads of her students. She should also feel free to think of new ones that will be even more beneficial to her students, their parents, and to the school.

THE WORKING PARENT

Sometimes people think of working parents as persons too busy to actively participate in school affairs. Nothing could be further from the truth. Head Start Day-Care Centers throughout the United States require both rules to be used: the mother must be in a full time educational program, job training, or employment, and she must serve the school in ways that are possible for her. The staff is expected to get to know every home situation so that some agreement can be reached on ways to serve that is satisfactory to the school and to the mother. Head Start fathers, too, are called on to become additional arms and legs for the school in many projects.

Educational research projects at universities have experimented to discover the differences that can be found in children in programs with no parent

Dear Dads:

On Saturday March 2, 7 a.m. to 10 a.m., at the Southside Mall, we will be setting up the school's exhibit of artwork made by the children. If you can help us move sawhorses, boards, and other heavy materials from the school to the Mall, please let Miss Williams know by Thursday noon.

It is great to know we can always depend on you. Thank you.

Mrs. Clara Olafsen,
Director

Fig. 19-1 Head Start fathers are encouraged to help.

participation projects and programs with maximum parent involvement. The general conclusion is that the benefits to school children and parents far outweigh the problems in developing a parent program that achieves the support of every mother and father by their personal services to the school.

Today most programs for children under six, public and private, have several forms of parent-school interaction. Options are included so the working parent may participate.

PARENTS HELP AT SCHOOL

It is not unusual to find a working parent in the classroom on his/her day off from work, serving beside a nonemployed parent. Parents have different skills. The teacher who knows the parents well enough can use their skills in the way that is most useful in the classroom.

For a food unit, a mother may be the ideal person to involve the children in a cooking experience, help take them on a trip to a grocery store, or supervise the "grocery store" in role-playing area. She may enjoy just observing how the teacher teaches lessons so that she can use better methods in teaching her children at home.

In some schools, water and rest rooms are at an impractical distance from the classroom. The mother who escorts children to these areas and back to the room is helping to avoid serious interruptions in the work of the other children. If a teacher must stop to take the child who "can't wait", it interrupts the learning experiences of her group.

The dad who supplies a male influence at the school on his day off is especially helpful to the child who has no father in his home. Some dads may wish to help with the indoor learning or to just converse

with the children. The language experience usually is very interesting to the children. Often new vocabulary is introduced and the children's concepts are broadened. Children truly enjoy having a man to whom they can talk.

On the playground, dads are truly at ease with the children. Their strength, endurance, and safety-consciousness make them valuable assets outdoors. Woodworking activities may be set up outdoors. A father may be asked to supervise, since woodworking may be done only under supervision.

Fathers have pooled their time and materials to make outdoor equipment. Sand piles, tire swings, seesaws, climbing ladders, and tree houses are some of the results. Dads can spade gardens for young gardeners. They may provide small tools at planting and weeding time.

Fig. 19-2 Volunteer fathers are an asset to the parent involvement program.

Parent Helpers for the Week Jan. 14-18				
Monday	**Tuesday**	**Wednesday**	**Thursday**	**Friday**
1. Mrs. Silas: observing	1. Mrs. Silas: observing	1. Mrs. Silas: observing	1. Mrs. Silas: read a book to small groups	1. Mrs. Schwartz: matzah crackers for snack
2. Mrs. Bloom: Story time	2. Mrs. Romero: review lessons, one-to-one	2. Mr. Sams: ball throwing	2. Mr. Schwartz: talking about his work: auto repair	2. Mrs. Schmidt: launder paint smocks
3. Mrs. Satterfield: refreshments for Debbie's birthday	3. Mr. Martinez: ball throwing for distance	3. Mrs. Brunson: review lessons		3. Mrs. Williams: mend doll clothes
		4. Mrs. Floren: make 10 beanbags at home		
		5. Mrs. Myles: make 10 bean bags at home		
		6. Mr. Lufkin: repair 3 tri-cycles at home		

Fig. 19-3   **This simple chart makes it easy for the teacher to schedule and keep a record of the services given the school by parents.**

Parents who are active in some of the ways just mentioned also usually attend parent-staff meetings at the school. These may or may not be conducted in a formal manner. They may be in the evening or on weekends. The system used is not important. It is important that the get-togethers are a source of pleasure and enrichment for all concerned. Parents must be given opportunities to make suggestions to help the school. They must be made aware of school needs that parents can meet. They must be made to feel accepted so that they will feel free to express criticism if they are feeling critical. (Schools are not perfect. Any school can profit from criticism made in the best interests of the children.)

The school that stays tuned in to the needs of the parents is usually in a position to meet some of the needs. Information may be given, resource lists supplied, community services referrals made, and needs "info" placed in the hands of those who can help.

Parents may have language problems. The school may be able to provide langauge instruction for parents who are learning to speak English. It is not unusual for a school to find a parent who is willing to help other parents — with language or by giving instructions in an art or craft, such as crocheting or woodworking.

Fig. 19-4   **The school and the community benefit when mothers can get together at the school.**

Fig. 19-5   A working parent may contribute items that add to the cultural enrichment of the curriculum.

Parents have social as well as instructional needs. A pleasant attractive place for get-togethers and coffee may be supplied by the school. Parents may wish to help by bringing refreshments. Mothers on all economic levels like to help with parties for adults and for children. A mother who can barely support her family is often still willing to come and serve and help clean up. She is serving the school just as those are who can afford to buy or make cookies.

Another important aspect of parent participation is in providing the schools with objects, materials, or ideas that are representative of their ethnic groups. Multiethnic classes provide children with wonderful opportunities for cultural enrichment. If parents bring special kinds of costumes, customs, musical instruments, foods, recipes, art objects, and stories that are unknown to some of the children of other ethnic groups, little children can develop appreciations of others who are different from themselves in some ways. There is a great advantage in having multiethnic groups of children. Even if one group is somewhat hostile to another, the opportunity for the teacher to develop understanding in all groups (and therefore to reduce hostility) can be a rewarding challenge. Most parents can be united in the best interests of their children.

Another important parent service to the school is participating in school evaluations. Parents can be prepared by the school so that their comments are reasonably objective. If possible, they should contain suggestions for the improvement of the school. This type of parent evaluation is really helpful.

PARENTS HELP AWAY FROM THE SCHOOL

Fathers and mothers are sometimes needed to drive their cars for field trips if a school cannot afford transportation. It is important that all drivers are licensed and that there is adequate insurance coverage on the children in such a situation. (Some schools have clauses in their regular insurance policies that cover these conditions.)

Occasionally materials are donated to schools. Parents may take lumber, plans, and paint home to make shelves, classroom dividers, and even tables.

Parents make excellent public relations (PR) personnel. They often handle publicity for fund raising affairs very well. Signs must be made and placed strategically in the community. Tickets must be sold or invitations made and mailed. Telephoning must be done. Many parents would rather do these tasks than cook and serve food.

In the home, parents can serve the school daily. If the school explains to parents simple ways to increase the child's learning at home, the everyday routines of eating, bathing, dressing, and housekeeping can become active learning for the child.

If parents can be helped to learn that discipline means "teaching", not "punishment", they can become excellent reinforcers at home of good behaviors the child is learning at school. If Mother sees her three-year-old pick up and put away all his blocks at school without a problem, she may be willing to learn the school's method of teaching him this good habit (especially if she sometimes must spank him to get him to do this at home). This is excellent involvement in the program of the school: both the learning and the using of the knowledge of teaching good behavior.

The teacher is responsible for seeing that parents are made aware of the many ways at school and

October 6,

Dear Mr. and Mrs. Brink:

Jimmy is learning the names of some shapes: circle, square, and triangle. Please have him point out to you any things at home that have these shapes, such as his ball, a square box, and a three-sided container. Thank you.

Mary Pauley

Fig. 19-6   Helping parents learn how to reinforce the school curriculum at home can be beneficial to them, the child, and the school.

away from school in which they can be more actively involved with the influence of the school on the lives of the children. When the school and home unite to help to work for the children, everyone gains; there are no losers. The first step to produce this objective is for the teacher to help parents become aware of the possibilities.

Another major responsibility of the teacher is that of expressing appreciation to parents for all that they do to cooperate with the school. Just a verbal "thank you" in person or on the phone is sometimes all that is needed. In other situations, brief "thank you" notes are better. Public recognition at meetings is often a good idea. A system of awards for hours of service and given according to a schedule is another way the teacher and school can say, "We appreciate your interest in the education of the children and in our school".

SUMMARY

For many years the PTA served as the parent involvement program for most schools. During World War II, many mothers entered the field of labor and business. This increasing trend made it impossible for mothers to attend afternoon PTA meetings.

Universities have discovered through research projects that it is highly beneficial to children, parents and schools to have parents actively participating in the child's learning and in school activities. Therefore, when government antipoverty programs began in the sixties, mothers were required to be full-time em-

ployees or students in order for their children to qualify for these educational day-care programs such as the Head Start Child Development Centers. Also, parents were required to actively serve the school their child attended—each parent in a way that was possible for him/her. Now such kinds of parent programs are becoming part of nearly all public and private schools for very young children.

Working parents may be just as interested and as actively involved in their child's school programs as those who are not employed. The classroom, the child, the school all have many needs. The teacher communicates these needs to parents and tries to find a satisfactory way for every parent to participate.

At the school, supervision of many children's projects, such as role-playing and woodworking, reading, demonstrating, and just saving the teacher many steps in filling noninstructional needs offer a variety of choices to each parent. Away from the school, field trips, PR work, making school equipment, fundraising, and teaching the child in the home are all ways for parents to be involved with the school.

Two of the teacher's responsibilities in the parent involvement program are to find appropriate opportunities for each parent and to see that all the parents receive a "thank you" message (verbal or written) or public recognition of some kind. When parents feel their work is appreciated by the teacher and the school, they are encouraged to continue being actively involved with the school and their child's education.

SUGGESTED ACTIVITIES

- Talk to a preschool teacher who has good parent participation in school activities. List some ways the parents are involved, and state how she interests parents in helping.

- Talk to a public school kindergarten teacher who does not have many parents who are actively involved with the school. Have her explain the problems she faces. List suggestions for handling problems like these.

- Talk to two mothers, one employed and one who is not working, who are active in their children's parent participation program. List the ways each one helps the school or is active in school affairs. Add any that were not mentioned in the unit to the ones given.

REVIEW

A. Briefly explain how present parent involvement programs came into being.

B. Briefly explain how parents of the very young child can be actively involved in school activities for parents.

C. Select each item which correctly completes each of the following statements.

1. A mother has just told her child's teacher that she is too tired to work for the school after she gets home and finishes taking care of her children. The teacher should then

   a. Tell her that she understands and will not bother her anymore.

   b. Tell her that she understands and ask her if she would be interested in a small project to help the children that she could do at home on the weekend if the teacher brought her the materials.

   c. Suggest that perhaps if she could visit her some evening at home when it would be convenient, she could talk over some of the possibilities for helping that are available to mothers who work.

   d. Tell her that even tired mothers need to save some energy for parent involvement at schools.

2. The teacher has just explained to a father of a student that the kindergarten is having a work-party for parents on Saturday. There will be many kinds of help needed. He has just said he is sorry but he has other plans for the day. The teacher should

   a. Tell him he will be missed but that there will be many tasks left after the work-party and ask him if he would like to help with one of them she thinks he can do well.

   b. Tell him she realizes not everyone can make it Saturday and ask when it would be convenient for him to help with some other tasks.

   c. Tell him that if he can change his plans it would be a good idea because everyone should do his share.

   d. Say "thank you anyway."

3. The teacher has just been refused by three parents she asked to help in the classroom. She has just said "Sometimes this parent involvement stuff is more trouble than it's worth." The assistant teacher should

   a. Agree that it's a lot of work and offer to help with some of the calling, stating "Maybe the next three will be able to help. Sometimes I really couldn't help when my child's teacher called on me."

   b. Say "You're probably right. If they don't want to get involved that is their problem."

   c. Say that she knows it is discouraging when parents refuse but perhaps another way can be found to involve those who are a little afraid to help in the room.

   d. Tell her she realizes she is discouraged today and that perhaps tomorrow will be a better day for asking parents.

unit 20 benefits of parent involvement

OBJECTIVES

After studying this unit, the student should be able to

- Explain the benefits to a child when his parent/parents are actively involved in serving the school.

- Explain the good effects on the parent who participates in parent activities.

- Explain how the school and the community at large may profit from a strong parent involvement program.

When parents participate in school activities at the school and away from the school, many benefits are received by the child, his parents, and the school. When the parent involvement is a planned part of the total school program, the benefits are much greater. When the school staff unites in a belief in the importance of having parents work directly with the school, wonderful things can happen.

If a school does not have a special plan and procedure for working with parents, there is still a possibility that individual teachers may develop their own goals for the parents of their students. The time-consuming part is the initial getting-acquainted process. Home visits by teachers and assistant teachers are good ice breakers. More than any other activity, they convince parents that the teacher is concerned, that she/he cares about their children. This encourages parents to cooperate, and home-school relationships are off to a good start. Consistent efforts to find ways for each parent to be helpful produce results. There are often a few parents who refuse to work with the school, but for those who do cooperate, a chain reaction of benefits begins.

BENEFITS TO THE CHILD

One of the highest affective goals that the school strives for in young children is the development of a positive self-concept. When a child likes himself as a person, he learns to like others and is open to learning experiences. He has enough self-confidence to try new activities, to accept challenges, and not to be crushed if he is not always successful.

Mothers and fathers can be helped to realize that their presence at the school in a helpful role makes a child very proud and pleased. It says to him, "My mom and dad care about me and my school".

Usually when parents first visit the school to observe, they are very surprised at how much their child has learned already. Comments to the child on this can further strengthen the child's natural inclination to learn and his attitude toward school. Both of these are extremely vital to the child's future. A firm home-school supportive interaction during early childhood is a solid foundation that makes it less likely that the child will become alienated from school in later years.

The parent who observes and/or serves as an assistant teacher learns some of the teaching tech-

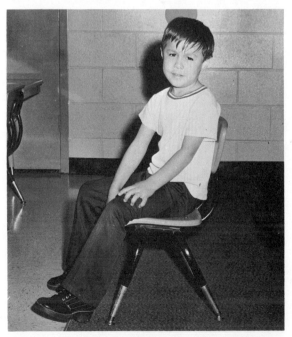

Fig. 20-1 Although a child may enjoy a "time-out" situation for a few moments, it soon becomes an effective method of discipline for many children.

niques that help her to become a better teacher at home. (Parents do teach at home daily though they may not realize this.) The teacher's method of disciplining may be new to the mother. If she sees it work effectively, she may be willing to give up her less effective methods and learn new ones. This simplifies life for the child (and the parents eventually). If the teacher's methods are good ones, the child will grow in self-discipline as he has similar situations handled in the same way at home. Often a double standard, if a home-school conflict exists, causes the child to have to make choices. If he is not alienated from school, he becomes unhappy at home. This can be prevented when schools work with parents to help them learn to be more effective teachers at home and to support the school in all that it teaches the child.

A mother's or dad's visit to a classroom of four-year-olds is often the topic of conversation for many days after. (A teacher often wishes the children would remember her words the way they do the words of a visiting parent!) Having an extra adult in the room gives a better pupil-teacher ratio. There can be more language development; more children will have an adult to listen to them. The child whose parent comes to school has many things to talk about with his family at home concerning the day's adventures.

Spending time in the classroom often gives a parent a new view of his child. A father who came for the first time states, "I had no idea my boy was learning so much. He's not just a five-year-old kid,

Fig. 20-2   A child becomes more important to his group as the teacher shows them new beanbags his mother made for them at home.

he's a real student!" He made his child aware of his admiration and appreciation of him.

When a child's parent is active for the school even in activities outside the classroom, all the children become aware that, somehow, the child's parent cares about them. This enhances any child's self-image. When children are told, "Aaron's mother made us these new beanbags," Aaron is a bit more important to his classmates.

Parent participation at the school and away from the school benefits the child in numerous ways. Some are instant and obvious. Others are more subtle and slower to take effect. Some of the effects are long lasting.

BENEFITS TO THE PARENT

In addition to the benefits the child receives, the parents themselves often have much to gain by giving their time to the school. The more they learn about their children, the better parents they can be. Parents often feel embarassed about their own lack of knowledge about children. When parents feel comfortable in the classroom, it helps to relieve their own feelings of inadequacy. The children make parents feel wanted and needed. This may fulfill an emotional need of the parents and give them needed self-confidence.

When the teachers learn the wishes and needs of parents, they can plan experiences to meet those needs. Parent meetings to provide knowledge that the parents request are a regular part of many parent programs. Parents have learned a variety of subjects—from how to crochet to advanced child psychology—through early childhood parent involvement.

When parents serve on a "Parent Policy Board", they benefit from the experience of learning to "make the wheels turn". Many federally funded programs in the seventies require that policy boards have parents as part of their membership. When given ample opportunity in a democratic atmosphere, many parents have proved to be valuable additions to policy boards.

When serving the very young child's school, parents derive satisfaction from knowing they are helping, each in his own way. Finding the appropriate way for each parent to serve is the key to this benefit to parents.

When a staff member respectfully listens to a parent's grievances, and finds solutions to the problem, the parent is being shown the respect that helps him achieve the dignity he needs.

By assisting the school in evaluating its staff and program, parents receive training in seeing things objectively and in making suggestions for improvement in acceptable ways. This behavior is a useful one in many other aspects of life. After a training session one mother explained, "No wonder our gripes don't get any attention sometimes. We don't always go about it the right way."

Parents who assist on field trips have as much fun as the children do. They often learn many new things as well. After a trip to a commercial bakery, one mother said, "No wonder bread is expensive. I had no idea that making bread is so complicated."

Parents who accept the public relations tasks for the school meet many new people. They sometimes make valuable contacts in the business world, as well.

The preschool parent involvement program provides many benefits to parents. Few of the benefits are economic ones, but the psychological ones are immeasurable and great.

BENEFITS TO THE SCHOOL

Since the child and his parent have much to gain when the parent takes an active part at the school, the snowball does not stop growing there. The center of it all, the school itself, becomes part of the large circle of benefits from the experience.

The teaching staff develops an adeptness in communications that was not included in teacher training. The teacher develops administrative skills in placing parents in their jobs, attaining cooperation from them, and training them in evaluation procedures.

The school receives services worth many dollars with no strain on the budget. The image of the school that was held by parents from another generation is slowly being erased. To them it was "the house of authority" from Monday till Friday, eight hours per day. Now it is becoming a center of education for adults and children together in the best interests of the children. It is sometimes a social center, a workshop, a learning center, a training center, and an evaluation center. With each additional activity, the role of the school grows in size and importance.

The introduction of kindergarten and nursery school classes in public schools has been stimulating to the parent programs that had dwindled to just a PTA. The whole school is awakening to the benefits of working more closely with all parents. This is no longer limited to programs for the economically

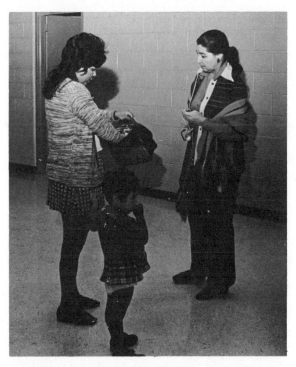

Fig. 20-3   It helps the home-school relationship when a parent can depend on having someone listen to her complaint at school.

disadvantaged child. It is in evidence in schools in a variety of neighborhoods. All of the schools can benefit from increased parent interest in school affairs.

BENEFITS TO THE COMMUNITY

When the child, his parents, and his school all profit from the many hours of service parents give a school, it is logical to assume that the whole community benefits from the action. They are a part of the community; other parts of the community as well, though, have much to gain.

When parents acquire self-confidence in their abilities to be of service at school, often the surrounding organizations and institutions are motivated to do more for the schools and to serve more in the community. There is often a healthful natural competition among schools. A school with good public relations work for its parent's activities can spur other schools and community clubs into greater programs to involve people in bettering their own community.

Parents who have preschoolers may become very involved with helping in the classroom and making some new equipment for the room. They may have older children in junior schools. Soon they become more attuned to the situation there. Possibly they can suggest ways to help with some of the junior school problems. If their first experience in helping is successful, they will probably attempt to be of service again. There is no limit to the amount of improvement in a community that can emerge from a strong parent participation program in an early childhood education class in a public or a private school.

SUMMARY

The school or teacher that initiates a program whereby each parent serves the school in some way begins a chain reaction of benefits. For the child, a better self-concept, more consistency between home and school standards of behavior, and improved communication with his parents may result. He develops a sense of mutual support between home and school that helps to maintain good attitudes toward education throughout life.

The parent who is active at school or for the school may have opportunities to learn more about being effective as a parent or about subjects of his choice. He may find his need for respect and dignity fulfilled and his self-confidence growing. The parent may find he can be influential if he serves on a school policy board or helps to evaluate the school, its program, and its staff.

The school receives many valuable hours of help from mothers and dads. A program can become a better one if it listens to constructive criticism from involved parents. The teachers who work with the parents develop administrative and communication skills in implementing the program. The natural interest in school affairs can be contagious until other schools and other community institutions are increasing and improving their own programs as a result of a good parent involvement program in an early childhood education class.

SUGGESTED ACTIVITIES

- Pretend you are a teacher of fifteen three-year-olds and you have an assistant teacher. Design a list of activities for yourself and your assistant to engage in to get the children's parents to volunteer their services. Place them in chronological order and list your part and hers.

- Attend a parent meeting in a day-care center. List all the parent services to the school that are mentioned in any way. Add others that you could suggest based on your observations.

- With another student, role-play a scene. Pretend you are an assistant teacher and she is a mother who is enrolling her four-year-old child in November. She is employed. Try to interest her in participating in the parent program of the school.

REVIEW

A. Explain how a child and his parent/parents benefit from having them actively participate in the school–parent program.

B. Explain how the school and community benefit when many parents are actively involved in school activities.

C. Make a list of ways to actively involve working parents of five-year-olds in public school kindergarten assuming that all of the parents work during school hours.

Section VII Finding A Job

unit 21 how to start

OBJECTIVES

After studying this unit, the student should be able to

- List at least nine kinds of places to go when seeking a job in early childhood education.
- List at least eight titles of positions of persons to see when seeking employment as an assistant teacher.
- List a series of at least eight steps a person might experience in seeking employment as an assistant teacher in an early childhood school.

Sometimes a person decides to find a job in early childhood education but does not know how to start. This person needs help in deciding where to look, whom to see, and what steps to take.

WHERE TO LOOK

Young people today often use the phrase "where the action is." This is the best place to look for employment in early childhood education: where the early childhood action is. This varies with the type of community, but even most small towns have some early childhood classes in church-related weekday schools. If they are day-care centers, the children may be as young as a few months of age. Some have first grade groups for children too young for

Fig. 21-1 Large cities offer excellent opportunities for employment in early childhood education.

public school grade one but apparently ready for grade one work. Nearly all public schools today have kindergarten classes for five-year-old girls and boys. Many of these schools employ assistants to work with the teachers.

Some private homes offer child care and may be licensed by the state if their facilities meet the criteria for licensing. In a very small town, most of the citizens can help someone who is trying to locate existing early childhood programs.

In larger towns or small cities, there are many more opportunities for employment although it may be a more time-consuming task to find them. A look at the telephone directory may be helpful. Under the heading "Schools" there may be numerous listings that give the job hunter needed information:

Bible Schools
Board of Education
Chamber of Commerce
Child Guidance Consultants
City Directory
Employment Agencies
Employment Services
Handicapped Children's Schools
Job Resume Service
Justices of the Peace

Schools:
Nursery and Kindergarten (Academic)
Parochial
Private
Public
Universities and Colleges

The larger towns often have a phone listing for local government under such headings as *Mayor, City Council, Sheriff's Office, Justice of the Peace, Town Hall.* If this is hard to determine, a phone call to "Information" will usually produce the phone number of a place where someone has the kind of information needed — where to go to find early childhood programs in the town. If one early childhood school can be located, the chances are good that the staff there knows where other programs for young children are to be found in the town. If the town is large enough, there may be a Chamber of Commerce, which usually has information to meet the needs of the job hunter.

Possibly the town may have a junior college. The two-year college — just as the four-year college does — maintains an employment service for its students. The placement office has lists of job openings which it posts on view for the public. Frequently, however, the openings may be in towns far away.

The small city may have state employment offices listed in the telephone directory. It may also have a private employment agency. Both offices would know of openings in early childhood schools in that city. The state office may also know of similar positions in other parts of the state.

Small cities may have professional organizations, such as a local chapter of The Association for Childhood Education (A.C.E.). A public school that has a kindergarten class probably has information on this and other professional groups. These groups usually have an employment service or at least exchange information on where help is needed. Attending a meeting of such an organization may produce answers about available positions.

Frequently child care associations have their own organization. They tend to feel that many of their problems are unique to all-day care. Therefore they have a separate group to meet their special needs. Attending one of the group's meetings should provide knowledge of openings on the day-care staffs. If there are Head Start child development or day-care centers, a visit or a phone call to one of them will reveal where to go to seek employment in local Head Start.

The newspaper want ads have competition from radio and television programs today. All of them should be given attention. Probably the last place to look for job opportunities in early childhood schools is the employment agency that is operated commercially — that charges applicants for finding jobs for them. However, all available options should be considered.

To the owner, director, and staff of all day-care centers:

> Our regular Child-Care Association meeting will be held Thursday, 7:30 P.M., Nov. 14 at the Miller Day-Care School, 4900 Wash St.
>
> Topics to be discussed:
>
> A.   Parents who are frequently late in picking up their child.
>
> B.   Curriculum reinforcement after nap time.
>
> Please come and share your solutions to these problems. Coffee and dessert will be served.
>
> Mrs. Tom Miller, Secretary
> Child-Care Association

Fig. 21-2 People in day-care frequently have their own organizations because many of their problems are unique to the day-care situation.

WHOM TO SEE

In seeking a position as a teacher or assistant teacher, the job hunter often finds that the person whom he should see may have one of several titles. If the position is with a large public school district, the personnel director interviews each applicant. In a small district, the principal of the school may give an initial interview. The personnel director/principal makes recommendations to the Board of Education. This Board actually does the hiring, but often the members just follow the recommendation of the interviewer. Where there are special programs in public schools for the handicapped and economically or language disadvantaged children, often the program director and the district personnel director must both interview and make recommendations to the Board.

A person who is seeking employment in a private school may request an interview with the school director. In some schools, a person who wishes a job may meet with the whole teaching staff who are given the right to accept or refuse a new person offered to the team by the administrator in charge. In a few day-care centers the director or teacher in charge may refer the person seeking employment to the owner of the business.

College employment services are under the direction of an employment director. Anyone in the office has information on whom to see. Public employment agencies usually have an information desk

Fig. 21-3 The personal interview is an important part of the employment procedure.

where forms are given to prospects and interviews are arranged.

Usually it saves time to ask immediately of the first person met in an organization the name or title of the person to see when applying for a job with the school. If the person asked does not know, he can probably find out for the applicant.

STEPS TO TAKE

- Before starting to find a job, it is best to spend some time carefully thinking through one's capabilities and limitations. It is essential that a job applicant be completely honest with his future employer. "Know thyself" is a good motto for one seeking a job.

- The applicant should visit early childhood schools and ask about staff openings.

- If a school has or knows that it will have a position available, the applicant requests an opportunity to observe for a day. This enables the person to determine if the philosophy of the school and her personal philosophy are compatible. It also reveals the emotional climate of the school. The degree of friendliness and freedom from tension may be determined.

- If no openings are discovered by visits, the newspaper want ads should be thoroughly checked. Sometimes there are local television and radio programs that help people find jobs or applicants for jobs.

- If possible, the job seeker should attend meetings of the local professional organization representing early childhood schools. The person

in charge may be aware of employment needs before the meeting, or if not, the prospect may be referred to others at the meeting who can be helpful.

- If no job openings have been discovered by the steps listed, the applicant should visit the employment agencies: first the local college, then the state employment agencies. Other free community employment service agencies may be discovered. As a last resort, commercial agencies may be used. The job hunter should be sure to have a clear understanding of the agency charges for their service before filling out any forms. (Some are known to charge high fees.)

- If a person in a hiring position has an opening, he usually asks an applicant a few questions about educational and work experience. If he is pleased with the answers given him, he may give the applicant an application form to fill out or he may make an appointment for a lengthier interview at another time. If he is displeased with the answers given him, he will probably explain that the experience stated does not meet that which is required to fill the position.

- If a person who is hiring has an applicant fill out an initial form stating general information, he will then try to determine more about the applicant's attitudes than the form reveals. He needs to know if the applicant is the kind of person who will get along well with the present staff. The applicant may be introduced to the teacher with whom she will work if she is hired. Seeing the two persons (teacher and applicant) interact is sometimes revealing. If a specific curriculum is used, the applicant may be asked to look at it and react to it. The least the applicant can expect is a lengthy conversation about herself with the person who hires. This is important to the school and to the prospective employee. It is better to discover serious differences before a new job is started than for a new employee to quit later, leaving both persons just where they were: one needing a job and the other needing an employee.

Hopefully, a person who is studying to become a teacher or assistant teacher will be guided into appropriate channels by the school. This is best accomplished before the end of the school year. If a student is not successful in acquiring a position by

Fig. 21-4 A teacher explains the curriculum to a prospective assistant teacher.

the end of the school year, it is advisable that he/she serve as a volunteer in a school that operates all year round. Several days per week volunteer service permits continuing to hunt for a job while staying "where the action is" to gain practical experience.

SUMMARY

A person looking for work for the first time in early childhood education has many places to look, persons to see, and steps to take. Going to early childhood programs in action is a highly recommended way to begin. After visiting several, the applicant can take the routine steps required by those of interest.

If the city is large, the telephone information service and directory are helpful in locating the places to visit or places known to need more staff. Colleges maintain employment services that are helpful to the public and the student. Newspapers, radio, and television sometimes have information for the job seeker. Public employment agencies are usually available in cities.

In public schools, the personnel director interviews applicants. In smaller school systems, the principal interviews and accepts applications. In daycare centers and private schools, the teacher in charge, director, or owner may be the person to see.

College employment services usually employ a director. Other agencies have varying titles for the person to see. Usually an information desk is available to give out instructions for the procedure of applying.

There are several steps to take after deciding to seek employment in early childhood education. It is necessary to be honest with those who hire. It is wise to get acquainted with a school before applying, if possible. The philosophy of education held by the school must be compatible with that of the applicant if there is to be harmony among the staff.

A systematic exploring of early childhood programs may be assisted by the phone directory, observations, public agencies, news media, and professional organizations. If a student has not secured a position at the end of the school year, it is practical for him/her to volunteer his/her services at an all-year school for a day or two per week while continuing to seek employment. By so doing, the prospective teacher is staying where the action is and learning and is also in constant touch with an employment situation.

SUGGESTED ACTIVITIES

- Using the telephone directory of the city nearest you, make a list of all the places where you may go to seek employment as an assistant teacher.
- On a basis of what you can discover by phone about ten specific schools, eliminate those you are sure do not interest you. Give reasons for excluding them.
- Compare your lists from the preceding activities with those of other students. Discuss the samenesses and differences among the lists.

REVIEW

A. List nine places a person might go in seeking a job in early childhood education.

B. List at least eight titles of positions of people whom an applicant might seek in finding a job in early childhood education.

C. List a series of at least eight steps a student might experience in seeking employment as an assistant teacher in an early childhood school.

unit 22 filling out forms

OBJECTIVES

After studying this unit the student should be able to

- Define the following terms: resume, job description, application, applicant.
- List six kinds of information that an employer looks for in a job description of an applicant's previous employment.
- List seven rules to observe in filling out application forms.

One of the most important skills needed in finding a job is the filling out of many kinds of forms. This activity precedes being hired in almost any kind of work. Correctly filled out forms open the door to the person seeking a position. Incorrectly filled out forms sometimes block the way. There are a few rules to remember and techniques to use in filling out forms that make a positive impression. Each person gains by using this knowledge.

RESUME

Often a teacher who has a degree or is certified is required to provide a resume of experiences when applying for a teaching position. The *resume* presents a thorough picture of the applicant's life experiences that would be helpful in the position being sought. Usually, assistant teachers are not required to do this. However, since there is a possibility that there will be a certification for assistant teachers in the near future, it is wise to be prepared. The following kinds of information are expected in a resume.

- *Current Statistical Information:* name, address, phone number, and age; present employer's name, address, and phone number; marital status and other members of immediate family.

- *Educational Achievement:* highest level of academic experience, degrees, certificates, academic honors received.

- *Employment Experience:* a history of work experience (beginning with current employment, if any, and listing in order each previous work experience back to the earliest one).

- *Other Personal Experiences:* Those activities that contribute to applicant's abilities or are related in some way to the kind of work being sought.

- *Professional Involvement:* a list of professional organizations to which applicant has belonged or belongs presently, showing number of years involved with each one.

- *Published Works:* any written material produced by applicant and published.

- *Other Written Work:* works produced by applicant that have not yet been published.

Probably the only one of the seven that may be difficult to understand is the fourth one: "Other Personal Experiences." Here the employer wants to know about things the applicant has done that are

---

Work experience:

May '73 - present: Assistant teacher, Playschool Day-Care Center, Taylor City, Ohio.

July '70 - May '73:   Part-time attendant, Playschool Day-Care Center, Taylor City, Ohio.

June '68 - July '70:   Part-time sales girl, children's wear, Sears, Taylor City, Ohio.

Fig. 22-1 In a resume, work experience is stated from present employment back to the applicant's earliest employment.

Correct	Incorrect
1. Planned and taught playground games to five-year-olds.	1. Had fun playing cute games outside with kindergarteners.
2. Played piano for musical activities for four-year-olds (2 classes).	2. Helped with the wonderful music hour the kids liked.
3. Taught fives to set tables and to help serve lunch and clean up after lunch.	3. Got the kids to love to help me at lunch time.
4. Was responsible for helping to contact mothers to serve as volunteers.	4. Got names to give us a lift and have fun at the school.

Fig. 22-2 In describing a previous job, statements should be objective, factual, and clearly stated.

not a part of his work (for pay) experience. Any hours that he has volunteered his services in any activity that can be considered related to early childhood education should be listed. Babysitting with younger sisters and brothers may be included. Teaching in church or Sunday school should be mentioned. Working with a recreational program with young children or at a church camp may be included. Under this point, there should be no duplication of any work experience listed.

JOB DESCRIPTIONS

When resumes are not expected, job applicants may be asked to give a thorough description of any previous jobs they have held where the work was similar to the work they are seeking. In writing a job description to fit past work experience, several thoughts should be kept in mind: (1) The person who reads the description is going to want answers to these questions from the information:

- What kinds of responsibilities has the applicant had?

- Which skills were used?

- Which abilities will be expected that were not shown in the previous job?

- Which ones are now needed but were not expected before?

- How many people did the applicant have to get along with before?

- How many children has the applicant worked with? Which ages? In which kinds of activities?

(2) It is vital that the job description contains information that the reader needs. It is distracting to the person who reads for information if there are irrelevant details throughout the statements. Each one should contain facts and should not contain a statement of the writer's feelings about the experience.

(3) In composing the job description, it is helpful to think of the daily routine in terms of the kind of duties performed. When a day's schedule is ready, duplication can be removed. For example, "Helped prepare and serve morning snack, lunch, afternoon snack" becomes "Helped prepare and serve foods for the children daily."

Fig. 22-3 A job description may state: "Helped serve children's food daily."

(4) When thinking of the weekly schedule, other specific tasks emerge, such as, "Had full responsibility for the children two hours weekly while teacher attended a teacher's meeting."

(5) After weekly tasks have been added, the applicant fills in any others, such as "Was responsible for monthly ordering of classroom supplies." Listing first daily, then weekly and finally other duties sim-

---

Application for Employment

A. PERSONAL:

   Name _____ Age _____ Sex _____ SS No. _____

   Address _____ Phone _____ Citizen _____

B. EDUCATION:

   High School _____ Grade Completed _____

   Other Training or Education _____

   _____

C. EMPLOYMENT:

   Work Experience _____

   _____

   _____

   _____

   Driver's License: Yes _____   No _____

   Do you have transportation?   Yes _____   No _____   Kind? _____

   Job Desired _____

   Date _____ Signature _____

   _____

Fig. 22-4 Some application blanks call for a minimum of essential information.

plifies making a complete list of activities to include in a job description.

When applying for a job, it is appropriate to ask to see the description of the job that is or will be available. It is not unusual however, to discover that it does not exist. Assistant teacher job descriptions are rare and if they are available, they are likely to be stated in general terms, such as "Helps to prepare lessons."

APPLICATIONS

At an employment agency or school office, a job applicant is asked to fill out an application blank. These vary considerably. One may ask for the barest essential information. Another may call for a much more comprehensive description of the applicant's experience and skills. The same rules apply in both instances.

- Write legibly; print, if possible, in ink.
- Follow instructions exactly. If it says "Check", use a check mark. If it says "Mark with an X", do so.
- Write something for every item. In some cases, write "None." Write "not applicable" if the item is inappropriate for the applicant.
- If the applicant does not understand what is meant by the direction given, he should ask someone in the office if the person who gave him the application has left the room.
- Do not use abbreviations except standard ones such as Mr./Mrs./Ms. If "languages spoken" is an item, write "Spanish", not "Span.".
- When the applicant's signature is required, write the name as it is written on official documents, such as bank checks.

- If the form seems messy when completed (has scratch-outs, writing in margins), ask for another form and copy the information neatly onto it.

- Be prepared to give references when applying. Have the names, addresses, and phone numbers of at least three persons for character references. If applicant was employed previously, he should have the names, addresses, and phone numbers of at least three people who knew him there: his employer and/or persons with whom he worked.

At the time an application is made, some agencies require the applicant to take a test for literacy or general intelligence. At a few schools, a test may be a requirement, but this is rare. Someone may ask the job prospect to observe at the school and then discuss the observations. Asking intelligent questions about the observations can be as desirable as answering them. It is better for the job seeker to be honest than to try to bluff his/her way into a job for which he/she may not be ready.

SUMMARY

Correctly filled out forms create a good impression on the reader, so it is essential to observe a few rules to achieve this. When assistant teachers achieve a certified status, they may be expected to provide a resume of personal information just as certified or teachers with degrees are asked to do. The applicant should know the kinds of information expected.

If an employer requests a description of a previous position held, the applicant must know the kinds of questions the employer will ask himself as he reads — so that appropriate objective statements are made. He should know how to make comprehensive but concise statements to describe the work.

There are general rules that apply to filling out all forms. They can be applied to produce the kind of forms that create a good impression on a prospective employer. Every job applicant can master these simple rules to help himself in securing a job.

SUGGESTED ACTIVITIES

- Create a resume giving current information about yourself. Compare yours with those of other students. Make additions if necessary.

- Create an imaginary job description for an assistant teacher in a class of three-year-olds with one teacher and twelve children. Pretend that she held the job during one school year (nine/ten months).

- Prepare a list of character references for yourself. If you have had work experience prepare a list of employment references for yourself, also.

REVIEW

A. Define the following terms: applicant, application, resume, job description.

B. List and briefly describe seven kinds of information to be included in a resume.

C. List the kinds of things a prospective employer wants to learn from a description of a previous job.

D. Briefly state the seven rules to be followed in filling out job applications.

unit 23 personal interviews

OBJECTIVES

After studying this unit, the student should be able to

- Briefly explain the value to an employer of a personal interview with a prospective employee.

- Briefly explain the employer's expectations when a job applicant is interviewed.

- Explain the preparation and conduct necessary to a successful personal interview for employment.

Very few persons are hired for any kind of work without experiencing a personal interview with the employer or his representative. In the process of seeking a job as a teacher or an assistant teacher in early childhood education, the personal interview is important although it is rarely enough on which to base a decision. The applicant must make a favorable impression during the meeting with the person who hires before being given another kind of opportunity to prove that he or she is the right person for the job. The applicant needs to understand fully the value of the personal interview and must take the time to prepare for it carefully in order to make as favorable an impression as possible.

VALUE

The interview in which the employer or his representative asks questions of the job applicant creates impressions in the minds of both persons. If both are positive, further tests of the suitability of the job seeker follow. If either person has negative feelings as a result of the meeting, the relationship may end there.

Usually a person does not keep an appointment for a personal interview unless he sincerely wants the job in question. So it is worthwhile to be properly prepared for the occasion.

Thorough questioning by the interviewer (the employer or his representative) is essential. Some of the attributes of the applicant are observable. Many others are not. Knowledge of the characteristics of little children at various ages, of how children learn, and of appropriate activities for them can be discussed. Even more important to the employer, however, are the attitudes of the applicant. The employer needs to know if the applicant is willing

Fig. 23-1 The exchange of information makes an interview valuable to both parties.

to learn, is flexible when change is desirable, and can get along well with other people. A skillfully conducted interview can give the interviewer some information on these points. If the impressions given are negative, the interview has saved the time it takes to examine further the applicant's suitability.

The applicant, too, at an appropriate time during the interview, may seek information on several factors that influence his desire to have the job. He may ask about school policies, philosophy, methods of discipline, attitude toward creativity, and working conditions including salary. He is entitled to know about these matters so that he will not later become an unhappy employee because of conflicts between his own ideas and those of the school.

The person seeking the position, as well as the interviewer, does not have time to waste interacting in a classroom of a school in which he cannot work happily. The interview can save him time by permitting him to obtain the information he needs. The attitude of the school toward parent involvement may be important to the applicant. It is appropriate to ask about this near the end of the interview if it is essential to the happiness of the applicant.

---

1. To get information from the applicant.
2. To give information to the applicant.
3. To form an opinion about the applicant.

Fig. 23-2 An employer has three main purposes in a personal interview with a prospective employee.

The personal interview gives the interviewer an opportunity to judge the applicant's appearance and demeanor. The chief value however lies in the exchange of information that is possible. The information is needed by both parties so that neither one will waste time on further activities if there are some points on which the two cannot agree.

EMPLOYER EXPECTATIONS

The employer or his representative sets the time for the personal interview. He expects the time to be spent determining first that the applicant has the needed qualifications (including attitudes) to perform well in the job. Secondly, he expects to find out if the applicant is still interested after he knows much more about the job.

Since time means money to any employer, he usually does not want the interview spent on irrelevant topics. It is highly desirable to have great personal compatibility among the members of a staff. In a very small school, an interview may branch into personal and noneducation subjects. In a large school, however, an administrator must be satisfied with professional compatibility. The interview then may be only on the subject of early childhood education. It should be remembered that the employer's expectations are to be met and respected in this matter.

The professional future of the job seeker may be affected by the personal interview. He must remember, though, that the employer has an already

established system to protect in most instances. Many children's lives may be touched by the person who is hired. The employer must be thorough in screening persons who want to accept this great responsibility. The applicant is expected to understand this and to willingly cooperate in helping with this decision. The employer expects the prospective employee to answer all reasonable questions as accurately and concisely as possible. After his questions have been answered, he expects the interviewee to mention any areas that are of significance to him if they were not satisfactorily explained to him earlier. Any vital information that can be obtained orally should be discussed. The interviewer expects to conclude whether the applicant is or is not a person who can do the job well — as far as this can be determined by discussion.

DOs AND DON'Ts

Every prospective employee is told by someone to "Just be yourself, stay relaxed, and answer the questions." While these are good suggestions, they are not enough. The following list of DOs and DON'Ts may be applied to any employment interview. The applicant should **DO** the following: (1) Be on time, (2) Be well groomed: have a neat, clean appearance; wear simple jewelry and clothes (at least moderately conservative); hair and nails are to be at their inconspicuous best, (3) Maintain good posture: sit up straight with legs crossed below the knees, (4) Shake hands (firmly) if an offer is made, (5) Sit down where and when she/he is asked to do so, (6) Listen without interrupting (Your turn to get information comes later.), (7) Answer clearly and with self-confidence, (8) Be frank about his/her qualifications (Be honest and you may expect honesty.), (9) State a willingness to learn: without this, there is small chance of being considered for the job, (10) Indicate flexibility and ability to adjust to new situations: this, too, is a prerequisite, (11) Ask for needed information after the interviewer has asked all of his questions (Before coming, make a list of what you wish to ask.), (12) Bring a list of character and other references — if these were not required before the interview. (13) Thank the interviewer and ask when she/he may expect to hear from him.

The applicant should not do the following: (1) Be aggressive, forward, impatient, (2) Make herself at home (You do not yet "belong" here.), (3) Interrupt the interviewer while he is asking questions, (4) Smoke cigarettes, cigars, or a pipe, (5) Brag or criticize anyone, (6) Dramatize statements in a loud voice, (7) Fail to express appreciation for receiving the interview.

The applicant who observes the DOs and DON'Ts listed passes the initial inspection of appearance and behavior. In addition to this, of course, knowledge and attitudes expressed are an important part of the job interview. After that there remains the demonstration of skills in interacting with very young children. This is crucial to success in such a position.

No applicant should feel offended because she/he is asked to show an ability to get along with children. After passing a test on knowledge of the rules, a driver's license seeker must drive the car and demonstrate skills before he receives his license. This is because lives are at stake when a driver takes the wheel. When a teacher takes the responsibility for the activities of a child at school, lives may not be at stake but the quality of life in that child's future may very well depend upon the experience. The fewer the changes made in the teaching staff during the school year, the greater are the chances for a smooth progression of learnings for the children.

To be asked to demonstrate interacting with children, an applicant must first have met the criteria expected in the personal interview. Therefore, preparing for it carefully is worth the effort.

SUMMARY

When filling out an application form results in a personal interview, it is of great importance to the employer and to the prospective employee. Each needs certain kinds of information before he can further pursue the relationship. This information can be exchanged during the interview. The interviewer, the employer or his representative, hopes to decide by the appearance, behavior, attitudes, and knowledge displayed if the candidate is a good choice for the job. The person interviewed hopes to learn if the school's philosophy and methods are compatible with hers. If both parties are favorably impressed, the applicant may expect to be asked to demonstrate her ability to interact with little children since this is a required skill for a teacher or assistant teacher.

Since the applicant must create a favorable impression first during the interview, it is important to prepare for it carefully and to approach it with an appropriate attitude. Making a good first impression in any employment interview can be assured by observing a few simple rules of courtesy and by looking one's best in an inconspicuous way. Being prepared to answer and then to ask questions related to the work and working conditions is advisable.

If the interview is successful, the applicant should expect to be asked to interact with children so that the interviewer can observe her skills. Since these skills are essential to being successful at the work, they must be demonstrated to maintain a stabilized staff with a minimum of changes during the school year. So much depends upon the success of the personal interview that the applicant should be prepared for it in every possible way.

SUGGESTED ACTIVITIES

- With another student, role-play having an interview for a position of assistant teacher in a day-care center. Have others observe and make suggestions for improvement. If possible, have the activity video-taped; write your own suggestions for ways to improve to assure a successful meeting.

- Write a list of questions for information you will want when you have a personal interview for a position of assistant teacher. (These are things you will ask after the interviewer has questioned you if they were not explained during the interview.)

- Make a list of topics you, a personnel director, would want to discuss with an applicant for a job as an assistant teacher in a public school kindergarten class.

REVIEW

A. Briefly discuss the value of a personal interview for employment.

B. Briefly explain the employer's expectations when a job applicant is interviewed.

C. In your own words, describe the rules for making a favorable impression at a personal interview for employment.

Section VIII Professional Development

unit 24 continuous education

OBJECTIVES

After studying this unit, the student should be able to

- Briefly explain the meaning and importance of continuous education.

- Name the kinds of "in school" educational opportunities that teachers may seek.

- List ten sources of "out of school" continuous education available to most teachers.

Many people are shocked at Alvin Toffler's description of American society in *Future Shock*. Some are amazed at his accurate picture of their own resistance to rapid change. Many are accepting his challenge to people all over the world — the global society. These persons are following his advice. They are engaging in *continuous education*. Toffler makes it clear that the only way a person can survive in the ever faster changing environment is to change with it.

For most persons this means making a deliberate effort to continually stay abreast of what is happening in their society, in their community, in their profession. In other words, people who survive without existing in a state of "future shock" will be intentionally learning something new daily — to help them adjust to the changing conditions, changing bodies of knowledge, changing technology, and changing interpersonal relationships of the times. They are undergoing continuous education by choice.

IN SCHOOL

It is said that the more a person learns, the more he realizes how little he knows. Most educators agree. Once embarked on a teaching career, the teacher begins a never ending search for what it takes to prepare students to live in the world of tomorrow. Some people may wonder how early childhood education can be affected since there are certain limits to what a preschooler can learn. Educators argue that those limits are not yet known. Scientists are finding out more every day about how children learn and about the effects of environment on learning. This is changing school settings and how teachers facilitate learning.

Colleges are increasing the number and kinds of course work available to those who work in early childhood education. Even experienced teachers are returning to study new research on teacher effective-

Fig. 24-1 Scientists are still learning how a child learns.

ness. Bilingualism in early childhood education is growing rapidly in the United States. Many areas do not have teachers who are prepared for this.

Compensatory education for economically disadvantaged children requires new studies. Programs for the culturally different children of ethnic minority groups send many teachers back to the classroom to learn to cope.

Many state governments are hearing pleas for public school programs for three- and four-year-old children. Most teachers know that three-year-olds cannot sit at primary desks in rows, but they are not prepared with alternatives.

Special education trends today are toward the integration of children with minor learning disabilities into the regular classroom on a part-time basis at least. So the regular classroom teacher must study how to handle the changing situation. In the school year, 1973-74, the Illinois public schools were mandated to find and provide schooling for all three-year-old and older preschoolers who may have disabilities of any kind. In several other states, including Texas, the same plan is being gradually implemented in the public schools. It must be preceded by the continuous education of the staff who are or will be responsible for the programs.

But what of the teacher who is in a traditional kindergarten program and whose children have done well each year in the first grade? First grade programs are rapidly becoming process-oriented instead of product-oriented. Kindergartens can prepare the child better if newer research is studied and applied. Appropriate uses of some structure under specific conditions can be justified. Teachers must know when and how. Some schools are changing totally to the discovery method. Many teachers need help to adjust to this idea; inservice training at the school is essential.

For the assistant teacher, change by continuous education is unlimited. Within the school itself there are many opportunities to study teaching techniques, the population served, and the improvement of curriculum. Getting to know the culture of the families in the community can be done through the parent involvement program at the school. Taking courses at neighboring schools may be helpful. Adult education classes can be helpful to teachers as well as to parents. Often they are less costly than academic college courses. A good preschool has a professional library of its own which contains many resource books that may be helpful to the assistant teacher.

Professional magazines publish many short helpful articles on practical matters for the classroom. There are usually several kinds of these periodicals available in a good teachers' library. Within the confines of the preschool itself and in academic and vocational classes in other schools, there are opportunities for a continuous education for the teacher and for the assistant teacher.

OUT OF SCHOOL

Some preschool personnel cannot be enticed into classrooms after school hours, although they are

Fig. 24-2 A child learns many things for himself at the "discovery learning table."

interested in learning. The world outside of schools is a never ending source of continuous education.

Today's newspapers, popular magazines, and book racks are no longer filled with only the spectacular, the noneducational, or the pornographic trivia they were once noted for. Most any of these sources of printed matter contain articles or whole books by well known authors accepted in educational circles: for example, Dr. Haim Ginott (*Teacher and Child*) and Dr. Thomas Gordon (*P.E.T., Parent Effectiveness Training*).

Educational television is slowly but surely gaining ground. Public interest programs often contain information that is relevant to early childhood schools. School financing and new laws affecting education are often explained on national networks and state and local news programs.

Most communities have some programs by creative artists in music, drama, and art that will enrich the

---

IMPORTANT!

"The Ballet de Folkerico" performs at the auditorium on Friday at 7 P.M. Car pools may be arranged at the office.

DON'T MISS THIS TREAT!

Fig. 24-3 A teacher's continuous education may include learning more about the cultural heritage of the children.

lives of all who see them and participate. Professional teachers' organizations often have workshop meetings open to the public. Public health authorities and medical schools frequently have public meetings to discuss topics of interest to the community. Many churches sponsor workshops and seminars for persons who work with children. College campuses are a rich source of interesting speakers; often lectures are free for students, with only a very small charge for nonstudents.

Radio still provides question and answer programs. Many people use their driving time to listen to interesting radio shows. Some are directly aimed at people in education. Others are for general information. All of them can be a part of the continuous education of teachers or assistant teachers who are vitally alive and interested in the world around them. They must have this genuine interest in almost everything if they hope to spark this kind of active interest in learning in the children they influence each working day.

SUMMARY

Continuous education refers to the planned effort of a person to increase his knowledge daily.

This is needed to enable him to escape shock in the future from the rapidity of change in his life. Education is undergoing a revolution that requires that every educator experience continuous education.

In most kinds of schools, teachers have learning goals. They may take college courses or other academic or vocational course work to improve skills. They may use the school library itself. So many new views of early childhood education are developing that all staffs must plan to study to be effective. Those new in the field at this time may expect to be studying from now on both in and out of school.

Outside the school in the community there are many good resources. Books, periodicals, radio, television, newspapers, and interesting programs are only a few of them.

A "good teacher" hopes to develop a love of learning in each very young child she helps to learn. She is most likely to do so if she models this love of learning herself by her own continuous education.

SUGGESTED ACTIVITIES

- From a Sunday issue of the newspaper of the city nearest you, list all the rich sources for learning that appeal to you.

- Make a list of your personal plans for continuous education when you are employed as a teacher or assistant teacher.

- Interview three teachers of very young children. Ask questions about the kinds of continuous education they enjoy.

REVIEW

A. Briefly explain the meaning and importance of "continuous education."

B. List five kinds of "in school" and five kinds of "out of school" sources for continuous education for teachers.

C. Select the items that correctly complete each of the following statements.

1. A teacher's group at an elementary school has mailed announcements to other neighboring schools that it is having a kindergarten science demonstration after school on Tuesday. A "K" teacher at one of the schools believes she has a good science center in her room. She should

    a. Decline on the grounds that she does not need help in science.

    b. Call and offer to help if it is needed.

c. Accept on the grounds that she might learn a few new good ideas to add to her own.

d. Decline because she plays bridge on Tuesdays.

2. A "K-3rd grade" art workshop is to be held at the school district teacher resource center. It is free to district employees. There is a two-dollar charge for nondistrict people. A teacher of four-year-olds in a private school is poor in creative art and needs ideas. She should

a. Pay the fee and go to get the ideas she needs.

b. Not go because it is unfair for some to pay and others not to pay.

c. Not go because the ideas will be too advanced for four-year-olds.

d. Go to see if one of her friends in the district can get her in free of charge.

3. A principal has asked that all his teachers listen at home to the one-hour educational television program on "Discipline in the Home and at School." They are to discuss it at a staff meeting later. The "K" teacher has excellent self-discipline developed in her pupils. She should

a. Watch a musical she prefers in order to relax.

b. Listen to the program to see if there are some ideas to use with the parents of her pupils.

c. Refuse to listen because she obviously does not need the information.

d. Listen to the show but suggest to the principal that it might be unwise to expect teachers to discuss a Tuesday evening television program since many of them have prior commitments for Tuesday evening hours.

unit 25 supervision

OBJECTIVES

After studying this unit, the student should be able to

- State the primary purpose of school supervision and list six ways in which to fulfill that purpose.
- Briefly discuss the role of the supervisor in a variety of kinds of schools.
- Compare the supervision process in a large public school system with that likely to be found in a small private preschool and list the advantages and disadvantages of both situations.

Supervision in public schools, like other aspects of educational systems today, is changing. It is no longer the largely evaluative process of observing teachers, writing reports on the things seen in the classroom, and giving the reports to the personnel department. A slow but sure evolution of the supervisory process has resulted in a much more personal relationship between teachers and supervisors. Teachers need to understand what they may expect in this relationship.

Private schools have a wide variety of types of supervision. The small day-care center may have a director who is not an educator but is a business person. Possibly a teacher need only meet the approval of the owner of the school. Sometimes the look of the school rates more highly than the quality of instruction for the children. (Parents are often more demanding as to the appearance of the school than of the education the child receives.) In some private schools, however, day care and others, the quality of instruction has a high priority on the list of goals. In these, the supervisory process is similar to that found in the public schools.

THE PURPOSE

The primary purpose of supervision in schools is to see that the instructional program is constantly improving. The instructional program includes these components of the system: teaching personnel, curriculum materials, supplementary materials, teacher training, evaluation, and interpersonal relationships. All these are vital parts of the instructional system. This gives a different view of supervision. Its purposes are to improve the educational product by

- Helping each teaching staff member as an individual to become a more effective teacher.

- Helping in the selection and improved uses of curriculum materials for the school.

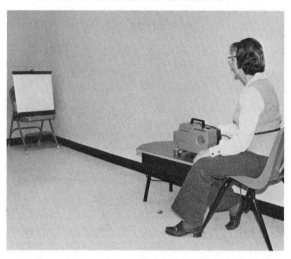

Fig. 25-1 **The supervisor helps in the selection of new materials for the curriculum and in planning creative ways to use them.**

- Providing supplementary materials or knowledge of resources for the teacher to add to the curriculum provided by the school.
- Arranging or giving training for each teacher that helps her with teaching techniques, use of materials, subject matter content, educational theory, or overcoming her personal faults.
- Analyzing instruction and objectively evaluating instructional materials.
- Coordinating with teaching and administrative staff members to help each group become more aware of the needs and expectations of the others.

Periodic Review of Day-Care Facilities

A representative of the State Department of Public Welfare will visit each day-care center periodically and may make a complete study at any time if indicated. A department representative will also revalidate the license to assure continual compliance. A license remains in force until it is suspended or revoked.

In this regard the Texas law states:

The State Department of Public Welfare shall have the authority to visit and inspect all such facilities embraced within this Act, whether licensed or unlicensed, at all reasonable times, to ascertain if same are being conducted in conformity with the law or if any conditions exist which need correction. (Section 8 (a) 4 of Article 695c, Vernon's Texas Civil Statutes)

Fig. 25-2 The Texas State Department of Public Welfare provides "minimum standards for day-care centers" in which the above paragraphs are found. The state retains the right to supervise all aspects of day-care facilities to insure that the children's best interests are served.

At one time school supervision was to find what, if anything, the teacher was doing wrong and to tell her to eliminate this behavior. The purpose of supervision today is to give help to every teacher, enabling her to capitalize on her strengths, strengthen her weaknesses, and eliminate her errors — in short, to become a more effective teacher.

THE PERSONS

In some very small schools, a minimum of supervision of teaching occurs. In state-licensed day-care centers, the licensing bureau sends representatives to evaluate each center. Custodial care only is no longer acceptable. Educational opportunity is required for all children in the licensed child development centers. The center may have other supervision as well.

In privately-operated schools for very young children, an owner, director, lead teacher, supervisor, or principal may perform the supervisory role. It is likely to be only a part of that person's responsibilities.

In public schools, the size of the school district, of the schools, and of the classes all affect the supervisory function. In general the wealthier the district, the more likelihood there is of every teacher having a "Supervisor." Districts with a lower "dollars per pupil" are more likely to have principals function as the only instructional leaders or resource persons.

Where a school district is fortunate enough to have principals responsible for the quality of the instruction in their schools and to have supervisors, also, these may be responsible for several grade levels.

A person may supervise K-3rd grade or grades 4-6, 7-9, or 10-12, for example.

In some systems, a supervisor is selected because of expertise in a specific field. One teacher may have a supervisor for language arts and a different one for science, social studies, and math. There may be still another for music and art. Sometimes these persons are titled consultants. Where there are public school programs for four- and five-year-old children, there may be a curriculum resource specialist, usually a very experienced former preschool teacher.

In a teaching team, the teacher serves as a supervisor to the assistant teacher in fulfilling some of the purposes of supervision. The teacher helps the assistant to improve her teaching techniques, to understand children, and to deal with them as individuals more effectively as the weeks pass. She also provides her with supplementary materials or provides resource information on what and where to find them. When a satisfying relationship develops among team members, the teacher is in a position to help each individual become a better teacher.

In accepting a position as a teacher or assistant teacher, one should request information on who is involved in the supervision process at the school. It is important to know to whom instructional problems should be addressed. It is not important that the person have a specific title, such as "supervisor".

THE PROCESS

The processes of school supervision vary greatly according to conditions. The ratio of teachers to supervisors controls the number of "in person" interactions between a teacher and the supervisor. This is true whether the supervisor has that title or is the school principal. The size of the geographical area a supervisor must travel also affects the number of times the teaching staff sees the supervisor. In very large school districts, after an initial visit with every teacher, the rest of the year may be spent solving problems and giving some kind of help only where it is requested. The teacher who does not have problems that are obvious or that are discussed at the initial observation period may not see the supervisor again until the end of the year — unless the teacher requests help of a specific kind. (She must not be timid in asking for help.)

In specially funded programs, there are often supervision and evaluation guidelines. These programs provide maximum service to the teaching staff. They also require some degree of accountability for the children's learning. Continued funding of special projects is dependent on obtaining adequate improvement in the child's abilities. Supervision may include giving much one-to-one attention to teachers. It is likely to give inservice training throughout the year on topics that are relevant to the needs of the teachers involved. The teaching staff is required to attend and to demonstrate the benefits in the classroom.

Fig. 25-3 The supervisory role includes providing inservice training to improve the quality of classroom instruction.

Personnel evaluations were once the work of supervisors. Today this administrative function is more often limited to the school principal. The teacher is entitled to know at the first of the year

the kinds of evaluations that will be made. If a checklist or form is to be used, she should be shown a copy of it at the beginning of the school year. She has a right to know what is expected of her by the person who is to fill out the forms. If the supervisor is to help the teacher improve instruction and the principal is to evaluate, it is essential to know that these persons agree on what is desirable teacher performance in the classroom.

To prevent problems from possible disagreements, a principal may have the whole staff meet with him before school starts. The difference in roles is explained and evaluation forms are shown. Teachers are given opportunity to ask questions about the forms and about what is expected of them.

During the year when an evaluation of a teacher's work has been made, she is usually given a brief conference in which to discuss the report. Then she signs the form or checklist, indicating that she is aware of the observations made on it. If she disagrees with the evaluator, she is permitted to write a statement giving her reasons: This is attached to the form and becomes part of her permanent record in the personnel file.

Evaluations are usually done two or three times per school year. At the later evaluations, the evaluator expects to find the results of the help provided by the supervisor.

In small schools or small school districts, the supervision process may be much more casual. There may be more frequent interactions between teachers and those who perform the supervisory functions. Conversation over coffee may be the time when much supervisory help is given to the teaching staff. In these schools inservice training may be as personal as a teaching demonstration by the supervisor in the classroom with the students. A principal may be the only instructional or resource person available. His/her time for inservice training may be limited. He/she may ask master teachers (good models) to conduct inservice training for the other teachers.

Very small schools may have no formal evaluation program. An owner or director may keep an eye on what goes on daily. A teacher may not hear any evaluation unless she is breaking some school rules or is not maintaining good discipline in the room. She may hear a friendly comment occasionally. This is minimal supervision. Some teachers prefer to work in such a situation. They prefer the "more personal, less pressured" condition. The teacher who is genuinely concerned about improving her effectiveness will probably search for ideas by herself. She will not grow to her greatest potential, however, until she experiences a comprehensive program of supervision.

SUMMARY

Today's trend in supervision is to separate the role of the supervisor from that of the evaluator wherever possible. In small schools of every kind, one person is often required to fill both roles. The new view shows the supervisor as a resource person for the teaching staff. He provides the services to the teacher that result in improved instruction in the classroom. This includes spotting weaknesses, suggesting helps, providing supplementary materials or knowledge of where to get them, seeing that interpersonal relationships among staff members improve, and preparing teachers for evaluations to be made of them.

State licensing bureaus provide their own supervisors for day-care centers to be sure that all licensing requirements are met. Usually, though, a supervisor is a school employee. It may be a principal, but wherever possible, the roles of supervisor and evaluator are performed by two persons. In a teaching team, the teacher supervises the work of the assistant teacher. She helps her to improve techniques, understand the children, and to communicate more effectively.

Some general rules for the supervision process are (1) the teacher should know who is to supervise and evaluate her, (2) she should know the criteria by which she will be evaluated, (3) she should be informed of what kinds of help she may expect to receive and the process for requesting it, (4) she should know that the supervisor and evaluator agree on curriculum and in interpreting any forms that are used, and (5) she should be able to expect that the instructional program in her classroom will improve because of the supervisory process in the school.

SUGGESTED ACTIVITIES

- Interview a public school kindergarten supervisor about her work. Write down any tasks that may not be included in the suggestions in this unit.

- Interview a principal who has a kindergarten class in his school and who is both supervisor and evaluator of the teachers. Compare the supervision given teachers in this situation with that in the preceding activity.

- In a large day-care center, discuss the supervision process with a teacher. List ways to improve supervision from the teacher's point of view.

REVIEW

A. State the primary purpose of supervision in schools. List six ways by which supervision fulfills its purpose.

B. Discuss the role of supervisor in a variety of kinds of schools.

C. Compare the supervision process in a large public school system with that likely to be found in a small private preschool. List the advantages and disadvantages of each situation regarding supervision.

unit 26 inservice training

OBJECTIVES

After studying this unit, the student should be able to

- Define and state the purpose of inservice training.

- Describe four ways in which a teacher may be involved in inservice training.

- Briefly state the purpose, methods, and uses of teacher evaluations of an inservice training session.

Some of the most important contributions to the professional growth of a teaching staff are made in inservice training. This is training provided through the school administration and during school hours (usually). It is the responsibility of those persons who assume the supervisory role. Often many other people are involved in the design, implementation, and evaluation of inservice training.

Since the inservice meetings are usually held during the work day, all teaching staff may be required to attend. This insures maximum benefits from the meetings if they have been designed to meet existing needs. If the meetings provide the kind of help needed by most of the teachers, they are a practical means of improving the instruction in the school.

Fig. 26-1 Many new schools are built with observation rooms behind one-way glass windows.

DETERMINING NEEDS

To design inservice training that is truly helpful to teachers, their needs must be determined. This is done in several ways. Experience shows that at the beginning of the year there are some topics that may be reviewed with benefit to everyone. Classroom discipline, transitions, and affective development are topics that are timeless and are never exhausted.

During the first few weeks of public school each year, a supervisor (consultant, principal, supervisor, curriculum specialist) is busy seeing that the curriculum is smoothly getting underway in the classes. Instructional materials take up much of her time. The traditional "repeat" inservice session may be planned and held. If new instructional materials are used, there will be many calls from teachers on how to use the materials correctly.

Soon most of the teachers will have the classrooms operating smoothly. The supervisor will begin her observations in the classrooms. She will be analyzing the instruction she observes. When she has visited each classroom for several hours she may find some problems common to several rooms. There may be enough rooms to justify having an inservice meeting on solutions to the problem.

Experience and observation are two ways to determine inservice needs. A third very popular way to decide is to have each teacher suggest three topics that would be helpful to her. When the supervisor tabulates the suggestions, she may have numerous requests for some of the same topics. This helps her to plan relevant, truly useful sessions.

In some instances, the school administration decides on the subjects for some of the training. The teachers select other subjects. In other school districts, a supervisor and teachers work together periodically to arrive at a consensus on the best plans for training.

Research shows that better results have been obtained when teachers have had some input in choosing the topics for inservice training. Probably the largest numbers of teachers' needs can be met by using democratic group processes to make the selections of the ideas to be explored. However, the supervisor is an objective observer of all the classrooms. Her analyses of teachers' needs must be considered. If she sees that there is very little creativity evident in many classrooms, she is obligated to provide training to eliminate this need.

If evaluations are based on competency in meeting behavioral objectives for teachers, choosing topics for inservice may be pinpointed just as children's needs are assessed in great detail if progress charts are kept on meeting behavioral objectives in lessons. (So much is expected of teachers that the list is a very long one.) A teacher evaluates a child's needs by looking at the daily progress chart. She can see which objectives the child needs next. The supervisor can sometimes decide on a teacher's needs by looking at a chart of behavioral objectives (competencies) for teachers in much the same way. By looking at her progress charts on the teachers, she can decide which areas of the instruction program are weak. These may be used as subjects for inservice meetings. All too often however, there are no detailed lists of competencies. State boards of education are helpful in providing suggested alternative models where these are requested.

Small schools and small school systems often rely on staff discussions to decide on topics for inservice training. Unfortunately, many schools do not provide these aids to better instruction. A teacher who needs help with classroom management, curriculum, parent involvement, or interpersonal relationships should not feel guilty about saying so to the

---

October 1,

Dear Mrs. Sloan:

My assistants and I feel that we would like to learn more about ways to use our volunteer parents so that they will feel wanted and needed. Parents in the classroom are new to us. What do you suggest?

Marilyn Harris
Kindergarten, Rm. 10

Fig. 26-2 A teacher may expect a response to any reasonable request for help from an administrator (supervisor/principal/director).

---

person to whom she is responsible. Any person charge of any school is expected to be concerned about the children. Therefore, a teacher who asks for help to make things better for children may expect a response. It may not be called inservice training but it is serving the same purpose if it meets the teacher's needs.

PLANNING AND SCHEDULING

At the start of each school year, a school has its own unique needs to be met. The first inservice groups held each year are to meet these needs. They may be on old problems, new "rules and regs", previewing new curriculum guides. After a while, new needs appear. Teachers may ask for help. The instructional leader at the site (principal/director) may see poor teaching methods. Supervisors may note problems in the rooms. Teachers may be asked to name topics for discussion. From all such sources needs are determined. Then plans are made to meet the needs and the schedule is drawn up.

Often the staff is asked to help plan the inservice training. Where there is a set schedule of available time periods, it is easier to make arrangements. In some schools, teachers are given planning time (45 minutes to two hours) each day. One day a week – or, possibly, every other week – planning time may be designated as an inservice training period. A committee may work with the person in charge to plan the type of activity best suited to the topic. The committee may help make the preparations and/or the presentation.

Many factors influence the plans. The time and money allotted, transportation of guests or other participants, available equipment, space, and materials needed are essential considerations. The planner or planners must always ask questions about the possibilities in order to make the best decisions. Planning an inservice is a learning experience in itself.

When the needs have been determined and the decisions have been made on what to do and how to do it, then the jobs may be assigned to those who are to help – unless there are enough volunteers. Before the meeting, the supervisor or other person in charge checks to see that everyone has done his part, all arrangements have been made, all equipment and materials are ready.

Where there are no set schedules of time periods for teacher training, the "powers that be" must make other arrangements. Sometimes there are days designated as Teacher Workdays. On these days

Guest speaker	Use of manipulatives
Panel discussion	Use of audio-visuals
Small group discussions	Multimedia presentation
Role-playing	Use of chalkboard, flannel board
Demonstrations	Intermix groups

Fig. 26-3 To keep participants eager to attend frequent inservice training meetings, a variety of formats and materials may be used.

teachers come to school, but students do not. In public schools, these days are used for completing reports, grade cards, and other paperwork. Sometimes a part of a teacher workday is used for inservice training sessions.

Some schools have very dedicated teaching staffs that come at night or on Saturdays when a need is great enough for help with problems in the instructional program. With teaching as in other endeavors, "where there's a will, there's a way". Usually help can be arranged when teachers make their needs known to those able to help them.

EVALUATING

Teaching must be evaluated before it can be improved. This is true whether the student is a child or a teacher. Good inservice training must meet these criteria:

- It must be relevant to the needs of the participants.
- It must not work a hardship on the teachers to participate.
- It must be practical.
- It must be interestingly presented.
- It must be a learning experience.

Each inservice meeting should be concluded with evaluations. The person responsible needs to know if the training meets the criteria. If it does not, he needs to know in what way it does not. Use of the helpful information the teachers give, can make the next inservice meeting a better one. It is the responsibility of each member of the teaching staff to give an evaluation after each session. Planners are obligated to try to meet the needs of the teachers. They cannot do this without the cooperation of those attending in filling out evaluation forms. If the forms may be filled out without names being signed, this

helps teachers to be critical without fear of reprisal. Honest evaluations by teachers help to improve the quality of the training.

When an inservice program is a good one, it is also valuable to write this on the evaluation form. It is always appropriate to express appreciation.

SUMMARY

Most schools aid the professional growth of the teaching staff by having training meetings during work hours. These inservice meetings are usually based on the needs of teachers as they are made known by the teachers, the instructional leader, and other supervisory observers.

At the beginning of the school year, each school staff has sessions to meet the unique needs of that school. Later as problem areas are noticed, meetings can be designed as soon as the needs are determined.

In very small schools and in small school systems, staff discussions may be the only way of deciding what kinds of help are needed by the teaching staff. There may be no inservice training planned. A teacher should still feel free to ask someone in charge for the help she needs with curriculum, classroom management, parent involvement, or interpersonal relationships. Hopefully, anyone responsible for children's welfare (in charge of a school) will try to get help for a teacher who requests it.

Teachers and administrators often share the job of planning and scheduling inservice meetings. Each situation may vary in time and resources available. Each meeting should be interesting and be useful to those who attend. Those who plan inservice training meetings wisely ask the participants to evaluate them. The evaluation forms need not be signed so that teachers will feel free to express criticism as well as appreciation. By being honest on evaluation forms, the teaching staff makes it possible for those in charge to plan better meetings for the future. In this way, the teachers and the administration work together for better professional development in early childhood education.

SUGGESTED ACTIVITIES

- Attend an inservice training meeting for teachers of young children. Write a brief evaluation of the meeting.

- At the library, review a film or filmstrip used in training preschool teachers. State why you think it may or may not be good material for inservice training of new teachers.

- Acquire two different evaluation forms used by teachers or supervisors for inservice training participants. Decide which one you think is more useful and state your reasons.

REVIEW

A. Define and state the purpose of inservice training.

B. Describe four ways in which a teacher or assistant teacher may be involved in inservice training.

C. Briefly state the purpose, methods and uses of teacher evaluations of an inservice training session.

Section IX Current Status

unit 27 growth of early childhood education

OBJECTIVES

After studying this unit, the student should be able to

- State five reasons why educational changes are needed today.

- Account for vast increases in the numbers of early childhood educational programs since 1965.

- Briefly state the status of early childhood education in the United States today.

Both public and private early childhood schools and programs are rapidly increasing in number. The rate of increase is greater than the rate of population growth. For numerous reasons early childhood education is gaining in popularity.

The rapid upsurge in day-care facilities during World War II was a necessity. Mothers were needed in defense plants. They were needed to fill job vacancies where men had gone to war. After the war, women were still needed to fill the places of men who did not return. Many other women kept their jobs because they had learned to enjoy them. Day-care centers were needed then and since then have continued increasing in number.

The great surge of humanism that followed the end of the war encouraged integration, gave attention to the needs of ethnic minorities, and fostered women's liberation. These changes are resulting in more educational day care, public school preschool programs, and more working mothers who need the services offered. Never before has early childhood education had the status it currently enjoys. Recent figures show that more than one-third of all preschool age children in the United States attend early childhood education classes of some kind.

PUBLIC SCHOOL PROGRAMS

By 1960 the Educational Policies Commission of the National Education Association recommended that all children aged four or over have the opportunity to attend public schools. Serious acceptance of this was not seen until 1965, the beginning of Head Start. From then until now there was and is a dramatic rise in career opportunities in early childhood education. Expansion of programs and educational research related to them has opened the field to many newcomers.

The public agrees that educational change is needed for several reasons:

- The current system has produced greater conflicts among persons than ever before.

- Social changes require a place in addition to the home for good care for very young children.

- Compensatory education is needed for equal opportunities for children of minority groups.

- Scientists and educators have proved that early intervention of cognitive growth is developmentally sound.

- Better cooperation between home and school is recognized as a desirable goal; it is best achieved through early childhood education programs.

The federal government gave impetus to preschool programs first by meeting the needs of socio-economically disadvantaged children. Since 1965 public spending for these and related research projects has spiraled to unbelievable heights. So have job opportunities in early childhood education.

Colleges and universities have not supplied the demand for people with degrees in the field. Therefore, the rise of the paraprofessional role has answered the need. Presently, national legislation is being considered that will require that at least part of every staff in charge of little children has college work in child development.

Public schools have increasingly introduced early childhood programs in three main areas: the handicapped child, the non-English-speaking child, and the "culturally different" child. However, numerous states including Texas only recently have added public school kindergarten for all five-year-olds who desire it. (In some states it is required for fives.) The variety of public school early childhood programs makes it possible for almost anyone who desires it and has minimum qualifications to find a job in heavily populated areas.

The present expansion of these programs to include three- and four-year-olds continues. The teacher, assistant teacher, and teacher's aide are found in abundance in city public schools. Soon, however, there will be more college-prepared students to fill the staffs. Those who are less well prepared may have a more difficult time finding work in public schools.

Staff expansions using assistant teachers have proved so successful that a certification for these workers is being considered on a national level (C.D.A.). Performance tests will be the major portions of the criteria used. If a person, male or female, can perform adequately in the role of assistant, this should be recognized. Hopefully, it will be soon.

PRIVATE SCHOOL PROGRAMS

Private school early childhood programs include playschools, parent cooperatives, nursery schools, demonstration schools, day-care centers, private elementary school kindergartens, and church-related schools. Since the great increase in the number of public school early childhood programs, the expected drop in the number of private schools having them has not occurred. Instead, the number of working mothers has continued the increase in day-care facilities.

KIDDIE KAMPUS

Good News! *Kiddie Kampus* is expanding its services in the fall:

1. *Educational Day-Care* will be available for two-year-olds.

2. Before- and after-school care will be offered for fives attending public school kindergarten.

Please register early. Thank you.

Fig. 27-1 Flexible day-care centers are expanding as they lose fives to new public school kindergartens.

(Very few public schools give care except during the regular school day schedule.)

In a few schools where the number of five-year-olds has been reduced, the slack in enrollment has been taken up by lowering the entrance age for children. Also, many more day-care facilities now give care before and after the public school day if transportation can be arranged. Thus, by better meeting the current needs of the public, private early childhood schools have acquired higher status than before.

The introduction of Head Start child development centers was the introduction of effective educational curriculum in all-day care. Soon other early childhood schools were made aware of the possibilities. State licensing bureaus became more rigid in their demands for appropriate learning environments for all children. The spread of early childhood professional organizations on the state and local levels adds greater status to both private and public preschools.

PROJECTIONS

The number and variety of programs for preschoolers are increasing. Much more research is needed on the long-range effects of early childhood education. Short-range effects are proved to be positive in many research projects. This is especially true in programs where there is much parent involvement. The growing humaneness in public attitudes is reflected in preschool intervention and compensatory programs for disabled children of many kinds.

Industry, especially where large numbers of women are hired, is establishing its own child care facilities for the children of employees. Institutions such as hospitals and universities are beginning to profit from having early childhood educational programs on campus for the children of employees. Many more such programs are being planned. Absenteeism of employees is reduced and morale is better. Children are profiting. Some women are now encouraged to work (who did not want to earlier) because of the nearness to their children. Also, fathers are relieved that the mothers are so close to the children.

At the present time, teacher's salaries all over the nation are considered low among those in the professions. The salaries of assistants and aides are not commensurate with what is expected of them in some schools. However, this condition is receiving public notice. There is a good chance that corrections will be made in the near future.

Fig. 27-2 The trend toward early childhood education increases.

There is no doubt that early childhood education is booming. The field is increasing in quantity and quality. A person who genuinely believes in the goals of educational opportunity for the young child and tries to learn will probably be able to find work, although it may mean a move to a densely populated site or to one far away. There will be some years yet before there is an excess of trained personnel in early childhood education. Now is the time to start. Years of experience make a difference in the pay scale for all levels of teaching. The prospect for a future in early childhood education is very bright today.

SUMMARY

Changing life styles and an increasing humanism in government and in the public at large have helped to elevate the status of early childhood education. The demands created by World War II for women in the working world have never abated. The women's liberation movement is adding to present needs for all-day care facilities for the children of women who work.

The greatest upsurge in the quantity of programs for the preschool child occurred with the creation of Head Start in 1965. Since then many federal, state, and local government programs have increased the need for personnel. The need for certified personnel in public school programs for the very young far outgrew the resources, thus opening the door for paraprofessional assistants and aides. Private schools have always used some noncertified persons and continue to do so in their expansions.

The paraprofessionals have earned such status in early childhood education that the government is researching a competency-based evaluation to permit a certification as a paraprofessional. Hopefully, this may become a reality in the near future. .

Public school preschool programs were centered on children with learning, physical, or emotional disabilities and the socioeconomically deprived. These are still a primary focus. Now, however, public school kindergarten for all children is rapidly becoming a major goal.

Gradually day-care facilities have become more educationally oriented. Industry and institutions have provided these services for their employees with beneficial results. Parents have better morale and employee absenteeism is reduced by these projects.

Current research is available showing positive short-range gains for most children in educational preschool programs. Much more research is needed on the long-range effects. Social needs, continued research, and general public interest all indicate continually rising status for early childhood education. They also indicate maximum job opportunities in the field for some years to come.

SUGGESTED ACTIVITIES

- From a chamber of commerce in a city, obtain a present city directory and one that is from three to five years old. Compare the early childhood facilities listed.
- Call the offices of a large school district. Ask about changes in their early childhood programs in the past few years.
- Interview a director of a private preschool in a city. Ask about fluctuations in the enrollment and how public school programs have affected it.

REVIEW

A. State five reasons why educational changes are needed today.

B. Briefly account for vast increases in the numbers of early childhood educational programs since 1965.

C. Briefly state the status of early childhood education in the United States today.

unit 28 status of the child care assistant teacher

OBJECTIVES

After studying this unit, the student should be able to

- Briefly explain why there are so many demands for assistant teachers in early childhood education today.
- Briefly explain the advantages of being a trained assistant teacher.
- Briefly compare the current status and future status of the assistant teacher in early childhood education.

Throughout this book the importance of the assistance teacher has been stated. Her specific role has been clearly defined, and the way it came into being has been explained. Only a brief discussion regarding the current and future status of the assistant teacher is still needed.

CURRENT NEEDS

In large cities there are not enough trained assistant teachers to fill the staffs. Preschool staff requirements in public schools must be kept as high as possible for the sake of all the boys and girls in them and because the public schools must answer to the taxpayers. Often, though, such numbers of qualified persons are not to be found. Staff positions are then filled with noncollege trained but experienced help from day-care schools (if any are available).

Inequities in school financing in some states give some school districts an advantage over poorer ones. It is only natural for a person to work where he can make the most money. Therefore, poorer districts are sometimes forced to hire some staff who lack both training and experience. These districts must count on systematic inservice training each week to improve their schools. The poorer district offers a rewarding challenge to the beginner, trained or untrained, in early childhood education.

Since many day-care centers are federally financed, salaries at these centers are sometimes comparable to those in public schools for inexperienced help. This has drained the small private day-care centers of experienced staff. Most of these cannot as yet compete with public schools or government funding in salaries. But they are expanding and they are making an effort to compete. In San Antonio, Texas, in 1965 it was not unusual for a teacher's aide to receive $100.00 per month at a half-day kindergarten at a small private school. Today, the position pays about $250 per month.

The public continues to demand more and better day-care facilities and educational programs. More mothers work and need a place for their very young children during the long working day. The better the school, the larger the number of people who take their children there. In turn, more assistant teachers are needed and salaries become higher.

Public school programs include many that are for children whose first language is Spanish. The teachers and assistants who teach these children must be bilingual. There are rarely enough bilingual staff members where bilingual education is provided. The bilingual Spanish-English staff member is in great demand in California, Arizona, Texas, Florida, Illinois (Chicago), New York, Colorado, and in Michigan (when the migrant farm workers are there).

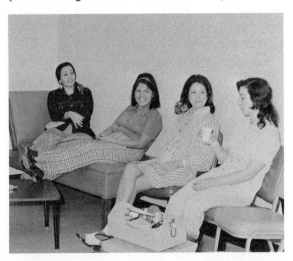

Fig. 28-1 The bilingual staff at an early childhood school relieve one another for a brief rest period while the children rest.

Program Director	Materials Evaluator
Program Coordinator	Parent Coordinator
Teaching Supervisor	Curriculum Writer
Principal	Curriculum Designer
Consultant	Researcher
Assistant Director	Documentation Specialist
College Instructor in E.C.E.	Program Evaluator
Early Childhood Magazine Writer	Center Coordinator

Fig. 28-2 Advancement opportunities in early childhood education.

Some day-care centers that have fewer five-year-olds now are licensed instead to accept infants of six months and older. These schools must now hire more assistants than they did when they had more older children. Licensing bureaus insist that there must be fewer children for each adult when the children are younger. (The ratio in Texas is one adult per four children under two years of age). This increases the total number of assistant teachers needed.

On all fronts in public and private schools of every kind for very young children, more teachers and assistant teachers are needed today. If training for early childhood work is effective, the more training an employee has, the better the situation is for the children. It is reasonable then to expect that better prepared staff will be paid better salaries than those who are less qualified. Current scenes reflect a great need for trained assistant teachers.

FUTURE NEEDS

According to figures from the National Education Association, in 1970 there were approximately 20 million children under age five in the United States. If the 1970 population trends continue, their prediction for 1980 is 28 million. During 1968, American colleges and universities graduated only 1200 teachers specifically trained to work as preschool teachers. This was three years after the Head Start programs were initiated! Such college programs have been increased but as yet cannot match the needs of the growing population.

There are limitless opportunities to advance in early childhood education today. Trained and experienced specialists are needed in college programs to prepare teachers and assistants. Consultants and super-

visors are needed now. There will be even greater need for these as early childhood education becomes universal throughout the nation. Program directors, day-care center operators, and research laboratory staffs will draw upon many who are now in the field. The trained assistant who is effective in the classroom will find educational opportunities made possible. These persons are the logical ones to step into many of the vacancies created by persons filling the new positions of leadership — now and in the very near future.

When behavioral criteria are used to fill certification requirements, many trained assistants will soon be ready to progress up the ladder in a successful career in early childhood education in public and private schools, government agencies, and parent cooperatives. A steadily increasing need for trained assistant teachers exists and will exist far into the future.

SUMMARY

Currently the assistant teacher enjoys a status never before accorded paraprofessional staff members. She is in great demand for several reasons: increased numbers of children in preschool programs and too few certified early childhood personnel. More mothers are employed and children are entering nursery schools at younger ages. The lower pupil-teacher ratio for younger children means more assistant teachers are needed.

Assistant teachers without college degrees have proved so valuable when properly trained that the government is exploring ways to give an assistant teacher certification based on performance in the classroom.

Salaries for assistant teachers are much higher than they were ten years ago, sometimes as much as

150% higher. Bilingual assistant teachers are in great demand wherever bilingual education is needed for Spanish-speaking students.

Federally-funded programs usually require the use of assistant teachers or aides in the classroom. Public and private schools are providing many more assistant teacher positions each year.

Predictions for population trends are greater than predictions for numbers of early childhood

certified staff. This in itself means that more assistants will be needed than are available today. Laboratory schools and other educational research projects are needed to determine the long-range effects of early childhood education. Many persons in the field today will move up into these new responsibilities, thus creating many more openings in present positions. The future holds possibilities of ever greater status for the assistant teacher.

SUGGESTED ACTIVITIES

- Review your philosophy of education. Make any changes needed to concur with your philosophy at this time.

- Review your statement of reasons why you wish to enter early childhood education. Make any changes needed today.

- Discuss competency based certification with your classmates. Make a list of statements for it and against it.

REVIEW

A. Briefly explain why there are so many demands for assistant teachers in early childhood education today.

B. Briefly explain the advantages of being a trained assistant teacher in early childhood education.

C. Briefly compare the current status and the future status of the assistant teacher in early childhood education.

BIBLIOGRAPHY

Association for Childhood Education International. *Feelings and Learnings.* Washington, D.C.: A.C.E.T., 1965.

Brisbane, Holly E. with Dr. Audrey Palm Riker. *The Developing Child.* Peoria, Illinois: Chas. A. Bennett Company, Inc., 1965.

Bruner, Jerome S. *Toward a Theory of Instruction.* Cambridge, Massachusetts: The Belknap Press of Harvard University Press, 1966.

Cohen, Dorothy H. *The Learning Child.* New York: Pantheon Books, 1972.

Cratty, Bryant J. *Active Learning.* Englewood Cliffs: Prentice-Hall, Inc., 1971.

Frost, Joe L. and G. Thomas Rowland. *Curricula for the Seventies.* Boston: Houghton-Mifflin Co., 1969.

Ginott, Haim. *Teacher and Child.* New York: The Macmillan Company, 1972.

Green, Marjorie M. and Elizabeth L. Woods, Ph.D. *A Nursery School Handbook for Teachers and Parents.* Sierra Madre, California: Sierra Madre Community Nursery School Association, 1972.

Gronlund, Norman E. *Stating Behavioral Objectives for Classroom Instruction.* London: The Macmillan Company, Collier-Macmillan Limited, 1971.

Hess, Robert D. and Doreen J. Croft. *Teachers of Young Children.* Boston: Houghton-Mifflin Company, 1972.

Hildebrand, Verna. *Introduction to Early Childhood Education.* New York: The Macmillan Company, 1971.

Hurlock, Elizabeth B. *Child Growth and Development, Fourth Edition.* New York: Webster Division, McGraw-Hill Book Company, 1970.

Landreth, Catherine. *Early Childhood: Behavior and Learning.* New York: Alfred A. Knopf, 1969.

Leeper, Sarah Hammond; Ruth J. Dales; Dora Sikes Skipper; and Ralph L. Witherspoon. *Good Schools for Young Children.* London: The Macmillan Company, Collier-Macmillan Limited, 1968.

McCandless, Boyd R. *Children, Behavior and Development.* New York: Holt, Rinehart and Winston, Inc., 1967.

Mindess, David and Mary Mindess. *Guide to an Effective Kindergarten Program.* West Nyack, New York: Parker Publishing Company, Inc., 1972.

Murphy, Lois B. and Ethel M. Leeper. *Caring for Children (Numbers One through Nine).* Washington, D.C.: United States Department of Health, Education and Welfare, 1973.

Rudolph, Marguerita. *From Hand to Head.* New York: Webster Division, McGraw-Hill Book Company, 1973.

Smart, Mollie S. and Russell Smart. *Children, Development and Relationships.* New York: The Macmillan Company, 1972.

Social Services Division, Texas State Department of Public Welfare. *Minimum Standards for Day-Care Centers.* Austin, Texas: Texas State Department of Public Welfare, 1971.

Southwest Educational Development Laboratory. *Bilingual Early Childhood Program.* Austin, Texas: National Educational Laboratory Publishers, Inc., 1974.

Spodek, Bernard. *Teaching in the Early Years.* Englewood Cliffs: Prentice-Hall, Inc., 1972.

Wadsworth, Barry J. *Piaget's Theory of Cognitive Development.* New York: David McKay Company, Inc., 1971.

Wills, Clarice Dechent, Ed.D. and Lucille Lindberg, Ed.D. *Kindergarten to Today's Children.* Chicago: Follett Educational Corp., 1967.

UNIT 1

A. Definitions in student's own words (from text material).

B. Specifically listed in introductory paragraphs.

C. 1. In recognizing normal and abnormal changes in children.

    2. In setting guidelines in planning curriculum.

    3. In measuring child growth and development.

    4. In guiding the child to his maximum development in each area.

D. 1. By providing skillful direction.

    2. Body size.

    3. His innate reflexive behaviors.

    4. No, that of girls exceeds that of boys.

    5. Delays in physical and cognitive development.

    6. Ulcers and psychosomatic illnesses.

    7. Critical period.

    8. Awareness and judgment.

    9. Create a stimulating environment, analyze children's needs, and meet children's needs.

E. 1. b, c, d   3. a, c, d

    2. c   4. a, b, c

F. 1. c   5. h

    2. f   6. g

    3. d   7. a

    4. e   8. b

UNIT 2

A. (In student's own words) this means that everything the child experiences all day long is perceived and recorded in his brain so that he is always learning.

B. 1. Assimilation means adding a new percept (sensory input) to a cognitive structure (in the mind) that already exists and to which it seems related.

    2. Accommodation means creating a new cognitive structure for a new percept because it seems unrelated to any existing cognitive structures (concepts).

    3. Equilibration means maintaining a balance between the amounts of assimilation and accommodation in a person's cognitive structures.

    4. a. Encouraged by giving him a positive self-image so he can think well of himself and feel competent.

         b. Discouraged by giving him a negative self-image through unnecessary criticism of him as a person.

    5. a. Encouraged by giving him an environment rich in opportunity for sensory experiences and letting him explore it.

         b. Discouraged by not allowing his curiosity to be satisfied by many sensory experiences daily.

    6. Jean Piaget

C. 1. Enactive processing: responding physically to visual motor stimuli.

    2. Iconic processing: responding perceptually to images which represent events.

3. Symbolic processing: responding perceptually to symbols — letters, words, numerals that have meaning.

D. 1. Exploring a new place.

2. Imitating a good model.

3. Making mistakes.

4. Being part of the action.

5. Communicating.

UNIT 3

A. 1. Having had all the previous experiences needed to be able to benefit or learn from the next activity.

2. A chart that shows the specific level of many skills that a child is likely to have at one specific age.

3. Activities that are designed to develop the larger leg, arm, and trunk muscles.

4. A period in which the child must have certain experiences for affective development; without them, his personality may be affected negatively throughout his life.

5. Behavior which reflects attitudes and emotions.

6. Playing beside another child but not with him.

7. Groups of objects, each group having the same (class) name and many common attributes.

B. 1. To determine which motor activities to teach a three-year-old girl, find several motor skills charts. List the skills and arrange them from easiest to hardest. Observe the child in the room and on the playground in self-selected activities. Determine which of the skills on the list she already has. Plan activities to test for any that are not observed. From the test results and the skills she has already demonstrated, plan games and practice activities to develop and expand her present skills. If necessary, fill in any gaps that are observed.

2. To determine the cognitive challenge for a four-year-old boy, list the skills found on several developmental skill charts for fours. Observe the child, determine which skills he has and plan to expand them. Determine which ones he lacks and plan lessons, games, or activities that will help him learn what he does not know but seems ready to learn.

3. Watch the five-year-old girl in self-selected activities. Notice her social skills in interaction with other children and with adults. Listen to her use of language and decide which kind of language experiences she is ready for. Plan ways to give her these opportunities daily. If she is ready for larger group experiences, plan these for story and discussion time.

UNIT 4

A. A theory of instruction is the complete set of ideas about teaching that represent what the teacher believes in (rationale) what she will do as a result of her beliefs (strategies) and how she will do these things (techniques). The strategies must be based on the rationale; the techniques must be based on the strategies. All together they form a theory of instruction.

B. 1. (g)   3. (f)   5. (d)   7. (i)   9. (e)
   2. (h)   4. (j)   6. (a)   8. (c)   10. (b)

C. There is no one specific correct answer. Possibilities are included in text.

UNIT 5

A. As listed on page 29.

B. Five of the following seven:

1. Self

2. Family

3. Home

4. Pets

5. Clothing

6. Foods

7. Toys

C. 1. Some of the puzzles   4. Some of the recordings

2. Some of the books   5. Some of the science items

3. Some of the pictures   6. Role-playing accessories

D. 1. Identifying same and different sounds

2. Ordering by size

3. Identifying by touching

4. How a plant grows

5. How water evaporates

E. Six of the nine listed on page 32.

F. In student's own words: (See figure 5-7, page 34.)

UNIT 6

A. 1. Mutual respect

2. Mutual high goals for children

3. Agreement on what to teach

4. Consistency in enforcing classroom rules

5. Willingness to share in preparing, teaching, etc.

B. In the student's own words:

The team members must daily prepare the room and materials in advance; be prepared to teach, present curriculum and evaluate it; evaluate the children's progress; plan for next day if changes are to be made and share administrative duties. Every team needs democratic leadership to focus on long-range goals and smoothly combine the efforts of all team members. The leader must see that all tasks planned by the team are assigned or assumed by team members.

C. In student's own words:

1. Change in curriculum activity because of lack of expected readiness

2. Change in daily schedule because of unexpected hospitality

3. Increase in daily schedule because of two levels of a skill needed

4. Arrange grouping to meet the social needs of children

5. Add new tasks because of additional help being available

D. 1. Greater resources of information
    2. Lighter workload per person
    3. More time for planning
    4. Greater continuity when teacher is absent
    5. Utilizes strong points of every person's abilities

E. 1. Be willing to share credit and/or blame.
    2. Accept other's ideas
    3. Realize others are equally dedicated to children
    4. Be able to accept constructive criticism
    5. Be very flexible to accommodate daily changes

UNIT 7

A. 1. a, c   2. a, c, d   3. b, c, d

B. An open classroom is a very large room leading to an outdoor learning area. The room is lined with interest centers and there are more in the middle of the room and outdoors. This is based on a belief in a need for every child to learn in his own way, making many choices of what he wants to learn, and how he wants to learn it.

C. 1. Tailoring curriculum to meet the needs of each individual.

    2. Discovery learning: given raw materials, the child uses them as he wishes and makes many discoveries as he does so.

    3. Open classroom schools in England for four- to seven-year-olds. They have unstructured curriculum and more children per adult than American open classrooms.

    4. Curriculum having a primary purpose of increasing the child's knowledge of facts.

    5. Curriculum having a primary purpose of developing processes for learning social, physical, and cognitive skills.

    6. Curriculum having a primary purpose of teaching the child to get along well with people, to communicate orally and to express emotions in acceptable ways.

UNIT 8

A. The long-range goals of process-oriented curriculum and those of a content-oriented curriculum are the same: to help the child develop maximally in every way. The daily goals differ in that the one focuses on the processes the child learns (respecting, valuing, associating ideas, discriminating same and not the same). The other focuses on the factual knowledge he learns about topics (community helpers, home, school, about school subjects such as language, music, math).

B. Besides planning lessons, the teacher must plan (1) supplementary materials, (2) grouping, (3) a daily schedule, and (4) teaching strategies and methods to use.

C. Five factors that influence children's success in attaining behavioral objectives are the following:

    1. The setting must be appropriate.

    2. There must be enough materials so a child does not have to wait a long time for his turn.

    3. The children must be ready for the skill or concept.

    4. The setting must be prepared in advance.

    5. The teacher must use teaching strategies that are appropriate.

D. 1. (a), (b), (c), (d)   2. (a), (c)   3. (b)

UNIT 9

A. A behavioral objective is a statement of the behavior expected of a child at the end of a specific learning experience. The characteristics are

   1. It is always stated in terms of the child's behavior.

   2. The conditions for learning are given in complete detail.

   3. The behavior must be one that can be seen.

   4. The child's behavior must be stated in terms of an amount (how many things or how many times).

B. Mastery learning is a kind of learning using sequences of objectives. A child must master an objective before he is given the next harder objective in the sequence. Advantages listed on page 59.

C. 1. Inadequate (No details on kind and number of pictures.)

   2. Adequate

   3. Adequate

   4. Inadequate (Behavior not observable.)

UNIT 10

A. Any five of the seven listed:

   1. Develops instant rapport with little children

   2. Is not sensitive to the emotional states of children

   3. Knows and understands self

   4. Is very flexible

   5. Has a sense of humor

   6. Constantly seeks more knowledge of children and of teaching

   7. Accepts responsibility for seeing that children learn

B. 1. Is motivated out of concern for children rather than for self. Has a strong desire to help children be and do their best.

   2. Wants to learn all she can about the children and how to teach them. Seeks opportunities to improve. Never reaches a state of self-satisfaction that permits ending of learning.

   3. Believes the "I'm OK, You're OK" philosophy. Has great tolerance for herself and all others as persons but will not tolerate bad behavior. Teaches children self-discipline, to like themselves, and to like others, also.

   4. Has confidence that her students will learn. This encourages her to find the ways to help every student learn.

   5. Is dedicated to the cause of early childhood education. Understands its importance in developing a child's intelligence, love of learning, and appropriate attitudes toward other persons.

C. Can become better qualified by reading many kinds of publications on early childhood, discussing matters with more experienced teachers, observing good teachers, accepting suggestions from a supervisor. College courses may be helpful even if not taken for college credit. Inservice training is sometimes more practical and specifically helpful.

D.   1. c, f   2. b, d, e

UNIT 11

A.   1. Uses a soft well-modulated voice.

2. Uses appropriate vocabulary and short sentences.

3. Speaks in a way that shows friendliness, positive attitudes, and no prejudices.

4. Uses good manners.

5. Is a good language model for the child.

6. Accepts the child's home language.

7. Praises the child's deeds sincerely and frequently.

8. Corrects in a way that is not belittling or embarrassing.

B.   Any eight of the ten following:

1. Listens daily to each child

2. Makes allowances for unusual circumstances.

3. Has high but realistic expectations for each child.

4. Is impartial

5. Gets down to the child's level when speaking to him.

6. Places child's artwork at his eye level.

7. Has an attractive orderly room each morning.

8. Welcomes child's parents at school.

9. Reflects child's interests in the curriculum.

10. Reflects child's ethnic background in the room; has a multicultural setting.

C.   1. c, e   2. a, b, d, e   3. b, c, d, e

UNIT 12

A.   1. Gives "mothering" when it is needed.

2. "Reaches" every child in her teaching.

3. Is consistently friendly and pleasant.

4. Handles a crisis calmly and efficiently.

5. Organizes the room and materials carefully.

6. Has happy independent learners in the room.

7. Shows appreciation of the efforts of each child.

8. Plans and teaches lessons designed for each child.

9. Uses appropriate methods of discipline (not corporal punishment).

10. Shows concern for the maximum development of every child.

B.   Any ten of the following:

1.   Communications with parents are friendly.

2.   Makes parents feel welcome in the room.

3.   Involves every parent in school cooperation in some activity.

4.   Explains the program and goals to all parents.

5.   Frequently informs parents of their child's progress.

6.   Helps parents as persons when possible.

7.   Shows respect for parents.

8.   Makes a friendly visit to each home by appointment but is not critical.

9.   Shows appreciation for help given by parents.

10.   Warmly greets and is responsive to parents whenever they meet, in and out of school.

11.   Reflects the cultures of the children's families in the classroom.

C.   The teacher interacts with both school and nonschool adult personnel in ways that affect the children. If her behavior with administrative persons, consultants, and volunteers, as well as with the school cafeteria and maintenance staff, always indicates that she sees them as members of one big team (working together in the best interest of the children), then she is effective in her relationships with these people.

D.   1.   b, d   2.   a   3.   a, c

UNIT 13

A.   Formal testing means giving a commercially written test in a prescribed way exactly alike to each child. It must be given and scored according to the directions that come with it to be valid. Informal testing means using developmental skills charts as checklists. The teacher may mark these or may make other written observations of the children in a natural play setting or in a contrived setting. A sequence of behavioral objectives may be used as an informal readiness test.

B.   Four questions to be asked in selecting a test:

1.   Is it necessary?

2.   What kind of information is needed?

3.   Is the test valid?

4.   Is it appropriate for the children?

C.   Any seven of the ten following DO's:

1.   Have parental permission if applicable.

2.   Determine need, validity, and appropriateness.

3.   See that tester is qualified and has good rapport with the child.

4.   Know and approve the uses to be made of the test scores.

5.   Test child only if he is well, rested, and in good spirits.

6.   Test for disabilities only if the child is well, rested, and in good spirits.

7.   Allow time to test leisurely.

8.   Make the testing like a game for the child.

9.   Test in a quiet private place.

10.   Date all tests and observations.

Any seven of the ten following DON'Ts:

1. Don't test unless you are capable and confident.

2. Don't make up your own rules for a prepared test.

3. Don't discuss test scores with parents (if possible).

4. Don't attach too much importance to any one test score.

5. Don't interpret a child's needs on the basis of test scores alone.

6. Don't tell a child how well he did or did not do on a test.

7. Don't trust your memory of your observations of children; write them down.

8. Don't test if you feel out of sorts or pressured. It may affect the results.

9. Don't be too quick to make placement decisions on the basis of a test. Consider the whole child.

10. Don't resent the time that testing takes. It is well worth it.

D.   1. c   2. b, c   3. c, d

UNIT 14

A. *Registration form:* information on the child needed to enter a school district for the first time.

Medical history: may be of immunizations only; is usually a complete record of the child's health from birth to the present.

PRC: permanent record card: comprehensive report of the child's total school experience, preschool through high school.

Progress chart: may be a list of behavioral objectives achieved, a developmental skills checklist, or a series of teacher's observations that reflect progress made by the child at intervals.

Permission slip: slip that a parent signs giving the school permission to do a specific thing considered worthwhile for the child.

Anecdotal record: a series of teacher observations of a child written on notecards or in a notebook about any behavior that is very unusual or may be a symptom of a problem the child has.

Pretest: any noncurricular test given to a child for some kind of evaluation at the beginning of the school year.

Posttest: a test which is the same pretest repeated at the end of a term or school year.

Behavioral objective: a statement that describes a behavior expected of a child at the end of a period of instruction and the conditions under which he is to perform the behavior.

B. Any ten of the following:

Registration form, Medical history, PRC, Forms for qualifying for special programs, Attendance, Lunch count, Emergency information, Class register, Financial records, Anecdotal records, Progress charts.

C.   1. Progress charts showing which behavioral objectives the child has attained.

2. Anecdotal records on a child showing the course of problem behavior.

3. Periodic teacher observations: skills checklists, developmental charts, observations in story form.

UNIT 15

A. *Self-evaluation:* the teacher evaluates her performance against a list of objectives of her own or against a checklist given her by the school.

Supervisory evaluation: someone on an administrative level evaluates the teacher's performance for the purpose of helping her improve her effectiveness.

Parent evaluation: parents report on the teacher's performance from their points of view.

Formal evaluation: an evaluation of a teacher's performance in a manner prescribed by the school, using specific forms and usually signed by the teacher and evaluator in acknowledgment. It becomes a part of her personnel record.

Informal evaluation: may be in anecdotal written form or in verbal conversational form. Its purpose is the same as that of a more formal evaluation: to improve the teacher's effectiveness.

"The whole teacher": refers to seeing the teacher subjectively and objectively from several points of view: her own, her supervisor's and that of the parents of her students.

Pragmatist: one who tries a strategy or procedure but if it is not successful keeps on trying others until he does find something that is effective.

Subjective information: personal opinion.

Objective information: statement of facts based on behaviors observed — uncolored by opinion.

Resource person: one to whom a teacher can go for help, advice, and materials.

B. 1. *Preparation:* evidence of planning, room appearance, convenience of materials, handling of emergencies.

2. *Teaching:* strategies and procedures used to insure that the children are learning.

3. *Classroom:* attractiveness, arrangement, furnishings, convenience, emotional climate.

4. *Discipline:* teaching, not punishment, is the desirable method of handling infractions of the rules; children should show evidence of self-discipline.

5. *Interpersonal relationships:* the teacher's rapport with children and her ability to get along with other persons.

C. 1. a, c   2. b, d   3. c

UNIT 16

A. All the members of a teaching team should have the same long-range goals for the children. For example, all may plan to see each child develop maximally in every possible way: cognitively, physically, socially, and in developing concepts. The same shorter range learning outcomes for each one should be desired by all team members. An example would be to agree that all the three-year-olds will be able to function well in small group activities within an eight-week period. The behavioral objectives for daily lessons should be planned together and agreed upon. Toward the learning goal mentioned, for instance, the team members should agree that the children should listen to a five-minute story daily in small groups and tell each other parts of the story they remember or answer questions about it.

B. If two members of a teaching team disagree upon a way to handle a classroom problem situation, they should spend a few minutes together discussing their points of view. If neither view in any way breaks any school rules or previously agreed on decisions, they may either agree to use one or the other or they may work out a compromise that satisfies both persons. If there are three or more members of the team and the matter is a purely arbitrary one, a majority vote may decide which way to go. If the matter is not arbitrary (involves a decision on right and wrong, a moral issue), then the teacher's decision must be respected and accepted graciously by the assistants.

C. 1. a. Analyze children's developmental levels.   b. Design and implement curriculum.

c. Communicate effectively with students, parents, and staff.

d. Administer evaluation tests.

e. Keep records.

f. Evaluate self-performance.

2. a. Accept responsibility for the accuracy of the records kept.

    b. Be accountable to parents and administrators for the learning environment, the emotional climate in the room, and the education of the children during school hours.

UNIT 17

A. 1. *Professional teaching staff member:* a salaried staff member who is educationally qualified to fulfill the role of teacher in charge of a class.

    2. *Paraprofessional teaching staff:* assistants or aides to the teacher who work with the children but are not usually qualified to be responsible for the room, the children, and the program.

    3. *Role acceptance:* a desirable attitude for a teacher or paraprofessional; it means that the person is willing to accept the duties and responsibilities in her job description or those assigned to her.

    4. *Teacher's accountability:* answering to parents and administrators for the quality of the children's learning, the learning environment, and the emotional climate in the classroom.

    5. *Professionalism:* having behaviors and attitudes that promote the best interests of the children and the adults with whom one works; selflessly doing all that is required to do the job well regardless of personal inconvenience or problems.

B. 1. Willingness to accept one's role of teacher, assistant teacher, or teacher's aide.

    2. Wanting to learn.

    3. Being open to constructive criticism and willing to give it to others.

    4. Being appreciative of parents who volunteer.

    5. Being loyal to your teaching team and to your school.

    6. Having loving concern for all the children.

    7. Assuming that others have good intentions.

C. 1. Be prompt.

    2. Be polite.

    3. Observe agreed-on rules.

    4. Try to see others' viewpoints.

    5. Carry your share of the load.

    6. Air grievances while they are small.

    7. Communicate often and well with other team members.

    8. Never neglect the children.

    9. Let others help you.

  10. Treat others as you would like to be treated.

UNIT 18

A. 1. In a day-care center when full-time employees go home, part-time employees stay with the children from rest time until parents pick them up.

    2. In public and private schools (other than day-care centers), a teacher's aide may be shared by two teachers. She may work mornings for one and afternoons for the other, or it may be preferable for her to work for each one full time during alternating weeks.

3. Volunteers may be scheduled one day per week or on special occasions for a single unique purpose, such as demonstrating a musical instrument.

B. Flexibility is needed because many teachers are set in their ways and will resist having "help", because of the many options available on how teachers can share the time of an aide, and because of the variety of skills volunteers may have. Many arrangements of schedules may have to be tried before a good one is found and compatible teams evolve.

C. 1. Teachers should be given inservice training on how an aide or volunteer can be helpful, what is expected of the teacher, and what may or may not be expected of the aide or volunteer.

2. An advertising campaign to attract volunteers should be undertaken.

3. Adequate information should be obtained from volunteers, parents, and nonparents.

4. Teachers should evaluate the information from parents and plan the best ways to use their skills.

5. A volunteer coordinator should classify the information from nonparent volunteers and coordinate it with the schools needs.

D. 1. Successful screening of volunteers for proper uses of their skills (parents and nonparents).

2. Providing inservice training on having an aide in the classroom for teachers who have not had the experience previously.

3. Foreseeing the positive effective development that is likely to occur for a child and his parent when the parent is a volunteer in the classroom.

4. Preparing assistant teachers and aides for having volunteer parents in the room.

5. Foreseeing the possible motivation in planning public recognition of volunteer service in the school by using an incentive awards system.

6. Providing adequate orientation for the volunteers before they serve in the classroom.

UNIT 19

A. The typical PTA was unable to involve all the working mothers after World War II. Research has shown that there are more benefits for the child, parent, and school if parents actively participate in school activities. The government antipoverty programs then required all parents with children in child development centers to give some kind of service to the school. This led to public schools initiating strong parent involvement programs at the preschool level.

B. Parents of the very young child can be actively involved in the school's activities for parents by serving in the classroom or school premises as another assistant to the teacher. The activities may be according to the skills of each parent. Many parents help the school by learning how the teachers teach and how to help their children learn at home. When this is done in the home, the parent reinforces what the child is learning in school. There are other school activities such as field trips, PR work, fund raising, and making equipment that parents can do away from the school. Parents can also permit the school to help them by attending learning experiences designed for parents by the school.

C. 1. b, c   2. a, b   3. a, c, d

UNIT 20

A. 1. Child benefits

a. Develops positive self-concept.

b. Teaches child his parents care about him and school.

c. Parent appreciates child more, strengthens rapport.

      d. Gives child good attitude toward school.

      e. Has fewer home-school conflicts.

      f. Has more language development.

   2. Parent benefits

      a. Learns how to teach at home, including discipline.

      b. Feels wanted, needed, appreciated.

      c. Learns about topics of his choosing.

      d. May have personal influence on school policy.

      e. May learn to be objective in evaluating others.

      f. Enjoys field trips and learns from them.

      g. May make valuable personal contacts.

B.   1. School benefits

      a. Staff develops administrative skills in communication, and in area of interpersonal relationships.

      b. Many dollars worth of free services.

      c. Improved image as a public facility.

      d. Receives support and reinforcement of curriculum in the home.

   2. Community benefits

      a. The community contains the child, parent, and school; therefore, if they benefit, the community benefits.

      b. Increases positive-type competition within the community.

      c. Promotes more and better communication among the parts of the community.

C. If parent's skills include them, these tasks may be performed by the working parents of public school kindergarten children.

   1. Attend evening meetings to learn more about subjects relating to the child, such as child development.

   2. Attend evening meetings to learn a new skill or to improve one, subjects to be elective.

   3. Help witn evening or Saturday repair of equipment for classroom or playground (doll clothes/swing).

   4. Help with evening fund raising events in some way: preparation/sales/PR/cleanup.

   5. Fill out evaluation forms on changes he sees in his child that are the result of school experience.

   6. Prepare child's garden (digging).

   7. Launder paint smocks, clean up cloths, similar tasks.

   8. Bake birthday cake/send valentines.

UNIT 21

A.   1. Public school kindergartens.   6. College employment office.

   2. Private preschools.   7. Private employment agencies.

   3. Local government offices.   8. Public (state) employment agency.

   4. Telephone "Information" number. 9. Professional organizations, such as A.C.E.

   5. Chamber of Commerce   10. Head Start Child Development Centers.

B.   1. Public school personnel director.   2. School principal.

3. Public school program director.

4. Private school owner.

5. Private school director or teacher in charge.

6. College director of employment services.

7. Information desk employee in public agencies.

8. Officer of early childhood professional organization.

C. 1. Know strengths and weaknesses.

2. Visit early childhood schools, inquire about staff openings.

3. Where there is a position open, ask to observe for a day. Try to determine the emotional climate and if the philosophy of the school and personal philosophy are compatible.

4. Check newspaper want ads, local radio, and television programs that help employers and employees find each other.

5. Attend any "open to the public" meetings of the local professional organizations for early childhood employees. Make your needs known to someone in charge.

6. Visit the employment agencies at the college, state agency, community service agencies, and as a last resort, commercial agencies.

7. Talk to the person who hires where there is an opening. Follow his directions for filling out forms, observing, discussing how you might fit into the school, or returning for an interview later.

8. Expect a lengthy interview and possibly some interaction with the present staff. This is important to insure getting the person best fitted for the job.

UNIT 22

A. *Applicant:* the person who is applying for the job and who fills out the application.

Application: form to be filled out by a person asking for employment.

Resume: a paper containing comprehensive personal and professional information about the job applicant that helps the employer to know the overall qualifications of the applicant.

Job description: a paragraph or paper that explains all the kinds of duties an applicant performed in his previous employment.

B. 1. Current statistical information on self, family, and employment.

2. Educational achievement: how much, what kind of education, honors received.

3. Employment experience: all the places you were previously employed, how long, job title.

4. Other personal experience: volunteer activities that helped to prepare you for the position you are seeking.

5. Professional involvement: professional organizations to which you have or do belong.

6. Published works: any papers or books you have written that have been published.

7. Other written work: anything of note that you have written that has not yet been published.

C. 1. The kinds of responsibilities you had.

2. The kinds of skills you used.

3. The activities expected of you that you experienced previously.

4. Activities that you have not experienced before but which are expected of the person in the new job.

5. The numbers of people in your interpersonal relationships on the job before.

6. The numbers of children you have worked with, their ages, and the kinds of learning experiences you had with them.

D. 1. Print or write legibly in ink.

2. Follow instructions exactly.

3. Fill in all the blanks.

4. If a direction is unclear, ask what is meant.

5. Do not use abbreviations, unless really necessary.

6. Sign with your business or official signature.

7. Copy over on a clean form if the first one is messy.

8. Be prepared to give both business and character references, three of each if possible.

UNIT 23

A. The value of the personal interview lies in the exchange of information between the interviewer and the person interviewed. The employer learns if the appearance, behavior, knowledge, and attitudes of the applicant are what is needed. The interviewee learns if the school's ideas are compatible with her own and if the working conditions (hours, schedule, salary, etc.) are acceptable.

B. In a job interview, the employer expects to learn if the applicant is qualified for the job, has acceptable appearance, manners, behavior, and if she is still interested after learning much more about the responsibilities of the job. He expects full cooperation in whatever kind of demonstration of skills is requested.

C. The rules for having a successful interview concern appearance, behavior, and preparedness. The applicant should be clean, neat, and conservative in appearance. Her manners should show courtesy and an awareness that it is she who is to convince the interviewer that she can be a good model for the children. She should be prepared to ask questions at the end of the interview about matters that are vital to her. She should bring references with her.

UNIT 24

A. Continuous education is the constant effort of a person to seek intellectual growth, skill development, and knowledge to meet his needs. It is important because of the speed with which changes occur in the world today. Education is affected just as are other professions. People must change daily in a progressive way to keep from suffering "future shock."

B. Continuous education in school may include

1. Inservice training

2. Using the teachers' resource library

3. Taking college courses

4. Taking adult education courses not in college

5. Interaction with parents at the school

Out of school resources may include any five of the following:

1. Newspapers	5. Creative arts programs in the school community
2. Radio	6. Community health facilities programs
3. Television	7. Church workshops and seminars
4. Books and periodicals	8. Public lectures

C. 1. b, c   2. a   3. b, d

UNIT 25

A. The primary purpose of school supervision is to improve the instructional program. It achieves this by

1. Helping teachers to become more effective.

2. Helping to select curriculum materials and to improve the uses made of them.

3. Providing supplementary curriculum materials or knowledge of resources so that teachers may get them.

4. Providing relevant effectiveness training for each teacher.

5. Analyzing instruction and evaluating instructional materials.

6. Coordinating with the teaching staff and the administrative staff.

B. 1. Licensed day-care centers may have their own supervisor (director/owner) and a state supervisor from the state licensing department.

2. Large public schools may have supervisors (supervisors/consultants) who serve only as resource persons to the teachers. They do not evaluate the results.

3. Small schools/school systems may have the school principal serve as teaching supervisor and principal.

4. Some private school systems may have supervisors who are to improve instruction. These persons may or may not also be evaluators.

C. In a large public school system a teacher may meet with the supervisor and principal (evaluator) at the beginning of the year. Methods and evaluation forms as well as what is expected of the teacher in the classroom may be stated. Later the supervisor observes, discusses her observations with the teacher and gives help as needed. The supervisor may provide inservice training for the staff as needed. The evaluator observes and reflects the results of the help. A teacher is shown the evaluation report and initials it. She may write a statement if she disagrees which is attached to the evaluation sheet. Supervision continues. The evaluation process is repeated near the end of the year.

In small schools, the principal may serve in both roles. In very small schools, formal evaluation may not be made. If a director, owner or principal observes that a teacher needs help he may give the help personally. He may just discuss the problem and let the teacher seek help wherever she wishes. This system may be easier to work under for people who prefer a lot of personal freedom to do their own thing or who are just beginning and do not feel ready for the formal evaluation system. The large public school system may seem less personal but it is more likely to help a teacher develop all her talents to the fullest. It is probably more demanding on her time but often it results in more effective teaching. Standards may be held very high in a large system. Many people must be pleased by the teacher. Competition is great.

UNIT 26

A. Inservice training is training for the teaching staff usually during hours of employment. Its purpose is to improve the instructional program by helping the teacher to learn better methods, techniques, or use of materials in the classroom.

B. Teachers may be involved in inservice training by (1) suggesting teacher needs, (2) planning the training, (3) helping with the implementing of the plans and (4) giving honest evaluations of the training.

C. The purpose of the evaluation is to let the supervisor or instructional leader know if the meeting meets the criteria for good inservice training. The methods used may vary just as classroom methods may vary. They may be given by the school staff or by someone outside the school. They may be lecture- or action-oriented. There may be mass participation or small group learning. There may be manipulatives and/or audiovisuals. There may be discussion groups or panels. The evaluations are properly used when the information is tabulated and serves as a basis for planning future training. Appreciations or criticisms of the arrangements, methods, approach to the topic, and preparation give the planners guidelines for further planning to help make the training as useful as possible.

UNIT 27

A.   Educational changes are needed today because

1.   The older systems have produced great conflicts.

2.   Social changes such as increased numbers of working mothers and increased humanism demand places in addition to the home for good care for very young children.

3.   Children of minority groups are entitled to educational opportunities equal to those of others.

4.   Scientists and educators have proved that very early school intervention is developmentally sound.

5.   Parents and schools need to work more actively together on educating the child and this is best accomplished through early childhood programs.

B.   Vast increases in the numbers of early childhood programs since 1965 are caused by

1.   More working mothers.

2.   More programs for the handicapped children.

3.   Schools for socioeconomically disadvantaged children provided by the federal government.

4.   Increase in educational standards required by state licensing bureaus for day-care facilities.

5.   More public school kindergarten available.

6.   Industry providing care for the children of its employees.

7.   Hospitals and universities providing schools for the children of their employees.

C.   Early childhood education in the United States enjoys greater status today than it has ever had before. It is generally accepted and is supported now at all levels of government and by many private institutions. Educational research is beginning long-range studies on its effects. It is a field that probably will continue to expand for many years to come. Job opportunities are plentiful and increasing.

UNIT 28

A.   Assistant teachers in early childhood education today are in great demand because

1.   There are more young children in schools.

2.   There is a shortage of teachers certified in early childhood education.

3.   More mothers are employed and are placing much younger children in nursery schools.

4.   Younger children require a lower pupil-teacher ratio than older children.

5.   There is an increase in bilingual education and a shortage of bilingual teachers.

6.   The federal government insists that assistant teachers are included in the staffs of early childhood schools and programs that are federally funded.

B.   The trained assistant teacher

1.   Will make more money than the untrained one.

2.   Will be more likely to be offered educational opportunities for advancement.

3.   Will be more likely to pass competency-based evaluations for certification when this becomes a reality.

4.   Will be more likely to be ready to assume jobs with greater responsibilities in early childhood education as opportunities present themselves.

C.   The current status of the assistant teacher in early childhood education is higher than it has ever been. Salaries are higher, demand is greater, attention is being given to certification for the position. The future looks even brighter. Many new high-level positions can be foreseen. As teachers accept them, there will be more opportunities for advancement for the trained assistant teacher of today.

INDEX